The Canoe
and the Saddle

A CRITICAL EDITION

Theodore Winthrop

Edited and with an introduction by
Paul J. Lindholdt

UNIVERSITY OF NEBRASKA PRESS • LINCOLN AND LONDON

Library of Congress Cataloging-in-Publication Data
Winthrop, Theodore, 1828–1861.
The canoe and the saddle : a critical edition / Theodore Winthrop,
edited and with an introduction by Paul J. Lindholdt.
p. cm.
Originally published: Boston : Ticknor & Fields, 1863 [c1862].
Includes bibliographical references and index.
ISBN-13: 978-0-8032-9863-7 (pbk. : alk. paper)
ISBN-10: 0-8032-9863-3 (pbk. : alk. paper)
1. Washington (State)—Description and travel. 2. Northwest,
Pacific—Description and travel. 3. Chinook jargon—Glossaries,
vocabularies, etc. I. Lindholdt, Paul J. II. Title.
F891.W79 2006
917.970444—dc22   2006001529

Set in Bulmer by Kim Essman.
Designed by Ray Boeche.

Contents

Illustrations

Following page 76

Acknowledgments

Many colleagues and friends have made this project possible. Dr. Charles Mutschler, director of Archives and Special Collections at Eastern Washington University's John F. Kennedy Library, scanned a copy of the book for me and chased down secondary materials. Lisa Scharnhorst of Special Collections at the University of Washington Libraries confirmed my collations of the text. Lynn Pankonin, collections manager for the Spokane Tribe, helped untangle the genealogical knots of Winthrop's Indian guide and furnished photos. David Robinson, Distinguished Professor of American Literature and director of American Studies at Oregon State University, corroborated the originality of key passages. Gary Williams, professor of English at the University of Idaho, generously loaned me his photocopies and transcriptions of Winthrop materials from the New York Public Library, which houses most Winthropiana today. Johannes Bergthaller in Germany shared his insightful graduate seminar paper on Theodore Winthrop, to which I am greatly indebted. Diane Schmitz, in Grant and Research Development at Eastern Washington University, helped me to prepare the manuscript and apply for support. Finally, I am grateful to the Northwest Institute for Advanced Study, which awarded me two research grants that allowed me to complete this project.

Introduction

In 1853, carrying money in his pocket and elegant attire in his saddlebags, a twenty-four-year-old New Englander named Theodore Winthrop toured the territories of California, Oregon, Washington, and British Columbia after his job as a clerk in the Panama jungle proved too taxing for his delicate health. His tour of the Northwest yielded two adventure books: a novel, *John Brent*, and a nonfiction travel account, *The Canoe and the Saddle*. Both books appeared posthumously in the 1860s and blazed through many printings. In 1890, the town of Winthrop in Washington's North Cascades would be named for him, as would the Winthrop Glacier on Mount Rainier that he described so vividly.

The Washington Territory, where he spent most time during his six-month tour of the Pacific Northwest, was a place of ecological and racial turmoil. Indians on both sides of the Cascades were dying from diseases, bullets, and drink; their economies had been transformed by white contact and their ancestral lands usurped and historic lore ridiculed. Lumber vessels loaded with fir trees to be sunk as piles to build San Francisco docks were already thronging the waters of Puget Sound. Miners were raking creek beds and hillsides for gold. Would-be cattle barons were carving out beef ranches. Winthrop acknowledges few of these historical transitions, even though he traveled some three hundred miles with the S'Klallams and Klickitats, whose tribal names he had planned to use as the title of the book that would become *The Canoe and the Saddle*, until a Confederate bullet fired in an early battle of the Civil War eclipsed his literary plans.

The Canoe and the Saddle, initially published in 1862 and edited anew here for the first time since 1957, reveals much about how European American privilege and presumption shaped the West. The book is a novelized memoir, and it has granted Winthrop standing as an ecological prophet who celebrated a pristine wilderness that was beginning already to yield to roads, farms, and harvests of timber and fish. Northwest historians—John H. Williams in 1913, Robert Cantwell in 1972, and Timothy Egan in 1990—have lavished praise on *The Canoe and the Saddle* for its appreciation of landscape. Winthrop wrote, in transcendental tones, "Our race has never yet come into contact with great mountains as companions of daily life, nor felt that daily development of the finer and more comprehensive senses which these signal facts of nature compel. That is an influence of the future." Unlike his celebrated New England contemporaries Ralph Waldo Emerson and Henry David Thoreau, however, racial and religious prejudices complicate his writing.

He was born in 1828 in New Haven, Connecticut, twenty-four years before his tour of the West commenced. He traced a genealogical line that stretched back on his father's side to John Winthrop, first governor of the Massachusetts Bay Colony. On his mother's side, he claimed among his forebears the evangelical Jonathan Edwards, who was the foremost theologian in America, and Timothy Dwight, of a literary coterie at Yale College known as the Connecticut Wits, later a Yale president. A scion of New England gentry, he graduated atop his small Yale class of 1848. Thereafter he lived and clerked abroad, tried his hand at legal practices in St. Louis and New York, socialized with famous landscape painters, and composed the four novels and three nonfiction books on which his slender reputation rests. He died young, in a botched Civil War battle he had helped to plan.

Poor health nagged him his whole life. He suffered from religious doubts, and constant stomach pains very nearly disabled him. His full red beard might have helped to swell his appearance beyond his meager but athletic 126 pounds. Still wobbly from the smallpox he contracted when he first came into the Oregon Territory five months before, he reported in his journal that he had managed to buy some laudanum and baking soda while traveling the Oregon Trail back toward New York. The baking soda was no doubt used to ease his indigestion or dyspepsia, but the laudanum—a concoction that contained opium or an opium derivative—must have been meant to assuage much greater pains.

Like many of his Puritan forebears, he struggled earnestly with his faith. During college he underwent a religious conversion and spent so many hours praying in his room that his sisters feared he was losing his mind. In his later years, nervous fatigue and recurring bouts of depression complicated brief and feverish jags of sociability. When he confessed in a letter to his widowed mother that his belief in Christianity was waning, she grieved openly to her family and friends, and he became the object of gossip in New York, New Haven, Newport, and Boston. One distant and elder relative,

George Templeton Strong, sniffed in his journal that the young Theodore, who at the time was home and making the rounds of New York salons and soirees, was overly prone to issue rank atheist opinions. Religious conflicts also seep into his books. The narrator of his ur-western *John Brent* laments that no one in America would offer prayers for him throughout his travails across the great basins and ranges of the western territories, but instead his countrymen reject him as a pagan.

By late August 1853, the sickly young aristocrat was wrapping up his Northwest excursion. He had enjoyed the hospitality of many community leaders including Jesse Applegate and William Fraser Tolmie. Now, though, a genuine challenge lay before him—a voyage across Washington Territory by water and land at the hands of Indian guides, a voyage that would suggest to his eventual editors an escapade of a title, *The Canoe and the Saddle*. So at rustic Port Townsend, on the northwest shore of Puget Sound, he harshly bartered with the S'Klallam Indians for help and hired a forty-foot dugout canoe and paddlers to transport him some eighty-five miles south to the inner reaches of the sound near present-day Tacoma.

Winthrop accepted the services of the "Duke of York," actually Chetzemoka, whom he characterized unfairly as "a drunken rascal, a shameless liar, a thief," but who actually led a large tribe and befriended the white settlers. One year after guiding Winthrop in 1853, Chetzemoka became hereditary chief of his people, an office he held till 1876. Two years afterward, Chetzemoka signed the Treaty of Point No Point, which in the late twentieth century became a compelling legal basis for removing the Elwha and Glines Canyon dams near Port Townsend. Chetzemoka's two wives, Seehem-itza and Chill'lil, had been satirically renamed "Queen Victoria" and "Jenny Lind" by white settlers. A photo reproduced in this edition shows Chetzemoka in black dress jacket and hat, his chest outthrust, his eyes appraising the photographer with a mix of distrust and pride. "Civilization came, with step-mother kindness," Winthrop wrote of Chetzemoka, "baptized him with rum, clothed him in discarded slops, and dubbed him the Duke of York." In a canoe with Chetzemoka, where his Indian hirelings were paddling hard to earn their blankets, Winthrop confiscated some of their rum. This seizure—in the interest, he alleged, of efficiency and speed—sparked an uprising that Winthrop deemed fit to subdue by flourishing his Colt six-shooter. And that's the way his expedition across the Washington Territory began.

After a two-day paddle trip, the entourage arrived at Fort Nisqually near present-day Tacoma, where Winthrop paid off his S'Klallam paddlers. Rising early the next day, he got busy trading and bartering, sizing up the horses and the men alike. He purchased pork, hardtack, and three mustangs; hired a young but seasoned Indian guide to take him across the Cascades; and hit the Naches Trail for Fort Dalles on the Columbia River, a journey of more than two hundred miles. An experienced horseman who lavished love upon his well-worn Indian steeds, Winthrop named them and made sure they had adequate water and feed. With his three horses and his guide, he ascended from sea level to the 4,800-foot summit of Naches Pass as swiftly as he dared to push the animals along trails often precipitous or laced with fallen trees. (Several months later the Longmire party had to butcher oxen for leather to lower wagons down those same cliffs.) Over the summit, with their rapport souring, Winthrop again confronted his companion with a pistol and was abandoned to wander lost, ailing, and alone on a desert prairie.

Throughout all of these exploits, he adopted the collar of a cultural minister and thus perhaps fulfilled the spirit of his Puritan ancestors by entirely secular means. He was self-inspired to deliver civilization in the territory and leaven every less-than-genteel act among his Indian companions. He commended nature's glories with great eloquence, waxing ecstatic in their fine light, inspiring later travelers and wilderness advocates. Instead of settling for hardtack and pork alone, he bought and shot fresh meat. Cooking up salmon and grouse on the trail, he demonstrated for the hungry Indians the finest in culinary arts. His showy shirts, breeches, and hats found room in his bags alongside more routine supplies. Newly returned from the continent, where he had spent a great deal of time in France, he tried to introduce his haute couture to the indigenous people. Convinced that he was enhancing race relations, he was actually damaging chances for effective intercultural communication between Indians and settlers in later years.

Ethnic tensions were already high when he visited the territories and took notes for his books. In 1847, six years before him, Cayuse Indians had murdered Marcus and Narcissa Whitman and their family in Walla Walla, an act that hardened extant animosities. The Mexican American War, which Henry David Thoreau had protested with his now-famous civil disobedience, had been decided in America's favor in 1848. At the same time as Winthrop's arrival in 1853, Congress created the Washington Territory, separating it from the Oregon Territory because so many immigrants had settled around Puget Sound. Isaac Stevens, territorial governor, initiated a survey for a rail route to extend from the Great Lakes to Puget Sound, a venture that brought 240 soldiers, surveyors, engineers, and naturalists tramping over Indian lands. Stevens also conducted a series of treaty councils on both sides of the Cascades to lubricate more fractious Indians for treaty signings. The Yakama chief Kamiakin, an estimable figure in Winthrop's narrative, soon led a coalition of interior tribes against the whites in what became known as the Yakima War of 1855-56. To cement his foundation for later settlement proceedings, Governor Stevens adopted the cramped and inadequate Chinook Jargon to translate treaty terms and answer questions, even though skilled bilinguals who spoke both English and the regional Salish dialects were available. Winthrop learned Chinook Jargon, the medium of commercial exchange in the Northwest, and in this eight-hundred-word pidgin he rendered much of the dialogue that passes for Indian-white parley in his book. Intrepid travelers he reasoned—absentee investors and leisurely travelers alike—would benefit from his knowledge of the jargon, which is composed mainly of tribal languages with later additions of English and French.

His overland guide, an Indian whom he knew only as Loolowcan, came to him at the demand of Owhi, Loolowcan's father, a Yakama chief. No other record of the name Loolowcan appears in regional histories, and one may conclude with A. J. Splawn that Winthrop's guide was actually Lo-kout, who enrolled ultimately in the Spokane Tribe as L'Quoit. (Some Indians refused to divulge their names to whites, either for reasons of security or for fear of vengeful deities.) Five years after Winthrop's visit, Lo-kout's brother, Qualchan, would be hanged near Spokane for an alleged murder, and their father, Owhi, would be captured and shot while trying to escape. But Lo-kout would slip the noose and live another sixty years. Dwelling at the confluence of the Columbia and Spokane rivers with his brother's widow in 1906, Lo-kout gave an interview that has been overlooked. In that interview, Lo-kout said he wished that he had murdered Theodore Winthrop when he had the chance. The reasons for Lo-kout's bitterness will come into fuller focus below, but it might suffice at this point to say that Winthrop abused those

Indians to whom he was the most indebted. He behaved like a man whose upper-class breeding made him especially partial to his own cultural values.

And yet Winthrop's exchanges with the Indians contained both give and take. No matter how rushed and abrupt, he had to navigate the contact zone that united Indian-white relations. He needed their help to cross the territory. His exchanges with Chief Owhi at Fort Nisqually demonstrate this interdependence best. Haunted by the clock, burning to make a meeting with fellow travelers at Fort Dalles, Winthrop had to parley politely all the same. To secure Owhi's son as a guide was his interest. To get his way, he had to compromise; he had to traverse the middle ground, as Richard White has termed it. Old Owhi translated into vivid language the landscape that the travelers needed to follow across the Cascades via Naches Pass. He delivered his narrative of the topography of the route in torturous drama and detail, Winthrop thought, but the old man had to be respected and indulged, and his several attendants needed to be deferred to courteously. Ultimately the epic sweep of Owhi's narrative, the grandeur of his dramatic oratory, won over Winthrop, who became an appreciative audience. "Owhhigh as a pantomimist would have commanded brilliant success on any stage," he wrote. "Would that there were more like him in this wordy world." When it came time to fix a price for the scouting and guiding services that Owhi had arranged, Winthrop offered generous compensation for that time and place. In grateful reciprocation, Owhi bestowed a gift on Winthrop—a handmade quirt girded with otter fur, an object Winthrop had admired. When Owhi attempted to append extras to the oral contract—shoes and clothing for his attendants and his son—Winthrop firmly told him no. To travel the middle ground required compromise. The Indians had to make concessions and press requests in turn.

It might be said the Indians took the tenderfoot traveler for a ride in more than the literal sense. Those whom Winthrop encountered were already Indians in the making, in Alexandra Harmon's fitting phrase for the natives in and around Puget Sound. They were learning the ropes and rewards of their persistence to survive among European American immigrants. When Winthrop drew his pistol in the canoe—to turn his paddlers back to the task of ferrying him down Puget Sound—they suspended their rebellion and fell asleep. This was a brilliant move, one worthy of a judo master, that took Winthrop's greatest strength and turned it to their immediate gain. They chose not to argue, mutiny, or comply submissively with his demand. Instead they gave him cause to think better of his impulsive power trip, his pistol flourish, as they drew his hasty journey to a temporary halt.

Recounting incidents like this one, Winthrop wrote in scenes. He rendered his exchanges with the Indians in dialogue, using Chinook Jargon and thereby simplifying complicated intercultural transactions in that facile tongue. He dramatized his journey by novelizing his memory of it. Histories have borne him out, though: he falsified none of the details. His wit and erudition, his readiness to ornament his Northwest excursion with classical and contemporary allusions, generated a charm that amounts to more than artifice. In milder moods, he might praise the Indians: "in every fact of our little world these children of nature found wonderment and fun," using language that can be read as condescending, while elsewhere the tone goes elegiac: "The same spirit of our darksome enlightenment that makes slavery possible," he wrote, "makes maltreatment of Indians certain." Guilt was another recurrent register in his emotional range regarding the native people of the Northwest. He was "mindful of the heavy mesne profits for the occupation of a continent, and the uncounted arrears of blood-money owed by [the white] race," an observation that presages twentieth-century talk of slave reparations. His original title for *The Canoe and the Saddle* was "Klalam and Klickatat," a title focusing wholly on the indigenous people.

Besides this travel account or memoir, his pioneering western books include one that explores aristocracy and religion on the Oregon Trail. To contemporary eyes, that equestrian saga of a novel, *John Brent*, is as vexed by anti-Mormonism as *The Canoe and the Saddle* is by its harsh judgments of the Indians. In his ethnocentrism and religious intolerance, then, Winthrop again fulfilled the spirit of his Puritan ancestry. If during his lifetime he had failed as a writer—all five books rejected by publishers—his death in the Little Bethel battle of the Civil War accorded him swift notoriety. Publishers contended for the same manuscripts they had at first spurned. By setting his best work in the West, he captured the imagination of English and American readers, so much so that fifty-five editions of his books appeared between 1861 and 1876, and Winthrop ranked as one of the most popular of American writers for that time. His insights into the American West may be traceable to his outsider's point of view. In this respect his work looked forward to Mark Twain's *Roughing It* (1872) and backward to Washington Irving's *A Tour on the Prairies* (1835) and dozens of colonial-era promotion tracts, histories, and ethnographies.

The nineteenth-century literary critic William Dean Howells, who called *The Canoe and the Saddle* "a fresh, vivid, and amusing book," might have been surprised to find the ways that later scholars used it. Winthrop's 1913 editor, John H. Williams, lathered his introduction and footnotes with antiquated praise and apologized for the many Indian names that, he said, must "inspire horror and disgust" in the civilized reader. Williams's other comments are rife with prejudice too. Winthrop proved "a useful tool for state-building," Williams wrote, a wrench for furthering manifest destiny. In his 1972 history *The Hidden Northwest*, Robert Cantwell praised Winthrop for his precocious recognition of ways the natural environment may shape character. The notion of nature as nurture, of the abstract wild as a fostering force, might seem romantically antiquated or confined to aficionados of the rural experience, but it still has followers. Journalist Timothy Egan, cowinner of a Pulitzer Prize, effectively lauded and adopted Winthrop as a spirit guide, a surrogate like Dante's Virgil, on his tour through the Northwest in *The Good Rain.* "He predicted," Egan noted of Winthrop, "that a regional style and outlook would evolve as the North Cascades were appreciated for their singular beauty." That prediction was right.

Winthrop instigated a Northwest aesthetic. If the Hudson River School of painters of his era showcased scenic mountain ranges—the Andes, Catskills, Adirondacks, Rockies, and the Sierras—Winthrop delivered the Cascades to the page. That chain of mighty mountains, which runs from southern British Columbia to northern California, includes the highest glaciated peak in the contiguous states, Mount Rainier. Its snowy reflection arrested Winthrop vividly on Puget Sound, and its presence loomed over much of his arduous trip around its flanks. His account of a thunderstorm, a model piece of nature writing, recalls Thomas Cole and Albert Bierstadt in its dense atmospherics: "A gloomy purple storm lay over the Cascades, vaster than they." Alongside his teenage Indian companion and their trio of mustangs—a packhorse, his own saddle horse, and one that Lo-kout rode bareback—all of them weary from the long day's ride, the author watched as dark clouds massed and advanced: "Beside that envelope of storm hiding the west from floor to cope, there was only to be seen, now softened with dull violet haze, the large, rude region of my day's gallop,—thirty miles of surging earth, seamed with frequent valleys of streams flowing eastward, where scanty belts of timber grew by the water-side." There was no cover to be had, and the cavalcade stood vulnerable to the storm. "Fitful bursts of weeping rain were now coming thicker, until control ceased, and the floods fell with no interval, borne on furiously, dashing against every upright object as great crushing wavewalls smite on walls of cliff by the sea-side." Such a living landscape possessed the power to transcend all military muscle and white dominion. Its scale must have astounded eastern audiences. This was the sublime, as landscape painters presented it—so vast, grand, and perilous that it had to inspire veneration and awe. "There were sudden clefts, and ravines with long sweeping flanks, and chasms where a cloud mountain-side had fallen in, leaving a precipice all ragged and ruinous, ready itself to fall." Magnificent and threatening at once, the scene recalls the many romantic paintings of storms and mountains of the nineteenth century, panoramas where the human figure is invariably swallowed by its surroundings, dwarfed by nature's force. No other period reporters, tourists, diarists, or Hudson's Bay Company employees acknowledged the qualities of those mountains so very thoroughly. Winthrop fed upon them, relished them.

Mount Rainier was known among the Indians only as Tacoma, for big peak. It measures 14,411 feet (4,392 meters). Winthrop zealously sanctioned the Indian name over the English name—bestowed by Captain Vancouver in honor of an admiral who had never seen the peak. The twenty-four-year-old Winthrop, viewing the mountain's reflection in a calm Puget Sound while his Indian guides plied their paddles, thought at first that he was seeing things. "It was a giant mountain dome of snow," Winthrop wrote of this glimpse of the peak from the Indian canoe, "swelling and seeming to fill the aerial spheres as its image displaced the blue deeps of tranquil water." Mountains exert an "ennobling influence" over humans he noted, and he seemed to have welcomed this majestic reminder of his own nobility in the presence of his S'Klallam guides. Camping in the peak's shadow, he wrote, "The summer evening air enfolded me sweetly, and down from the cliffs and snowy mounds of Tacoma a cool breeze fell like the spray of a cascade." As if he had become a member of nature's elect, a transcendental descendent of his Puritan forebears, he fantasized that the mountain was shedding the grace of its breeze for him and him alone. In the serene season when he passed through, late August, the mountain shared both male and female qualities. There was "feminine beauty in the cones, and more of masculine force and hardihood in the rough pyramids." In much the way that Ralph Waldo Emerson had called for the emergence of a poet who would celebrate America, Winthrop predicted the Northwest would inspire later generations of writers and artists, as it has. His literary renditions of the Cascades contributed most powerfully to his reputation as an advocate of the Pacific Northwest's environment.

Removing himself from his Indian companions, Winthrop studied Mount Rainier from many angles, as landscape painters do, while he circumnavigated it on his journey to Fort Dalles. Here is a painterly description of what would be named, after his explicit description, the Winthrop Glacier on the mountain: "The blue haze so wavered and trembled into sun-light, and sunbeams shot glimmering over snowy brinks so like a constant avalanche, that I might doubt whether this movement and waver and glimmer, this blending of mist with noontide flame, were not a drifting smoke and cloud of yellow sulphurous vapor floating over some slowly chilling crater far down in the red crevices." Ethereal and permanent, Olympian and austere, the peak distanced Winthrop from his circumstances, allowing him to transcend territorial history and his participation in it.

He had a more gut-level regard for the salmon. This icon of the Pacific Northwest whose populations ran as strong as sixteen million in the Columbia River drainage in 1853, gave him occasion to explore his signature themes of wildness and civility, of beauty and offense, linking the salmon to the people whom he met, saying the west-side Indians "were oozier with [salmon's] juices than I could wish of people I must touch and smell for a voyage of two days," but he nonetheless bought some big fish near Puyallup from members of a resident tribe. He transformed the silver migratory fish, through his cultured touch, into objects fit for admiration. If the Indians did not warrant his full respect, the noble salmon did. On the Naches Trail, preparing dinner, he gave painterly detail to a salmon he propped up to roast: "The colors that are encased within a salmon, awaiting fire that they may bloom, came forth artistically. On the toasted surface brightened warm yellows, and ruddy orange; and delicate pinkness, softened with downy gray, suffused the separating flakes." His subtle touch transformed the fish. Yet in a callous passage that tried to justify European American dominion, by making the indigenous people somehow alien, he wrote, "how much better than feeding foul Indians it was to belong to me, who would treat his proportions with respect, feel the exquisiteness of his coloring, grill him delicately, and eat him daintily!" Salmon were indeed impressive creatures, even if he had purchased them from "a singularly fishy old gentleman, his wife an oleaginous hag, [and] an emotionless youth." The salmon demonstrated his ability to gild the facts by refining coarse and clashing particulars of his frontier experience.

Ecologically speaking, Winthrop disappoints today. Praising roads and rail lines, he defended the undeniable harm they bring, explaining that "the unenlightened" always have resisted "the destruction that precedes reconstruction." This language is as chillingly rich in implications for the Indians as it is for the frail fabric of ecological relations. Some individual Indians might need to be destroyed, some big trees too, before they can be renewed. Like the Hudson River painters who influenced him, particularly his good friend Frederic Edwin Church, Winthrop's observations resided somehow out of time, as if shuttering history, as if privileging only the present moment and the private perceiver.

And yet his sensitivity to language redeems him to a degree. Especially in the matter of onomastics—the study of proper names—Winthrop was ahead of his time. Again and again he honored the Indians by sanctioning their tongue. They knew Puget Sound as Whulge, and he wrote that the "Tides in Whulge, which the uneducated maps call Puget's Sound, rush with impetus, rising and falling eighteen or twenty feet." He is history's champion of Tacoma, over against "Mount Regnier [as] Christians have dubbed it, in stupid nomenclature perpetuating the name of somebody or nobody." The mighty Rainier, object of meditation in *The Canoe and the Saddle*, remained one of the sole sources of civility for him, in a world so swiftly shifting ecologically and culturally.

Savagery and civilization were always at odds in Winthrop. Salted pork or bacon, a staple of the trail, was his foodstuff of choice. He lavishly commended its fumes, wafting across the West,

as the essence of a civilizing European American culture. By contrast, "the rude, dangerous forces of nature," he wrote, stood ready
always to seduce a man of quality into barbarism. The Hudson's
Bay Company forts, where he found conversation and comfort, were
still involved in the dwindling trade of exporting furs to Europe,
a fact he mentions only in passing. Transcendental tones elevate
his narrative, as in the stunning opening of chapter 5, "Forests of
the Cascades," and in the following memorable sequence that concludes with a telltale Thoreauvian paradox: "I was going homeward across the breadth of the land, and with the excitement of this
large thought there came a slight reactionary sinking of heart, and a
dread lest I had exhausted onward life, and now, turning back from
its foremost verge, should find myself dwindling into dull conservatism, and want of prophetic faith. I feared that I was retreating
from the future into the past. Yet if one but knew it, his retreats are
often his wisest and bravest advances." As did Thoreau, Winthrop
believed that the preservation of the civilized world resides within
its wildness—if that wildness can be kept at arm's length.

By today's standards, Winthrop seems brutally regressive in
his attitudes toward ethnicity and race. He impaled the Indians
with cruel epithets. His overland guide, "low-browed Loolowcan,"
more specifically "a half-insolent, half-indifferent, jargoning savage,"
had a "superstitious soul." Prospective visitors to the territory, he
believed, may benefit from his prior prudence and wisdom, if and
when the "attempt is made to manage Pagan savages." The opening of *The Canoe and the Saddle* explains his need to cross the territory and join his companions swiftly. He hired Indian paddlers and
demanded that they depart at once. Instead, they wanted to sleep
off some liquor, which enraged Winthrop: "I became wroth, and,
advancing where the king of all this region lay, limp, stertorous, and

futile, I kicked him liberally." With triumph he reported it. "Yes! I have kicked a king!" Such a *coup de pied* was accounted a deadly insult to Indians there and then. Heedless of their cultural practices, though, Winthrop exulted in his temerity and made a mock of the occasion. And of course he got his way. Some Indians packed and paddled him, even sticking with him in the canoe when he took their rum and trained his pistol on them: "Look down this muzzle as I whisk it about and bring it to bear on each of you in turn. Rifled you observe. Pleasant, well-oiled click that cylinder has." Bravado lards his story, aiming to engage his stay-at-home readers in England and back east.

Neglected research by Washington legislator and historian A. J. Splawn helps assess Winthrop's involvement in the cultural collisions that were closing the Northwest frontier. In 1906, Splawn found and interviewed Lo-kout, the guide who had broken his commitment and abandoned Winthrop fifty-three years before. The experience of guiding him helped to make a warrior out of Lo-kout, who would live till at least 1913, his sadness palpable when Edward Curtis photographed him. Splawn asked if he was Winthrop's Loolowcan. The man rose to his feet quickly and, "with flashing eyes, he said, 'Yes, I was then Loolowcan, but changed my name during the war later.'" By 1906, he was living with his hanged brother's widow, whom he had embraced as his wife. After his brother and father were killed in 1858, Lo-kout had fought against the white militias. Seven bullets had passed through him. During one battle, wounded badly, he fainted and went into shock. A passing military volunteer slowed down long enough to club him with a rifle butt in the forehead, crushing in his skull and leaving him for dead. In 1906, when Splawn interviewed Lo-kout, his forehead had a dent that, Splawn said, "would have held an egg." Photographic evidence corroborates Splawn's claim. In language that *The Canoe and the Saddle* precisely confirms, Lo-kout noted:

> *I did not like the man's looks and said so, but was ordered*
> *to get ready and start. He soon began to get cross and*
> *the farther we went the worse he got, and the night we*
> *stayed at the white men's camp who were working on the*
> *road in the mountains, he kicked me with his boot as if*
> *I was a dog. When we arrived at Wenas Creek, where*
> *some of our people were camped, I refused to go farther;*
> *he drew his revolver and told me I had to go with him to*
> *The Dalles. I would have killed him only for my cousin*
> *and aunt. I have often thought of that man and regret-*
> *ted I did not kill him. He was me-satch-ee (mean).*

Acting moody, reviling his guide, delivering him a kick while he slept, and wielding his pistol to get his way—these details are consistent with Winthrop as he profiled himself in his book. No wonder he needed to turn away narratively from his behavior, from his Indian guides and the domination over them by his own kind, toward nature as a transcendent space that could relieve him and allow him to exercise control with his command of language.

In much the same way that a beauty strip of standing trees beside a highway may camouflage clear-cut logging scars on distant hills, the splendid scenery of Winthrop's travel narrative camouflages dramas of the U.S. territorial imperative in full swing. Reading *The Canoe and the Saddle* less for its environmental prophecy than for its contributions to culture studies may bring the man into fuller focus for twenty-first-century readers. A fortunate son of New England gentry, he enjoyed the privilege and education that helped him valorize landscapes so memorably. As a social commentator on the nineteenth-century West, he brought proficient language skills to bear, and in doing so he constructed his Indian subjects in partial and partisan terms. He boasted, in rhetoric meant to entice nineteenth-century readers, that "the story of a civilized man's solitary onslaught at barbarism cannot lose its interest." His rhapsodic attitude toward nature, his esteem for the Northwest's overlooked potential to shape character, helped him to screen off the ethnic and ecological violence taking place in the Washington Territory.

Note on the Text
and Printing History

My copy text for this critical edition is a printing from 1863 in the Archives and Special Collections division of the John F. Kennedy Library at Eastern Washington University. I say "printing" because it is not an edition that differed from the 1862 version. A single edition or setting of this book served the British and American reading public until 1913 when John H. Williams published his lavish volume of the Winthrop narrative and added "SIXTEEN COLOR PLATES AND MORE THAN ONE HUNDRED OTHER ILLUSTRATIONS." Williams's subtitle wisely restored the alliterative working title from Winthrop's holograph manuscript: "Klalam and Klickatat. Nature and Natives of the Northwest." Winthrop's original publisher, the Boston-based Ticknor and Fields, chose to disregard Winthrop's intentions, though, and instead imposed as a title "The Canoe and the Saddle," a title to appeal to readers hungry for action over analysis, adventure over ethnography. In 1957, Alfred Powers presented another edition of this book, the Nisqually Edition, which is now long out of print and, like the Williams edition, a collector's item. Indeed, it is a measure of Winthrop's enormous popularity in his own century that printings of his book from its original plates are more widely available and affordable than the Williams and Powers editions.

Emendations

The Canoe and the Saddle

1. An Entrance

A wall of terrible breakers marks the mouth of the Columbia, Achilles of rivers.

Other mighty streams may swim feebly away seaward, may sink into foul marshes, may trickle through the ditches of an oozy delta, may scatter among sand-bars the currents that once moved majestic and united. But to this heroic flood was destined a short life and a glorious one,—a life all one strong, victorious struggle, from the mountains to the sea. It has no infancy,—two great branches collect its waters up and down the continent. They join, and the Columbia is born to full manhood. It rushes forward, jubilant, through its magnificent chasm, and leaps to its death in the Pacific.

Through its white wall of breakers Captain Gray, with his bark, the Columbia, first steered boldly to discover and name the stream. I will not invite my reader to follow this example, and buffet in the wrecking uproar on the bar. The Columbia, rolling seaward, repels us.

Let us rather coast along northward, and enter the Northwest by the Straits of De Fuca, upon the mighty tides of an inland sea. We will profit by this inward eddy of ocean to float quietly past Vancouver's Island, and land at Kahtai,[1] Port Townsend, the opening scene of my narrative.

The adventures chronicled in these pages happened some years ago, but the story of a civilized man's solitary onslaught at barbarism cannot lose its interest. A drama with Indian actors, in Indian costume, upon an Indian stage, is historical, whether it happened two hundred years since in the Northeast, or five years since in the northwest corner of our country.

2. A Klalam Grandee

The Duke of York was ducally drunk.[1] His brother, King George, was drunk—royally. Royalty may disdain public opinion, and fall as low as it pleases. But a brother of the throne, leader of the opposition, possible Regent, possible King, must retain at least a swaying perpendicular. King George had kept his chair of state until an angular sitting position was impossible; then he had subsided into a curvilinear droop, and at last fairly toppled over, and lay in his lodge, limp and stertorous.

In his lodge lay Georgius Rex, in flabby insensibility. Dead to the duties of sovereignty was the King of the Klalams. Like other royal Georges, in palaces more regal than this Port Townsend wigwam, in realms more civilized than here, where the great tides of Puget's Sound rise and fall, this royal George had sunk in absolute wreck. Kings are but men. Several kings have thought themselves the god Bacchus. George of the Klalams had imbibed this ambitious error, and had proved himself very much lower than a god,

much lower than a man, lower than any plebeian Klalam Indian,—
a drunken king.

In the great shed of slabs that served them for palace sat the
Queen,—sat the Queens,—mildeyed, melancholy, copper-colored
persons, also, sad to say, not sober. Etiquette demanded inebriety.
The stern rules of royal indecorum must be obeyed. The Queen
Dowager had succumbed to ceremony; the Queen Consort was sinking; every lesser queen,—the favorites for sympathy, the neglected
for consolation,—all had imitated their lord and master.

Courtiers had done likewise. Chamberlain Gold Stick, Black
Rod, Garter King at Arms, a dozen high functionaries, were prostrate by the side of prostrate majesty. Courtiers grovelled with their
sovereign. Sardanapalus[2] never presided, until he could preside no
longer, at a more tumble-down orgie.

King, royal household, and court all were powerless, and I was a
suppliant here, on the waters of the Pacific, for means of commenc-
ing my homeward journey across the continent toward the Atlan-
tic. I needed a bark from that fleet by which King George ruled the
waves. I had dallied too long at Vancouver's Island, under the hospitable roof of the Hudson's Bay Company, and had consumed invalu-
able hours in making a detour from my proper course to inspect the
house, the saw-mill, the bluff, and the beach, called Port Townsend.
These were the last days of August, 1853. I was to meet my overland
comrades, a pair of roughs, at the Dalles of the Columbia on the first
of September. Between me and the rendezvous were the leagues of
Puget's Sound, the preparation for an ultramontane trip, the passes
of the Cascades, and all the dilatoriness and danger of Indian guidance. Moments now were worth days of common life.

Therefore, as I saw those winged moments flit away unharnessed
to my chariot of departure, I became wroth, and, advancing where

the king of all this region lay, limp, stertorous, and futile, I kicked
him liberally.

Yes! I have kicked a king!

Proudly I claim that I have outdone the most radical regicide. I
have offered indignities to the person of royalty with a moccasined
toe. Would that that toe had been robustly booted! In his Sans
Souci, his Oeil de Boeuf, his Brighton Pavilion,[3] I kicked so much
of a first gentleman of his realm as was George R., and no scalping-
knife leaped from greasy seal-skin sheath to avenge the insult. One
bottle-holder in waiting, upon whose head I had casually trodden,
did indeed stagger to his seat, and stammer truculently in Chinook
jargon, "Potlatch lum!—Give me to drink," quoth he, and inconti-
nently fell prone again, a poor, collapsed bottle-holder.

But kicking the insensible King of the Klalams, that dominant
nation on the southern shores of Puget's Sound, did not procure
me one of his canoes and a crew of his braves to paddle me to
Nisqually, my next station, for a blanket apiece and gratuities of
sundries. There was no help to be had from that smoky barn or its
sorry inmates, so regally nicknamed by British voyagers. I left them
lying upon their dirty mats, among their fishy baskets, and strode
away, applying the salutary toe to each dignitary as I passed.

Fortunately, without I found the Duke of York, only ducally
drunk. A duke's share of the potables had added some degrees
to the arc of vibration of his swagger, but had not sent it beyond
equilibrium. He was a reversed pendulum, somewhat spasmodic
in swing, and not constructed on the compensation principle,—
when one muscle relaxed, another did not tighten. However, the
Duke was still sober enough to have speculation in his eyes, and
as he was Regent now, and Lord High Admiral, I might still by his
favor be expedited.

It was a chance festival that had intoxicated the Klalams, king and court. There had been a fraternization, a powwow, a wah-wah, a peace congress with some neighboring tribe,—perhaps the Squaksnamish, or Squallyamish, or Sinahomish, or some other of the Whulgeamish, dwellers by Whulge,—the waters of Puget's Sound. And just as the festival began, there had come to Port Townsend, or Kahtai, where the king of the Klalams, or S' Klalams, now reigned, a devil-send of a lumber brig, with liquor of the fieriest. An orgie followed, a nation was prostrate.

The Duke was my only hope. Yet I must not betray eagerness. A dignitary among Indians does not like to be bored with energy. If I were too ardent, the Duke would grow coy. Prices would climb to the unapproachable. Any exhibition of impatience would cost me largess of beads, if not blankets, beyond the tariff for my canoe-hire. A frugal mind, and, on the other hand, a bent toward irre-sponsible pleasure, kept the Duke palpably wavering. He would joyfully stay and complete his saturnalia, and yet the bliss of more chattels, and consequent consideration, tempted him. Which shall it be, "lumoti" or "pississy,"—bottle or blanket? revel and rum, or toil and toilette?—the great alternative on which civilization hinges, as well among Klalams as elsewhere. Sunbeams are so warm, and basking such dulcet, do-nothing bliss, why overheat one's self now for the woolen raiment of future warmth? Not merely warmth, but wealth,—wives, chiefest of luxuries, are bought with blankets; with them canoes are bought, and to a royal highness of savages, blan-kets are purple, ermine, and fine linen.

Calling the Duke's attention to these facts, I wooed him cautiously, as craft woos coyness; I assumed a lofty indifference of demeanor, and negotiated with him from a sham vantage-ground of money-power, knowing what trash my purse would be, if he refused to be tempted. A grotesque jargon called Chinook is the lingua-franca of the whites and Indians of the Northwest. Once the Chinooks were the most numerous tribe along the Columbia, and the first, from their position at its mouth, to meet and talk with strangers. Now it is all over with them; their bones are dust; small-pox and spirits have eliminated the race. But there grew up between them and the traders a lingo, an incoherent coagulation of words,—as much like a settled, logical language as a legion of centrifugal, marauding Bashi Bazouks,[4] every man a Jack-of-all-trades, a beggar and blackguard, is like an accurate, unanimous, disciplined battalion. It is a jargon of English, French, Spanish, Chinook, Kallapooya,[5] Haida, and other tongues civilized and savage. It is an attempt on a small scale to nullify Babel by combining a confusion of tongues into a confounding of tongues,—a witches' caldron in which the vocable that bobs up may be some old familiar Saxon verb, having suffered Procrustean docking or elongation, and now doing substantive duty; or some strange monster, evidently nurtured within the range of tomahawks and calumets. There is some danger that the beauties of this dialect will be lost to literature,

"Carent quia vate sacro."[6]

The Chinook jargon still expects its poet. As several of my characters will use this means of conveying their thoughts to my reader, and employ me only as an interpreter, I have thought it well to aid comprehension by this little philological preface.

My big talk with the Duke of York went on in such a lingo, somewhat as follows—

"Pottlelum mitlite King Jawge; Drunk lieth King George," said I. "Cultus tyee ocook; a beggarly majesty that. Hyas tyee mika; a mighty prince art thou,—pe kumtux skookoom mamook esick; and knowest how robustly to ply paddle. Nika tikkry hyack klatawah copa Squally, copa canim; I would with speed canoe it to Squally. Hui pississy nika potlatch pe hui ikta; store of blankets will I give, and plenteous sundries."

"Nawitka siks; yea, friend," responded the Duke, grasping my hand, after two drunken clutches at empty air. "Klosche nika tum tum copa hyas Baasten tyee; tender is my heart toward thee, O great Yankee don. Yaka pottlelum—halo nika—wake cultus mann Dookeryawk; he indeed is drunk—not I—no loafer-man, the Duke of York. Mitlite canim; got canoe. Pe klosche nika tikky klatawah copa Squally; and heartily do I wish to go to Squally."

Had the Duke wavered still, and been apathetic to temptation of blankets, and sympathetic toward the joys of continued saturnalia, a new influence now brought to bear would have steadied him. One of his Duchesses, only duchessly intoxicated, came forth from the ducal lodge, and urged him to effort.

"Go, by all means, with the distinguished stranger, my love," said she, in Chinook, "and I will be the solace of thy voyage. Perchance, also, a string of beads and a pocket-mirror shall be my meed[7] from the Boston chief, a very generous man, I am sure." Then she smiled enticingly, her flat-faced grace, and introduced herself as Jenny Lind,[8] or, as she called it, "Chin Lin." Indianesque, not fully Indian, was her countenance. There was a trace of tin in her copper color, possibly a dash of Caucasian blood in her veins. Brazenness of hue was the result of this union, and a very pretty color it is with eloquent blushes mantling through it, as they do mantle in Indian cheeks. Her forehead was slightly and coquettishly flattened by art, as a woman's should be by nature, unless nature destines her for missions foreign to feminineness, and means that she shall be an intellectual roundhead, and shall sternly keep a graceless school, to irritate youthful cherubim into original sinners. Indian maids are pretty; Indian dames are hags. Only high civilization keeps its women beautiful to the last. Indian belles have some delights of toilette worthy of consideration by their blonde sisterhood. O mistaken harridans of Christendom, so bountifully painted and powdered, did ye but know how much better than your diffusiveness of daub is the concentrated brilliance of vermilion stripes parting at the nose-bridge and streaming athwart the cheeks! Knew ye but this, at once ye would reform from your undeluding shams, and recover the forgotten charms of acknowledged pinxit.[9]

At last, persuaded by his own desires and the solicitations of his fair Duchess, the Duke determined to transport me. He pointed to a grand canoe on the beach,—that should be our Bucentaur,[10] and now he must don robes of ceremony for the voyage. For, indeed, both ducal personages were in deshabille. A dirty shirt, blue and short, was the Duke's chief habiliment; hers, a shirt longer, but no cleaner.

Within his palace-curtains now disappeared the second grandee of the Klalams, to bedeck himself. Presently I lifted the hanging mat that served for door to his shed of slabs, and followed him. His family and suite were but crapulous[11] after their less than royal potations. He despatched two sleepy braves to make ready the canoe, and find paddles.

"Where is my cleanest shirt, Chin Lin?" he asked.

"Nika macook lum; I buy grog with um," replied the Duchess.

"Cultus mamook; a dastardly act," growled the Duke, "and I will thwack thee for't."

Jenny Lind sank meekly upon the mud-floor, and wept, while the Duke smote her with palm, fist, and staff.

"Kopet! hold!" cried I, rushing forward. "Thy beauteous spouse has bought the nectar for thy proper jollity. Even were she selfish, it is uncivilized to smite the fair. Among the Bostons, when women wrong us, we give pity or contempt, but not the strappado."[12] Harangues to Indians are traditionally in such lofty style. The Duke suffered himself to be appeased, and proceeded to dress without the missing article. He donned a faded black frock-coat, evidently a misfit for its first owner in civilization, and transmitted down a line of deformed wearers to fall amorphous on the shoulders of him of York. For coronet he produced no gorgeous combination of velvet, strawberry-leaves, and pearls; but a hat or tile,[13] also of civilization, wrinkled with years and battered by world-wandering, crowned him frowzily. Black dress pantaloons of brassy sheen, much crinkled at the bottom, where they fell over moccasins with a faded scarlet instep-piece, completed his costume. A very shabby old-clo' Duke. A virulent radical would have enjoyed him heartily, as an emblem of decay in the bloated aristocracy of this region. Red paint daubed over his clumsy nose, and about the flats surrounding his little, disloyal, dusky eyes, kept alive the traditional Indian in his appearance. Otherwise he might have been taken for a decayed priest turned bar-tender, or a colporteur[14] of tracts on spiritualism, or an ex-constable pettifogger in a police court. Commerce, alas! had come to the waters of Whulge, stolen away his Indian simplicity, and made him a caricature, dress, name, and nature. A primitive Klalam, clad in skins and undevoured by the flames of fire-water, he would have done well enough as a type of fish-fed barbarism. Civilization came, with step-mother kindness, baptized him with rum, clothed him in discarded slops, and dubbed him Duke of York. Hapless scarecrow, disreputable dignitary, no dukeling of thine shall ever become the Louis Philippe of Klalam revolutions. Boston men are coming in their big canoes over sea. Pikes have shaken off the fever and ague on the banks of the muddy Missouri, and are striding beyond the Rockys. Nasal twangs from the east and west soon will sound thy trump of doom. Squatters will sit upon thy dukedom, and make it their throne.[15]

Tides in Whulge, which the uneducated maps call Puget's Sound, rush with impetus, rising and falling eighteen or twenty feet. The tide was rippling winningly up to the stranded canoes. Our treaty was made; our costume was complete; we prepared to embark. But lo! a check! In malignant sulks, King George came forth from his mal-perfumed lodge of red-smeared slabs. "Veto," said he. "Dog am I, and this is my manger. Every canoe of the fleet is mine, and from this beach not one shall stir this day of festival!"

Whereupon, after a wrangle, short and sharp, with the Duke, in which the King whipped out a knife, and brandished it with drunken vibrations in my face, he staggered back, and again lay in his lodge, limp and stertorous. Had he felt my kick, or was this merely an impulse of discontented ire?

How now? Could we not dethrone the sovereign, and confiscate his property? There are precedents for such a course. But savage life is full of chances. As I was urging the soberish Duke to revolutionary acts, or at least to a forced levy from the royal navy, a justifiable piracy, two canoes appeared rounding the point.

"Come unto these yellow sands, ye brass-colored braves," we cried. They were coming, each crew roving anywhither, and soon, by the Duke's agency, I struck a bargain for the leaky better of the two vessels.

No clipper that ever creaked from *status quo* in Webb's shipyard,[16] and rumbled heavily along the ways, and rushed as if to drown itself in its new element, and then went cleaving across the East River, staggering under the intoxicating influence of a champagne-bottle with a blue ribbon round its neck, cracked on the rudderpost by a blushing priestess,—no such grand result of modern skill ever surpassed in mere model the canoe I had just chartered for my voyage to Squally. Here was the type of speed and grace to which the most untrammelled civilization has reverted, after cycles of junk, galleon, and galliot building,—cycles of lubberly development, but full of instruction as to what can be done with the best type when it is reasoned out or rediscovered. My vessel was a black dug-out with a red gunwale. Forty feet of pine-tree had been burnt and whittled into a sharp, buoyant canoe.[17] Sundry cross-pieces strengthened it, and might be used as seats or backs. A row of small shells inserted in the red-smeared gunwale served as talismans against Bugaboo.[18] Its master was a withered ancient; its mistress a haggish crone. These two were of unsavory and fishy odor. Three young men, also of unsavory and fishy odor, completed the crew. Salmon mainly had been the lifelong diet of all, and they were oozier with its juices than I could wish of people I must touch and smell for a voyage of two days.

In the bargain for canoe and crew, the Duke constituted himself my courier. I became his prey. The rule of tea-making, where British ideas prevail, is a rough generalization, a spoonful for the pot and one for each bibber. The tariff of canoe-hire on Whulge is equally simple,—a blanket for the boat, and one for each paddler. The Duke carefully included himself and Jenny Lind among the paddling recipients of blankets. I ventured to express the view that both he and his Duchess would be unwashed supernumeraries. At this he was indignant. He felt himself necessary as impresario of the expedition.

"Wake closche ocook olyman siwash; no good that oldman savage," said he, pointing to the skipper. "Yaka pottlelum, conoway pottlelum; he drunk, all drunk. Wake kumtux Squally; no understand Squally. Hyas tyee Dookeryawk, wake pottlelum,—kumtux skookoom mamook esick, pe tikky hyack klatawah copa Squally; mighty chief the Duke of York, not drunk, understand to ply paddle mightily, and want to go fast to Squally."

"Very well," said I, "I throw myself into your hands. My crew, then, numbers six, the three fishy youths, Olyman siwash,[19] Jenny Lind, and yourself. As to Olyman's fishy squaw, she must be temporarily divorced, and go ashore; dead weight will impede our voyage."

"Nawitka," responded the Klalam, "cultus ocook olyman cloocheman; no use that oldman woman." So she went ashore, bow-legged, monotonous, and a fatalist, like all old squaws.

"And now," continued the Duke, drawing sundry greasy documents from the pocket of that shapeless draggle-tail coat of his, "mika tikky nanitch nika teapot; wilt thou inspect my certificates?"

I took the foul papers without a shudder,—have we not all been educated out of squeamishness by handling the dollar-bills of civilization? There was nothing ambiguous in the wording of these "teapots." It chanced sometimes, in days of chivalry, that spies bore missions with clauses sinister to themselves, as this: "The bearer is a losel vile,—have you never a hang man and an oak for him?" The Duke's testimonials were of similar import. They were signed by Yankee skippers, by British naval officers, by casual travellers,— all unanimous in opprobrium. He was called a drunken rascal, a shameless liar, a thief; called each of these in various idioms, with plentiful epithets thrown in, according to the power of imagery possessed by the author. Such certificates he presented gravely, and with tranquil pride. He deemed himself indorsed by civilization, not branded. Men do not always comprehend the world's cynical praise. It seemed also that his Grace had once voyaged to San Francisco in what he called a "skookoom canim copa moxt stick; a colossal canoe with two masts." He did not state what part he played on board, whether cook, captain, stowaway, or Klalam plenipo to those within the Golden Gate. His photograph had been taken at San Francisco. This he also exhibited in a grandiose manner, the Duchess, Olyman siwash, and the three fishy siwashes examining it with wonder and grunts of delight.

Now it must not be supposed that the Duke was not still ducally drunk, or that it was easy to keep him steady in position or intention. Olyman siwash, also, though not patently intoxicated, wished to be,—so did the three unsavory, hickory-shirted, mat-haired, truculent siwashes. Olyman would frequently ask me, aside, in the strange, unimpassioned, expressionless undertone of an Indian, for a "lumoti," Chinook jargon for *la bouteille*, meaning no empty bottle, but a full. Never a lumoti of delay and danger got Olyman from me. Our preparations went heavily enough. Sometimes the whole party would squat on the beach, and jabber for ten minutes, ending always by demanding of me liquor or higher wages. But patience and purpose always prevail. At last, by cool urgency, I got them all on board and away. Adieu Port Townsend, then a town of one house on a grand bluff, and one saw-mill in a black ravine. Adieu intoxicated lodges of Georgius Rex Klalamorum! Adieu Royalty! Remember my kick, and continue to be happy as you may.

3. Whulge

According to the cosmical law that regulates the west ends of the world, Whulge is more interesting than any of the eastern waters of our country. Tame Albemarle and Pamlico, Chesapeake and Delaware, Long Island Sound, and even the Maine Archipelago and Frenchman's Bay, cannot compare with it. Whulge is worthy of the Scandinavian savor of its name. Its cockney misnomer should be dropped. Already the critical world demands who was "Puget," and why should the title be saved from Lethe and given to a sound. Whulge is a vast fiord, parting rocks and forests primeval with a mighty tide. Chesapeakes and the like do very well for oyster "fundums" and shad-fisheries, but Whulge has a picturesque significance as much greater as its salmon are superior to the osseous shad of the east. Some of its beauties will appear in this my voyage.

I sat comfortably amidships in my stately but leaky galley, Bucentaur hight for the nonce. Olyman siwash steered. The Duke and Duchess, armed with idle paddles, were between him and me. The fishy trio were arranged forward, paddling to starboard and port. It was past noon of an August day, sultry, but not blasting, as are the summer days of that far Northwest. We sped on gallantly, paddling and spreading a blanket to the breeze.

The Duke, however, sogered[1] bravely, and presently called a halt. Then, to my consternation, he produced a "lumoti"[2] and passed it. Potations pottle-deep ensued. Each reveller took one sixth of the liquor, and, after the Duke's exhaustive draught, an empty bottle floated astern. A general stagger began to be perceptible among the sitters. Their paddling grew spasmodic.

. After an interval I heard again a popping sound, not unknown to me. A gurgle followed. I turned. The Duke was pouring out a cupful from his second bottle. He handed me the cup and lumoti for transmission to the fishy, forward. This must stop. I deposited the bottle by my side and emptied the cup into Whulge. Into an arm of the Pacific in the far Northwest I poured that gill of fire-water. Answer me from the northeast corner, O Neal Dow,[3] was it well done?

Then raged the siwashes all, from Olyman perched on high and wielding a helmsman paddle aft, to a special blackguard in the bow with villain eyes no bigger than a flattened pea, and a jungle of coarse black hair, thick as the mane of a buffalo bull. All stowed their paddles and talked violently in their own tongue. It was a guttural, sputtering language in its calmest articulation, and now every word burst forth like the death-rattle of a garroted man.

Finally, in Chinook, "Kopet; be still," said the Duke. "Keelapi; turn about," said he.

They brandished paddles, and, whirling the canoe around, tore up the water violently for a few strokes. I said nothing. Presently they paused, and talked more frantically than before. Something was about to happen.

Aha! What is that, O Duke? A knife! What are these, O dirty siwashes? Guns are these, flint-locks of the Hudson's Bay pattern. "Guns for thee, O spiteful spiller of enlivening beverage, and capturer of a lumoti. Butchery is the order of the day!"

"Look you, then, aborigines all. I carry six siwash lives at my girdle. This machine—mark it well!—is called a six-shooter, an eight inch navy revolver, invented by Col. Sam Colt, of Hartford, Conn.[4] God bless him! We are seven, and I should regret sending you six others to the Unhappy Hunting-Grounds of the Kicuali Tyee, Anglice Devil, the lowermost chieftain. Look down this muzzle as I whisk it about and bring it to bear on each of you in turn. Rifled you observe. Pleasant, well-oiled click that cylinder has. Behold, also, this other double barrelled piece of artillery, loaded, as you saw but now, with polecat-shot, in case we should see one of these black and white objects skulking along shore. Unsavory though ye be, my Klalams, I should not wish to identify you in your deaths with that animal."

Saying this, with an air of indifference, but in expressive pantomime, I could not fail to perceive that the situation was critical. Three drunken Indians on this side, and two and a woman on that, and I playing bottle-holder in the midst,—what would follow? Their wild talk and threatening gestures continued. I kept my pistol and one eye cocked at him of the old clo', the teapots, and the daguerrotype; my other eye and the double-barrel covered the trio in the bow. This dead lock lasted several minutes. Meantime the canoe had yielded to the tide, and was now sweeping on in a favorable course.

At last the Duke laid down his knife, Olyman siwash his gun, the three fishy ones theirs, and his Grace, stretching forth an eloquent arm, made a neat speech. Fluency is impossible in few-worded Chinook jargon, but brevity is more potent.

"Hyas silex nika; in wrathful sulks am I. Masatche nika tum tum copa mika; bitter is my heart toward thee. Wake cultus tyee Dookeryawk; no paltry sachem, the Duke of York. Wake kamooks, halo pottlelum; no dog, by no means a soaker. Ancoti conoway tikky mamook iscum mika copa Squally,—alta halo; but now, all wished to conduct thee to Squally; now, not so. Alta nesika wake tikky pississy, pe shirt, pe polealely, pe Kaliaton, pe hiu ikta,—tikky keelapi; now we no want blankets and shirts and powder and shot and many traps,—want to return. Conoway silex,—tikky moosum; all in the sulks,—want to sleep."

Whereupon, as if at a signal, all six dived deep into slumber,— slumber at first pretended, perhaps to throw me off my guard, perhaps a crafty method of evading the difficulty of a reconciliation, and the shame of yielding. So deep did they plunge into sham sleep, that they sunk into real, and presently I heard the gurgle of snores.

While they slept, the canoe drifted over Whulge. Fleet waters bore me on whither they listed, fortunately whither I also listed, and, if ever the vessel yawed, a few quiet strokes with the paddle set her right again. The current drew me away from under shore, and to the south, through distancing haze of summer, the noble group of the Olympian Mountains[5] became visible,—a grand family of vigorous growth, worthy more perfect knowledge. They fill the southern promontory, where Whulge passes into the Pacific, at the Straits of De Fuca. On the highest pinnacles of this sierra, glimmers of perpetual snow in sheltered dells and crevices gave me pleasant, chilly thoughts in that hot August day. After the disgusting humanity of King George's realms, and after the late period of rebellion and disorganization, the calming influence of these azure luminous peaks, their blue slashed with silver, was transcendent.

So I sat watchful, and by and by I heard a gentle voice, "Wake nika moosum; I sleep not."

"Sleepest thou not, pretty Duchess, flat-faced one, with chevrons vermilion culminating at thy nose-bridge? Wilt thou forgive me for spilling thy nectar, Lalage of the dulcet laugh, dulcet-spoken Lalage? Would that thou wert clean as well as pretty, and had known but seldom the too fragrant salmon!—would that I had never seen thee toss off a waterless gill of fire-water! Please wake the Duke."

The Duke woke. Olyman woke. Woke Klalams one and all. Sleep had banished wrath and rancor. All grasped their paddles, and, soon warming with work, the fugleman[6] waked a wild chant, and to its stirring vibrations the canoe shook and leaped forward like a salmon in the buzz of a tideway.

We careered on for an hour. Then I suggested a pause and a picnic. Brilliant and friendly thought,—"Conoway tikky muckamuck;" all want to eat. Take then, my pardoned crew, from my stores, portions of dried cod. Thin it is, translucent, and very nice for Klalam or Yankee. Take also hardtack at discretion,—"pire sapolel," or fired corn, as ye name it. Our picnic was rumless, wholesome, and amicable, and after it paddling and songs were renewed with vigor. We were not alone upon Whulge. Many lumber vessels were drifting or at anchor under the opposite shore, loaded mainly with fir-trees, soon to be drowned as piles for San Francisco docks. Those were prosperous days in the Pacific. The country which goes to sea through Whulge had recently split away from Oregon, and called itself Washington, after the General of that name. Indian Whulgeamish and Yankee Whulgers were reasonably polite to each other, the Pacific Railroad was to be built straightway, Ormus and

Ind were to become tributary. It was the epoch of hope, but frui-
tion has not yet come. Savages and Yankees have since been scalping each other in the most uncivil way, the P. R. R. creeps slowly
outward, Ormus and Ind are chary of tribute. Dreams of growth
are faster than growth.

The persons of my crew have been described. They all, according to a superstition quite common among Indians, declined to give
their names, or even an alias, as other scamps might do, except
the Duke and Duchess, proud in their foreign appellatives. I will
substitute, therefore, the names of the crew of another canoe in
which I had previously voyaged from Squally to Vancouver's Island,
with Dr. Tolmie, factor of the Hudson's Bay Company at the former
place. These were, 1. Unstu or Hahal, the handsome; 2. Mastu or
La Hache; 3. Khaadza; 4. Snawhaylal; 5. Ay-ay-whun, briefly A-wy;
6. Ai-tu-so; 7. Nuckutzoot; 8. Paicks; and two women, Tlai-whal
and Smoikit-um-whal, "Smoikit" meaning chief. They were of several different tribes, Squallyamish, Skagets, members of the different "amish" that dwell along the Sound, and two, Ai-tu-so and Nuckutzoot, proudly distinguished themselves as Haida, a generic name
applied to nations northward of Whulge. These few type names, not
without melody or drollery, may be interesting to the philo-siwash.
It would be inappropriate to the method of this sketch to go into
detail with regard to Indians of Whulge. But literature has taken
little notice of those distant gentry, and before they retreat into the
dim past, to become subjects of threnody with other lost tribes, let
me chronicle a few surface facts of their life and manners.

It seems a sorry thing, but is really a wise admonition of Nature,
that we should first distinguish in people their faults and deformities. The first observation when one of the Whulgeamish appears
is, "Lo the flat-head!" Among them a tight-strapped cushion con-

trols the elastic skull of childhood, crushing it back idiotic. Now a forehead should not be too round, or a nose too straight, or a cheek too ruddy, or a hand too small. Nature, however, does quite well enough by those she means to be flat-head beauties. Indians do not recognize this, and strive to better Nature. Civilization, beholding the total failure of the skull-crushing system, is warned, and resolves to discard its coxcombries and deformities, and to strive to develop, not to distort, the body and soul.

Are thoughts equally profound to be suggested by other corporeal members of Klalams and their brethren? All are bow-legged. All of a sad-colored, Caravaggio brown,[7] through which salmon-juices exude, and which is varnished with fish-oil. All have coarse black hair, and are beardless. Old people of either sex are hardly to be distinguished, man from woman. The young ladies are not without charms, and blush ingenuously. The fashion of fish-ivory ornaments, hung to the lower lip, has retreated northward, and glass beads and necklaces of hiaqua, a shell like a quill tooth-pick, conchologically known as a species of Dentalium, have replaced the disgusting labial appendages. Hickory shirts and woolen blankets are worn instead of skin raiment, mat aprons, and Indian blankets, woven of the hair of the fleecy dog. In fact, except for paint, these Indians might pass well enough for dirty lazzaroni.[8]

Gigantic clams, cod, and other maritimes, but chiefly salmon, are the food of the Whulgeamish. Ducks and geese visit their shores, and are bagged. No infrequent polecat skulks about their unsavory cabins, and meets the fatal arrow. Grasshoppers and crickets, dried, yield them pies. They cultivate a few potatoes, pluck plentiful berries, and dig sweet kamas bulbs[9] in the swamps. Few things edible are disdained by them.

Once, the same summer, as I voyaged with a crew of the Lummi tribe toward Frazer's River, they discerned a dead seal grotesquely floating on the water. Him they embarked, with roars of laughter, as his unwieldiness slipped through their fingers; and they supped and surfeited unharmed on rancid phoca[10] that evening. But salmon, netted, hooked, trolled, speared, weired, scooped,—salmon taken by various sleight of savage skill,—is the chief diet of Whulge. In the tide-ways toward the Sound's mouth, the Indians anchor two canoes parallel, fifteen feet apart, and stretch a flat net of strips of inner bark between them, sinking it just below the surface. They don a head-gear like a "rat's nest," confected of wool, feathers, furry tails, ribbons, and rags, considered attractive to salmon, and "hyas tamanous," highly magical. Salmon, either wending their unconscious way, or tuft-hunting for the enchantments of the magic cap, come swimming in shoals across the suspended net. Whereupon every fisher, with inconceivable screeches, whoops, and howls, beats the water to bewilder the silver swimmers, and, hauling up the net, clutches them by dozens. Sometimes fleets of canoes go a trolling, one fisherman in each slight shallop. He fastens his line to his paddle, and as he paddles trolls, A pretty sight to behold is a rocky bay of Whulge, gay with a fleet of these agile dug-outs, and ever and anon illumined with a gleam when a salmon takes the bait. In the voyage I have mentioned with Dr. Tolmie, a squadron of such trollers near the Indian village of Kowitchin crowded about us, praying to be vaccinated, and paying a salmon for the privilege. Small-pox is the fatalest foe of the Indian.

Spearmen also for food are the siwashes. In muddy streams, where Boston eyes would detect nothing, Indian sees a ripple, and divines a fish. He darts his long wooden spear, and out it ricochets, with a banner of salmon at its point. But salmon may escape the coquettish charms of the trolling-hook, may safely run the gauntlet of the parallel canoes and their howling, tamanous-cap wearers;[11] the spear, misguided in the drumly[12] gleam, may glance harmless from scale-armed shoulders: still other perils await them. These aristos[13] of the waters need change of scene. Blubberly fish may dwell through a life-long pickle in the briny deep, and grow rancid there like olives too salt, but the delicate salmon must have his bubbles from the brunnen.[14] Besides, his youthful family, the Parrs,[15] must be cradled on the ripples of a running stream, and in innocent nooks of freshness must establish their vigor and consistency; before they brave the risks of cosmopolitan ocean life. For such reasons gentleman salmon seeks the rivers, and Indian, expecting him there, builds a palisade of poles athwart the stream. The traveller, thus obstructed, whisks his tail, and coasts along, seeking a passage. He finds one, and dashes through, but is stopped by a shield of wicker-work, and, turning blindly, plunges into a fish-pot, set to take him as he whirls to retreat, bewildered.

At the magnificent Cascades of the Columbia, the second-best water bit on our continent, there is more exciting salmon-fishing in the splendid turmoil of the rapids. Over the shoots, between boulders and rifts of rock, the Indians rig a scaffolding, and sweep down stream with a scoop-net. Salmon, working their way up in high exhilaration, are taken twenty an hour, by every scooper. He lifts them out, brilliantly sheeny, and, giving them, with a blow from a billet of wood, a hint to be peaceable, hands over each thirty-pounder to a fusty *attache*, who, in turn, lugs them away to the squaws to be cleaned and dried.

Thus in Whulge and at the Cascades the salmon is taken. And now behold him caught, and lying dewy in silver death, bright as an unalloyed dollar, varnished with opaline iridescence. "How shall he be cooked?" asks squaw of sachem. "Boil him, entoia, my beloved" (Haida tongue), "in a mighty pot of iron, plumping in store of wapatoo, which pasaiooks, the pale-faces, name potatoes. Or, my cloocheman, my squaw, roast of his thicker parts sundry chunks on a spit. Or, best of all, split and broil him on an upright framework, a perpendicular gridiron of aromatic twigs. Thus by highest simple art, before the ruddy blaze, with breezes circumambient and wafting away any mephitic kitcheny exhalations, he will toast deliciously, and I will feast thereupon, O my cloocheman, whilst thou, O working partner of our house, art preparing these brother fish to be dried into amber transparency, or smoked in a lachrymose cabin, that we may sustain ourselves through dry-fish Lent, after this fresh-fish Carnival is over." Such discussions occur not seldom in the drama of Indian life.

In the Bucentaur, after our lunch on kippered cod and biscuits, we had not tarried. Generally in that region, in breezeless days of August, smoke from burning forests falls, and envelops all the world of land and water. In such strange chaos, voyaging without a compass is impossible. Canoes are often detained for days, waiting for the smoke to lift. To-day, fortunately for my progress, there was a fresh breeze from China-way. Only a soft golden haze hung among the pines, and toned the swarthy coloring of the rocky shores.

All now in good humor, and Col. Colt in retirement, we swept along through narrow straits, between piney islands, and by sheltered bays where fleets might lie hidden. With harmonious muscular throes, in time with Indian songs, the three stoutly paddled. The Duke generally sogered, or dipped his blade with sham vehemence, as he saw me observing him. Olyman steered steadily, a Palinurus skilful and sleepless.[16] Jenny Lind, excusable idler, did not belie her musical name. She was our prima donna, and leader of the chorus. Often she uttered careless bursts of song, like sudden slants of rays through cloudiness, and often droned some drowsy lay, to which the crew responded with disjointed, lurching refrain. Few of these airs were musical according to civilized standards. Some had touches of wild sentiment or power, but most were grotesque combinations of guttural howls. In all, however, there were tones and strains of irregular originality, surging up through monotony, or gleams of savage ire suddenly flashing forth, and recalling how one has seen, with shudders, a shark, with white sierras of teeth, gnash upon him not far distant, from a bath in a tropic bay. I found a singular consolation in the unleavened music of my crew. Why should there not be throbs of rude power in aboriginal song? It is well to review the rudiments sometimes, and see whether we have done all we might in building systems from the primal hints.

The songs of Chin Lin, Duchess of York, chorused by the fishy, seemed a consoling peace-offering. The undertone of sorrow in all music cheats us of grief for our own distress. To counteract the miseries of civilization, we must have the tender, passionate despairs of Favorita and Traviata;[17] for the disgusts of barbarism I found Indian howls sufficient relief.

By and by, with sunset, paddle-songs died away, and the Bucentaur slowed. The tide had turned, and was urgently against us. My tired crew were oddly dropping off to sleep. We landed on the shingle for repose and supper. Twilight was already spreading downward from the zenith, and pouring gloom among the sombre pines. Grotesque masses of blanched drift-wood strewed the shore and grouped themselves about,—strange semblances of monstrous shapes, like amorphous idols, dethroned and waiting to perish by the iconoclastic test of fire. Poor Prometheus may have been badly punished by that cruel fowl of Caucasus, but we mortals got the

unquenchable spark.[18] I carried a modicum of compact flame in a
match-box, and soon had a funeral pyre of those heathenish stumps
and roots well ablaze,—a glory of light between the solemn wall of
the forest and the dark glimmering flood.

On the romantic shores of Whulge, illumined by my fire, I had
toasted salt pork for supper, while the siwashes banqueted to repletion on dried fish and the unaccustomed luxury of hardtack, and
were genially happy. But when, with kindly mind, I, their chieftain, brewed them a princely pot of tea, and tossed in sugar lavishly, sprinkling also unperceivedly the beverage with forty drops
from the captured lumoti, and gave them tobacco enough to blow
a cloud, then happiness capped itself with gayety and merriment.
They heaped the pyre with fuel, and made it the chief jester of their
jolly circle, chuckling when it crackled, and roaring with laughter
when the frantic tongues of flame leaped up, and shot a glare, almost
fiendish, over the wild scene.

I sat apart with my dhudeen,[19] studying the occasion for its lesson.
"Would I be an Indian,—a duke of the Klalams?" I asked myself. "As
much as I am to-night,—no more, and no longer. To-night I am a
demi-savage, jolly for my rest and my supper, and content because
my hampers hold enough for to-morrow. I can identify myself thoroughly, and delight that I can, with the untamed natures of my comrades. I can yield myself to the dominion of the same impulses that
sway them out of impassiveness into frantic excitement. They sit
here over the fire, now jabbering lustily, and now silent and drifting along currents of association, undiverted by discursive thought,
until some pervading fancy strikes them all at once, and again all
is animation and guttural sputter of sympathy. I can also let myself
go bobbing down the tide of thoughtless thought, until I am caught
by the same shoals, or checked by the same reef, or launched upon

the same tumultuous seas, as they. These influences are primeval, aboriginal, fresh, enlivening for their anti-cockney savor. Wretchedly slab-sided, and not at all fitting among the many-sided, is he who cannot adapt himself to the dreams and hopes, the awes and pleasures of savage life, and be as good a savage as the brassiest Brass-skin.

"However, it is not amiss," continued my soliloquy, puffing itself away with the last whiffs of my pipe, "to have the large results of the world's secular toil *in posse.*[20] It is sometimes pleasant to lay aside the resumable ermine.[21] It is easy to linger while one has a hand upon the locomotive's valve. I will, on the whole, remain an American of the nineteenth century, and not subside into a Klalam brave. Every sincere man has, or ought to have, his differences or his quarrels with *status quo,*—otherwise what becomes of the millennium? My personal grudge with the present has not yet brought me to the point of rupture and reaction."

Had I uttered these reflections in a prosy lecture, my fishy suite could not have been sounder asleep than they now were. They had coiled themselves about the fire, in genuine slumber, after labor and overfeeding. Without dread of treachery, I bivouacked near them. I was more placable and less watchful than I should have been had I known that the Kahtai Klalams, under the superintendence of King George and the Duke, were in the habit of murdering. They sacrificed a couple of pale-faced victims within the year, as I afterwards was informed. However, the lamb lay down with the wolf, and suffered no harm. From time to time I awoke, and rolled another log upon the pyre, and then returned to my uneasy naps on the pebbles,—uneasy, not because the pebbles dimpled me somewhat harshly through my blankets, not because the inextinguishable stars winked at me fantastically through ether, nor because my scalp occasionally gave premonitions of departure; but because I did not wish, when offered the boon of a favorable tide, to be asleep at my post and miss it.

A new flood-tide was about to be sent whirling up into the bays and coves and nooks of Whulge when I shook up my sobered hero of the libelous teapots, shook up Olyman and his young men, and touched the Duchess lightly on the shoulder, as she lay with her red-chevroned visage turned toward the zenith. The Duke alone grumbled, and shirked the toil of launching the Bucentaur. We others went at it heartily, dragging our vessel down the shingle to the chorus of a guttural *De Profundis*.[22] It was an hour before dawn. We reloaded, and shoved off into the chill, star-lighted void,—a void where one might doubt whether the upper stars or the nether stars were the real orbs. Our red fire watched us as we sailed away, glaring after us like a Cyclops sentinel[23] until we rounded a point and passed out of his range, only to find ourselves sadly gazed at by a pale, lean moon just lifting above the pines. With the flames of dawn a wind arose and lent us wings. I succeeded in inspiring my crew with a stolid intention to speed me. A comradery grew up between me and the truculent blackguard who wielded the bow paddle, so that he essayed unintelligent civilities from time to time, and when we landed to breakfast, at a point where a giant arbor-vitae stood a rich pyramid of green, he brought me sallal-berries, and arbutus-leaves[24] to dry for smoking; meaning perhaps to play Caliban to my Stephano,[25] and worshipping him who bore the lumoti. The Duke remained either "hyas kla hye am," in the wretched dumps, or "hyas silex," in the deep sulks, as must happen after an orgie, even to a princely personage. I could get nothing from him, either in philology or legend,—nothing but the Klalam name of Whulge, K'uk'lults. However, thanks to a strong following wind and a blan-

ket-sail, we sped on, never flinching from the tide when it turned
and battled us.

We had rounded a point, and opened Puyallop Bay, a breadth
of sheltered calmness, when I, lifting sleepy eyelids for a dreamy
stare about, was suddenly aware of a vast white shadow in the water.
What cloud, piled massive on the horizon, could cast an image so
sharp in outline, so full of vigorous detail of surface? No cloud, as
my stare, no longer dreamy, presently discovered,—no cloud, but
a cloud compeller.[26] It was a giant mountain dome of snow, swelling and seeming to fill the aerial spheres as its image displaced the
blue deeps of tranquil water. The smoky haze of an Oregon August
hid all the length of its lesser ridges, and left this mighty summit
based upon uplifting dimness. Only its splendid snows were visible,
high in the unearthly regions of clear blue noonday sky. The shore
line drew a cincture of pines across the broad base, where it faded
unreal into the mist. The same dark girth separated the peak from
its reflection, over which my canoe was now pressing, and sending
wavering swells to shatter the beautiful vision before it.

Kingly and alone stood this majesty, without any visible comrade
or consort, though far to the north and the south its brethren and
sisters dominated their realms, each in isolated sovereignty, rising
above the pine-darkened sierra of the Cascade Mountains,—above
the stern chasm where the Columbia, Achilles of rivers, sweeps,
short-lived and jubilant, to the sea,—above the lovely vales of the
Willamette and Umpqua. Of all the peaks from California to Frazer's River, this one before me was royalest. Mount Regnier Christians have dubbed it, in stupid nomenclature perpetuating the name
of somebody or nobody.[27] More melodiously the siwashes call it
Tacoma,—a generic term also applied to all snow peaks. Whatever
keen crests and crags there may be in its rock anatomy of basalt,

snow covers softly with its bends and sweeping curves. Tacoma, under its ermine, is a crushed volcanic dome, or an ancient volcano fallen in, and perhaps as yet not wholly lifeless. The domes of snow are stateliest. There may be more of feminine beauty in the cones, and more of masculine force and hardihood in the rough pyramids, but the great domes are calmer and more divine, and, even if they have failed to attain absolute dignified grace of finish, and are riven and broken down, they still demand our sympathy for giant power, if only partially victor. Each form—the dome, the cone, and the pyramid—has its type among the great snow peaks of the Cascades.

And now let the Duke of York drowse, the Duchess cease awhile longer her choking chant, and the rest nap it on their paddles, floating on the image of Tacoma, while I ask recognition for the almost unknown glories of the Cascade Mountains of Oregon. We are poorly off for such objects east of the Mississippi. There are some roughish excrescences known as the Alleghanies. There is a knobby group of brownish White Mountains. Best of all, high in Down-East is the lonely Katahdin. Hillocks these,—never among them one single summit brilliant forever with snow, golden in sunshine, silver when sunshine has gone; not one to bloom rosy at dawn, and to be a vision of refreshment all the sultry summer long; not one to be lustrous white over leagues of woodland, sombre or tender; not one to repeat the azure of heaven among its shadowy dells. Exaltation such as the presence of the sublime and solemn heights arouses, we dwellers eastward cannot have as an abiding influence. Other things we may have, for Nature will not let herself anywhere be scorned; but only mountains, and chiefest the giants of snow, can teach whatever lessons there may be in vaster distances and deeper depths of palpable ether, in lonely grandeur without desolation, and in the illimitable, bounded within an outline. Therefore, needing all these emotions at their maximum, we were compelled to make pilgrimages back to the mountains of the Old World,—commodiously as may be when we consider sea-sickness, passports, Murray's red-covers, and h-less Britons everywhere.[28] Yes, back to the Old World we went, and patronized the Alps, and nobly satisfying we found them. But we were forced to inspect also the heritage of human institutions, and such a mankind as they had made after centuries of opportunity,—and very sadly depressing we found the work, so that, notwithstanding many romantic joys and artistic pleasures, we came back malcontent. Let us, therefore, develop our own world. It has taken us two centuries to discover our proper West across the Mississippi, and to know by indefinite hearsay that among the groups of the Rockys are heights worth notice.

Farthest away in the west, as near the western sea as mountains can stand, are the Cascades. Sailors can descry their landmark summits firmer than cloud, a hundred miles away. Kulshan, misnamed Mount Baker by the vulgar, is their northernmost buttress up at 49° and Frazer's River. Kulshan is an irregular, massive, mound-shaped peak, worthy to stand a white emblem of perpetual peace between us and our brother Britons. The northern regions of Whulge and Vancouver's Island have Kulshan upon their horizon. They saw it blaze the winter before this journey of mine; for there is fire beneath the Cascades, red war suppressed where the peaks, symbols of truce, stand in resplendent quiet. Kulshan is best seen, as I saw it one afternoon of that same August, from an upland of Vancouver's Island, across the golden waves of a wheat-field, across the glimmering waters of the Georgian Sound, and far above its belt of misty gray pine-ridges. The snow-line here is at five thousand feet, and Kulshan has as much height in snow as in forest and vegetation. Its name I got from the Lummi tribe at its base, after I had dipped in

their pot at a boiled-salmon feast. As to Baker, that name should
be forgotten. Mountains should not be insulted by being named
after undistinguished bipeds, nor by the prefix of *Mt.* Mt. Chim-
borazo, or Mt. Dhawalaghiri, seems as feeble as Mr. Julius Caesar,
or Signor Dante.

South of Kulshan, the range continues dark, rough, and somewhat unmeaning to the eye, until it is relieved by Tacoma, *vulgo*
Regnier. Upon this Tacoma's image I was now drifting, and was
about to make nearer acquaintance with its substance. One cannot know too much of a nature's nobleman. Tacoma the second,
which Yankees call Mt. Adams, is a clumsier repetition of its greater
brother, but noble enough to be the pride of a continent. Dearest
charmer of all is St. Helen's, queen of the Cascades, queen of Northern America, a fair and graceful volcanic cone. Exquisite mantling
snows sweep along her shoulders toward the bristling pines. Sometimes she showers her realms with a boon of light ashes, to notify
them that her peace is repose, not stupor, and sometimes lifts a
beacon of tremulous flame by night from her summit. Not far from
her base the Columbia crashes through the mountains in a magnificent chasm, and Mt. Hood, the vigorous prince of the range rises
in a keen pyramid fourteen or sixteen thousand feet high, rivalling
his sister in glory.[29] Mt. Jefferson and others southward are worthy snow peaks, but not comparable with these; and then this mas-
terly family of mountains dwindles ruggedly away toward California and the Shasta group.

The Cascades are known to geography,—their summits to the
lists of volcanoes. Several gentlemen in the United States Army,
bored in petty posts, or squinting along Indian trails for Pacific
railroads, have seen these monuments. A few myriads of Orego-

nians have not been able to avoid seeing them, have perhaps felt their ennobling influence, and have written, boasting that St. Helen's or Hood is as high as Blanc. Enterprising fellows have climbed both. But the millions of Yankees—from codfish to alligators, chewers of spruce-gum or chewers of pig-tail, cooks of chowder or cooks of gumbo—know little of these treasures of theirs. Poet comes long after pioneer. Mountains have been waiting, even in ancient worlds, for cycles, while mankind looked upon them as high, cold, dreary, crushing, as resorts for demons and homes of desolating storms. It is only lately, in the development of men's comprehension of nature, that mountains have been recognized as our noblest friends, our most exalting and inspiring comrades, our grandest emblems of divine power and divine peace.

More of these majesties of the Cascades hereafter; but now meseems that I have long enough interrupted the desultory progress of my narrative. We have floated long enough, my Klalam braves, on the white reflection of Tacoma. To thy paddle, then, sluggard Duke. Dip and plough into Whulge, ye salmon-fed. Squally and blankets be the war-cry of our voyage.

But first obey the injunction of an Indian ditty, oddly sung to the air of Malbrook:—

> *Klatawah ocook polikely,*
> *Klatawah Steilacoom;*

"Go to-night,—go to Steilacoom." Steilacoom was a military post a mile inland from Whulge. It had a port on the Sound, consisting of one warehouse, where every requisite of pioneer life was to be had. Thither I directed my course, pork and hardtack to buy, compact prog[30] for my mountain journey. Also, because I could not ride the leagues of a transcontinental trip, barebacking the bonyness of prairie nags, a friend had given me an order for a capital saddle of his, stored there. The crafty trader at Port Steilacoom denied the existence of my friend's California saddle, a grandly roomy one I had often bestrode, and substituted for it an incoherent dragoon saddle. He hoped, the scamp, that my friend would never return to claim his property, and he would be left residuary legatee.

Some strange Indians lounging here gave me a helpful fact. The Klickatats, so the Sound Indians name generally the Yakimahs and other ultramontane tribes, had just arrived at Nisqually, on their annual trading-trip. Horses and a guide I could surely get from them for crossing the Cascades into their country. Here I heard first the mighty name of Owhhigh, a chief of the Klickatats, their noblest horse-thief, their Diomed.[31] He was at Nisqually, with his tail on,—his tail of bare-legged highlanders,—buying blankets and sundries, with skins, furs, and stolen steeds.

Squally, euphonized to Nisqually, is six or seven miles from Steilacoom. We sped along near the shore, just away from the dense droop of the water-wooing arbor-vitae pyramids.[32]

"How now, my crew? Why this sudden check? Why this agitated panic? What, Dookeryawk! Are ye paralyzed by Tamanous, by demoniacal influence?"

"By fear are we paralyzed, O kind protector," responded the Klalam. Foes to us always are the Squallyamish. But more cruel foes are the mountain horsemen. We dare not advance. Conoway quash nesika; cowards all are we."

"Fear naught, my cowards. The retinue of my high mightiness is safe, and shall be honored. Ye shall not be maltreated, nor even punished by me for your misdeeds. Have a mighty heart in your breasts, and onward."

Panic over, we paddled lustily, and soon landed at a high bluff,—the port of Nisqually. We hauled up the Bucentaur, grateful to the talisman shells along its gunwale, that they had guarded us against Bugaboo. I looked my last, for that time, upon the sturdy tides of Whulge, and led the way under the oaks toward the Fort.

4. Owhhigh

It was harsh penance to a bootless man to tramp the natural Macadam[1] of minced trap-rock on the plateau above the Sound. The little pebbles of the adust[2] volcanic pavement cut my moccasined feet like unboiled peas of pilgrimage. I marched along under the oaks as stately as frequent limping permitted. My motley retinue followed me humbly, bearing "ikta,"[3] my traps, and their own plunder. Their demeanor was crushed and cringing, greatly changed since the truculent scene over the captured lumoti, which I still kept as a trophy, hung at my waist to balance my pistol.

After a walk of a mile, with my body-guard of shabby S'Klalam aristocrats, I entered the Hudson's Bay Company's fort of Nisqually. Disrepute draggled after me, but my character was already established in a previous visit. I had left Dr. Tolmie, the factor, at Vancouver's Island; Mr. H., his substitute, received me hospitably at the postern.[4] Nisqually is a palisaded enclosure, two hundred feet square. Bartizan towers protect its corners. Within are blockhouses for goods and furs, and one-story cottages for residence.[5]

Indian leaguers have of yore beset this fort. Indians have lifted Indians up toward the fifteenth and topmost foot of the fir palisades. Shots from the loopholes of the bartizans dropped the assailants, and left them lying on the natural Macadam without. Whereupon the survivors retired, and consulted about fire; but that fatal foe was also defeated by the death of every incendiary as he approached.

To visit such a place is to recall and illustrate all our early New-England history. Our forefathers fled, in King Philip's[6] time, to just such refuges. Personal contact with a similar state of facts makes their forgotten perils real. In that recent antiquity, pioneers exposed to the indiscriminate revenge of the savage flew from cabin and clearing to stockades far less defensible than this. Better its insecure shelter for wife and child than the terror of a forest forever seeming aglare with cruel eyes,—where the forester could never banish the curdling consciousness of an unseen presence, watching until the assassin moment came; where the silence might hear other sounds than the hum of insects or the music of birds,—might hear the scoffing yell of Indians, contemptuous victors over the race that scorned them. What wonder that the agonies of such suspense stirred up the settlers to cowardly slaughter of every savage, friend or foe? A frightened man becomes a barbarian and a brute. Fear is a miserable agent of civilization. We can hardly now connect ourselves with that period. No longer, when twigs crackle in the forest, do we shrink lest the parting leaves may reveal a new-comer, with whom we must race for life. Larceny is disgusting, burglary is unpleasant, arson is undesirable, murder is one of the foul arts; Indians were adepts in all of these trades at once. Any reminiscence of a condi-

tion from which we have happily escaped is agreeable. This palisade fort was a monument of a past age to me. It made me two hundred years old at once.

A monument, but not a cenotaph; on the contrary, it was full of
bustling life. Rusty Indians, in all degrees of frowziness of person
and costume, were trading at the shop for the three *b*'s of Indian
desire,—blankets, beads, and 'baccy,—representatives of need,
vanity, and luxury. The Klickatats had indeed arrived. To-morrow
Owhhigh[7] and the grandees were to come in from their camp to buy
and sell. All the squaws purchasing to-day were hags beyond the
age of coquetry in costume, yet they were buying beads and hanging them in hideous contrast about their baggy, wrinkled necks, and
then glowering for admiration with dusky eyes. These were valued
customers, since they knew the tariff, and never haggled, but paid
cash or its equivalent, otter, beaver, and skunk skins, and similar
treasures. The pretty girls would come afterward, as money failed,
and try to make their winsome smiles a substitute for funds.

In contrast to these unpleasant objects, a very handsome and gentlemanly young brave entered just after me, and came forward as
I was greeting Mr. H. He was tall and loungingly graceful, and so
fair that there must have been silver in the copper of his blood. This
rather supercilious personage was, he told me, of Owhhigh's band,
not by nation but by adoption. He was a Spokan from the Upper
Columbia, a volunteer among the Klickatats, perhaps because their
method of filibusterism was attractive, perhaps because there was a
vendetta for him at home. He wore a semi-civilized costume,—coat
of black from some far-away slop-shop of Britain, fringed leggins
of buckskin from the lodge of a Klickatat tailoress. A broad-beaded
band crossed his breast, like the ribbon of an order of nobility. The
incongruity in his costume was redeemed by his cool, dignified

bearing. He was an Adonis of Nature, not a rubicund Adonis of the D'Orsay type.[8] While we talked, he kept a cavalier's advantage, not dismounting from his fiery little saddleless black.

Him, by Mr. H.'s advice, I prayed to be my ambassador to the great Owhhigh. Would that dignitary permit me an interview to-morrow, and purvey me horses and a guide for my dash through his realm? My Spokan Adonis, with the self-possessed courtesy of a high-bred Indian, accepted the office of negotiator, and ventured to promise that Owhhigh would speed me. But in case Adonis should prove faithless, or Owhhigh indifferent, Mr. H. despatched a messenger at once for one of the Company's voyageurs, now a quiet colonist, who could resume the rover, and guide me, if other guidance failed, anywhere in the Northwest.

I now conducted the Duke and my party to the shop, and served out to them one two-and-a-half-point blanket apiece, and one to Olyman for the Bucentaur, accompanying the boon with a lecture on the evils of intemperance and the duty of faithfulness. They seemed quite pleased now that they had not butchered and scalped me, and expressed the friendliest sentiments, perhaps with a view to a liberal "potlatch" of trinkets. They also besought permission to encamp in the fort, lest pillage should befall them. It was growing dark, and the different parties of Indians admitted within the palisades were grouped, gypsy-like, about their cooking-fires. Some of these unbrotherly siwashes cast wolf's-eyes upon my Klalams, now an enviable and plunderable squad. These latter, wealthy and well-blanketed, skulked away into a corner, and when I saw them last, by their fire-light, the Duke, more like a degraded ecclesiastic than ever, was haranguing his family, while Jenny Lind sat at his feet, and bent upon him untruthful eyes. At morn they were not to be seen; the ducal pair, Olyman and the fishy, all had vanished. A few unconsidered trifles, such as a gun, a blanket, and a basket of kamasroots, property of the unbrotherly, had vanished with them. Unconsidered trifles will stumble against the shins of Indians, stealing away at night.

As these representatives of Klalam civilization now make final exit from my narrative, I must give them a proper "teapot." They may be taken as types of the worse character of the coast Indians,— jolly brutes, with the bad and the good traits of savages, and much harmed by the besettings of civilized temptations.

I cannot omit from the Duke of York's teapot facts within my own observation,—that he was drunken, idle, insolent, and treacherous,—nor the hearsay fact that he has since been beguiled into murders;[9] but I must notice also his apologies of race, circumstance, the bad influence of Pikes by land and profane tars by sea, and governmental neglect, a logical result of slavery.

Mr. H. had had great success in converting the brown dust of a dry swamp without the fort into a garden of succulent vegetables. As we were inspecting the cabbages and onions next morning, we heard a resonance of hoofs over the trap pavement. A noise of galloping sounded among the oaks. Presently a wild dash of Indian cavaliers burst into sight. Their equipment might not have borne inspection: few things will, here below, except such as rose-leaves and the cheeks of a high-bred child. Prejudice might have called their steeds scrubby mustangs; prejudice might have used the word *tag-rag* as descriptive of the fly-away effect of a troop all a-flutter with ribbons, fur-tails, deerskin fringes, trailing lariats, and whirling whip-thongs. It was a very irregular and somewhat ragamuffin brigade. But the best hussars[10] of the Christendom that sustains itself by means of hussars are tawdry and clumsy to a critical eye, and certainly not so picturesque as these Klickatats, stampeding toward us from under the gray mossy oaks.

They came, deployed in the open woods, now hidden in a hollow, now rising a crest, all at full gallop, loud over the baked soil,— a fantastic cavalcade. They swept about the angle of the fort, and we, following, found them grouped near the open postern, waiting for permission to enter. Some were dismounted; some were dashing up and down on their shaggy nags,—a band of picturesque marauders on a peaceful foray.

Owhhigh and his aides-de-camp stood a little apart, Spokan Adonis among them. At a sign from Mr. H., they followed us within the fort, and entered the factor's cottage. Much ceremony is observed by the Hudson's Bay Company with the Indians. Discipline must be preserved. Dignity tells. Indians, having it, appreciate it. Owhhigh alone was given a seat opposite us. His counselors stood around him, while three or four less potent members of his suite peered gravely over their shoulders. The palaver began.

Owhhigh's braves were gorgeous with frippery, and each wore a beaded order. The Murats[11] of the world make splendid fighting-cocks of themselves with martial feathers; the Napoleons wear gray surtouts. Owhhigh was in stern simplicity of Indian garb. On ordinary occasions of council with whites, he would courteously or ambitiously have adopted their costume; now, as he was master of the situation and grantee of favors, he appeared in his own proper style. He wore a handsome buckskin shirt, heavily epauletted and trimmed along the seams with fringe, and leggins and moccasins of the same. For want of Tyrian dye,[12] these robes were regalized by a daubing of red clay. A circlet of otter fur served him for coronet. He was a man of bulk and stature, a chieftainly personage, a fine old Roman, cast in bronze, and modernized with a fresh glaz-

ing of vermilion over his antiquated duskiness of hue. And certainly
no Roman senator, with adjuncts of whity-brown toga, curule chair,
and patrician ancestry, seated to wait his doom from the Gauls, ever
had an air of more impassive dignity than this head horse-thief of
the Klickatats.

In an interview with a royal personage, his own language should
be used. But we, children of an embryo civilization, are trained in
the inutilities of tongues dead as Julius Caesar, never in the living
idioms of our native princes. I was not, therefore, voluble in Klickatat and Yakimah. Chinook jargon, however, the French of Northwestern diplomatic life, I had mastered. Owhhigh called upon one
of his "young men" to interpret his speeches into Chinook. The
interpreter stepped forward, and stood expectant,—a youth fraternally like my Spokan Adonis, but with a sprinkle more of intelli-
gence, and a sparkle less of beauty.

My suit, already known, was now formally stated to the chief. I
wanted to buy three quadrupeds, and hire one biped guide for a trip
across the Cascade Mountains, and on to the Dalles of the Columbia. The distance was about two hundred miles, and I had seven
days to effect it. Could it be done?

"Yes," replied Owhhigh; and then—his bronze face remaining
perfectly calm and Rhadamanthine[13]—he began, with most expressive pantomime, an oration, describing my route across the mountains. His talk went on in swaying monotone, rising and falling with
the subject, while with vigorous gesture he pictured the changeful journey. The interpreter saw that I comprehended, and did not
interfere. Occasionally, when I was posed, I turned to him, and he
aided me with some Chinook word, or a sputtered phrase of concentrated meaning. Meanwhile the circle of councillors murmured
approval, and grunted coincidence of opinion.

My way was to lead, so said the emphatic recital of Owhhigh, first through an open forest, sprinkled with lakes, and opening into great prairies. By and by the denser forest of firs would meet me, and giant columnar stems, parting, leave a narrow vista, where I could penetrate into the gloom. The dash of a rapid, shallow, white river, the Puyallop, where was a salmon-fishery, would cross my trail. Then I must climb through mightier woods and thicker thickets, where great bulks of fallen trees lay, and barricaded the path; must follow up a turbulent river, the S'Kamish,[14] crossing it often, at fords where my horses could hardly bear up against the current. Ever and anon, like a glimpse of blue through a storm, this rough way would be enlivened by a prairie, with beds of fern for my repose, and long grass for my tiring beasts,—grass long as macaroni, so he measured it with outstretched hands. Now the difficulties were to come. He depicted the craggy side of a great mountain,—horses scrambling up stoutly, riders grasping the mane and balancing carefully lest a misstep should send horse and man over a precipice. The summit gained, here again were luxurious tarrying-places, and oases of prairie, and perhaps, in some sheltered nook, a bank of last winter's snow. Here there must be a long nooning, that the horses, tied up the night before in the forest, and browsing wearily on bitter twigs, might recruit. Then came the steep descent, and so, pressing on, I should arrive for my third night's camp at a prairie, low down on the eastern slope of the mountains, where a mighty hunter, the late Sowee,[15] once dwelt. Up before dawn next morning,—continued Owhhigh's vivid tale, vivid in gesture, and droning ever in delivery,—up at the peep of day, for this was a long march and a harsh one, and striking soon a clear river flowing east, the Nachchese,[16] I was to follow it. The river grew, and went tearing down a terrible gorge; through this my path led, sometimes in the bed of the stream,

sometimes, when precipices drew too close and the gulf too profound, I must climb, and trace a perilous course along the brink far
above, where I might bend over and see the water roaring a thousand feet below. At last the valley would broaden, and groves of pine
appear. Then my horses, if not too wayworn, could gallop over the
immense swells of a rolling prairie-land. Here I would encounter
some of the people of Owhhigh. A sharp turn to the right would
lead me across a mass of wild, bare hills, into the valley of another
stream, the Atinam, where was a mission and men in long robes who
prayed at a shrine.[17] By this time my horses would be exhausted; I
should take fresh ones, if possible, from the priests' band, and riding hard across a varied region of hill, prairie, and bulky mountains
thick with pines, and then long levels where Skloo a brother-chief-
tain ranged, I would arrive, after two days from the mission, at a
rugged space of hills, and, climbing there, find myself overlooking
the vast valley of the Columbia. Barracks and tents in sight. Scamper down the mountain. Fire a gun at river's bank. Indians hear,
cross in canoe, ferry me and swim my horses. All safely done in six
crowded days. So said Owhhigh.

This description was given with wonderful vivacity and verity.
Owhhigh as a pantomimist would have commanded brilliant success on any stage. Would that there were more like him in this wordy
world.

He promised also a guide, his son, now at the camp, and as to my
horses, I might choose from the cavalcade. We went out to make
selection,—all the Klickatats, except Owhhigh, Adonis, and the
interpreter, following in bow-legged silence. These three were vocal,
and of better model than their fellows. No Indian wished to sell
his best horse; each his second-best, at the price of the best. Their
backs were in shocking condition. Pads and pack-saddles had galled

them so that it was painful to a humane being to mount; but I felt that any one of them, however maltreated, would better in my service. I should ride him hard, but care for him tenderly. Indians have too much respect for "pasaiooks," blanketeers, Caucasians, to endeavor to cajole us. They suppose that, in a horse-trade, we know what we want. No jockeying was attempted; there were the nags, I might prove them, and buy or not, without solicitation.

The hard terrace without the fort served us for race-course. We galloped the wiry nags up and down, while the owners waited in an emotionless group, calm as gamblers. Should anyone sell a horse, he would not only pocket the price, but be spurred to new thefts from tribes hostile or friendly to fill the vacancy; yet all were too proud to exhibit eagerness, or puff their property.

At last, from the least bad I chose first for my pack animal a strawberry roan cob, a "chunk of a horse," a quadruped with the legs of an elephant, the head of a hippopotamus, and a peculiar gait;— he trod most emphatically, as if he were striving to go through the world's crust at every step. This habit suggested the name he at once received. I called him Antipodes,[18] in honor of the region he was aiming at,—a name of ill omen, suggesting a spot where I often wished him afterwards. My second choice, the mount for my guide, was Antipodes repeated, with slight improvements of form and manner. Gubbins[19] I dubbed him, appropriately, with a first accolade,— accolade often repeated, during our acquaintance, with less mildness. Hard horses were Antipodes and Gubbins,—hard trotters, hard-mouthed, hardhided brutes. Each was delivered to me with a hair rope twisted for bridle about his lower lip, sawing it raw.

And now the most important decision remained to be made. It was nothing to me that a misty phantom, my guide, should be jolted over the passes of Tacoma on a Gubbins or an Antipodes, but my own seat, should it be upon Rosinante or Bucephalus,[20] upon an agile caracoler or a lubberly plodder? Step forward, then, cool and careless Klickatat, from thy lair of dirty blanket, with that black pony of thine. The black was satisfactory. His ribs, indeed, were far too visible, and there were concavities where there should have been the convex fullness of well-conditioned muscle, but he had a plucky, wiry look, and his eye showed spirit without spite. His lope was as elastic as the bounding of a wind-sped cloud over a rough mountain-side. His other paces were neat and vigorous. I bought him at more dollars than either of his comrades of clumsier shape and duller hue. Indians do not love their horses well enough to name them. My new purchase I baptized Klale. Klale in Chinook jargon is Black,—and thus do mankind, putting commonplace into foreign tongues or into big words of their own, fancy that they make it uncommonplace and original.

There are several requisites for travel. First, a world and a region of world to traverse; second, a traveller; third, means of convey-ance, legs human or other, barks, carts, enchanted carpets, and the like; fourth, guidance by man personal, or man impersonal acting by roads, guide-boards, maps, and itineraries; fifth, multifarious wherewithals. The first two requisites seem to be indispensable in the human notion of travel, and existed in my case. The third I had provided; my stud was complete. A guide was promised; after an interview with Owhhigh I could give credence to his unseen son, and believe that the fourth requisite of my journey was also ready. I must now arrange my miscellaneous outfit. For this purpose the resources of Fort Nisqually were infinite. Mr. H. approached the dusty warehouses; he wielded the wand of an enchanter, and forth from dim corners came a pack-saddle for Antipodes, a pad-sad-dle for Gubbins, and great hide packs for my traps. Forth from the shelves of the shop came paraphernalia,—tin pot, tin pan, tin cups, and the needful luxuries of tea and sugar. My pork and hardtack had been already provided at Steilacoom, and Mr. H. added to them what I deemed half a dozen gnarled lignum-vitae roots.[21] Experimental whittling proved these to be cured ox-tongues, a precious accession. My list was complete.

I was lodged in a small cabin adjoining the factor's cottage. All my sundries had been piled here for packing, and I was standing, somewhat mazed, in the centre of a group of tin pots, gnarled tongues, powder-horns, papers of tea, blankets, bread-bags, bridles, spurs, and toggery,[22] when in walked Owhhigh, followed by several of his suite.

Owhhigh seated himself on the floor, with an air of condescension, and for some time regarded my preparations in grave silence. Mr. H. had told me that his parade of an interpreter during the council was only to make an impression. Some men regard an assumption of ignorance as lofty. Now, however, Owhhigh, dropping in unceremoniously, laid aside his sham dignity with a purpose. We had before agreed upon the terms of payment for my guide. The ancient horse-thief sat like a Pacha[23], smoking an inglorious dhudeen, and at last, glancing at certain articles of raiment of mine, thus familiarly, in Chinook, broke silence.

Owhhigh. "Halo she collocks nika tenas; no breeches hath my son" (the guide).

I. (in an Indianesque tone of some surprise, but great indifference). "Ah hagh!"

Owhhigh. "Pe halo shirt; and no shirt."

I. (assenting, with equal indifference). "Ah hagh!"

Owhhigh smokes, and is silent, and Spokan Adonis fugues in, "Pe wake yaka shoes; and no shoes hath he."

Another aide-de-camp takes up the strain. "Yahwah mitlite shoes, closche copa Owhhigh tenas; there are shoes (pointing to a pair of mine) good for the son of Owhhigh."

I. "Stick shoes ocook,—wake closche copa siwash; hard shoes (not moccasins) those,—not good for Indian." Owhhigh. "Hyas tyee mika,—hin mitlite ikta,—halo ikta mitlite copa nika tenas,— mika tikky hill potlatch; great chief thou,—with thee plenty traps abide,—no traps hath my son,—thou wilt give him abundance."

I. "Pe hyas tyee Owhhigh,—conoway ikta mitlite-pe hin yaka pot-latch copa liticum; and a great chief is Owhhigh,—all kinds of property are his, and many presents does he make to his people."

Profound silence followed these mutual hints. Owhhigh smoked in thoughtful whiffs, and the pipe went round. The choir bore their failure stoically. They had done their best that their comrade might be arrayed at my expense, and if I did not choose to throw in a livery, I must bear the shame and the unsavoriness if he were frowzy. At last, to please Owhhigh, and requite him for the entertainment of his oratory, I promised that, if his son were faithful, I would give him a generous premium, possibly the very shirt and other articles they had admired. Whereupon, after more unwordy whiffs and ineffectual hints that they too were needy, Owhhigh and his braves lounged off, the gloomy bow-legged ones, who had not spoken, bringing up the rear. I soon had everything in order, tongues, tea, and tin properly stowed, and was ready to be off.

Experienced campaigners attempt no more than a start and a league or two the first day of a long march. To burst the ties that bind us to civilization is an epoch of itself. The first camp of an expedition must not be beyond reclamation of forgotten things. Starts, too, will often be false starts. Raw men and raw horses and mules will condense into a muddle, or explode into a centrifugal stampede, a "blazing star," as packers name it. Then the pack-horse with the flour bolts and makes paste of his burden, up to his spine in a neighboring pool. The powder mule lies down in the ashes of a cooking fire. The pork mule, in greasy gallop, trails fatness over the plain. In a thorny thicket, a few white shreds reveal where the tent mule tore through. Another beast flies madly, while after him clink all the cannikins,[24] battering themselves shapeless upon his flanks. It is chaos, and demands hours perhaps of patience to make order again.

Such experience in a minor degree might befall even my little party of three horses and two men. I therefore, for better speed, resolved to disentangle myself this evening, and have a clear field to-morrow. Recalcitrant Antipodes, therefore, suffered compulsion, and was packed with his complex burdens. Leaving him and Gubbins with Owhhigh to follow and be disciplined, Mr. H. and I galloped on under the oaks, over the trap-rock, toward the Klickatat camp. Klale, with ungalling saddle, and a merciful rider of nine stone[25] weight, loped on gayly.

The Klickatats were encamped on a prairie near the house of a settler, five miles from the Fort. Just without the house was a group of them gambling. Presently Owhhigh followed Mr. H. and me into the farmer's kitchen, bringing forward for introduction his son, my guide. He was one of the gambling group. I inspected him narrowly. My speed, my success, my safety, depended upon his good faith. Owhhigh bore no very high character,—why should son be honester than father should? To an Indian the temptation to play foul by a possessor of horses, guns, blankets, and traps was enormous.

My future comrade was a tallish stripling of twenty, dusky-hued and low-browed. A mat of long, careless, sheenless black hair fell almost to his shoulders. Dull black were his eyes, not veined with agate-like play of color, as are the eyes of the sympathetic and impressionable. His chief physiognomical characteristic was a downward look, like the brown study of a detected pickpocket, inquiring with himself whether villainy pays; his chief personal and seemingly permanent characteristic was squalor. Squalid was his hickory shirt, squalid his buckskin leggins, long widowed of their fringe. Yet it was not a mean, but a proud uncleanliness, like that of a fakir,[26] or a voluntarily unwashed hermit. He flaunted his dirtiness in the face of civilization, claiming respect for it, as merely a different theory of the toilette. I cannot say that this new actor in my drama looked trustworthy, but there was a certain rascally charm in his rather insolent dignity, and an exciting mystery in his undecipherable phiz.[27] I saw that there was no danger of our becoming friends. There existed an antagonism in our natures which might lead to defiance and hostility, or possibly terminate in mutual respect.

Loolowcan was his name. I took him for better or for worse, without questions.

Owhhigh fully vouched for him,—but who would vouch for the voucher? Who could satisfy me that the horse-thieving morality of papa might not result in scalp-thieving principles in the youth? At least, he knew the way unerringly. My path was theirs, of constant transit from inland to seaside. As to his conduct, Owhhigh gave him an impressive harangue, stretching forth his arm in its fringed sleeve, and gesturing solemnly. This paternal admonition was, for my comprehension, expressed in Chinook jargon, doubly ludicrous with Owhhigh's sham stateliness of rhetoric. His final injunctions to young hopeful may be condensed as follows:—

"Great chief go to Dalles. Want to go fast. Six days. Good pay. S'pose want fresh horses other side mountains,—you get 'em; Get everything. Look sharp. No fear bad Indian at Dalles; great chief not let 'em beat you. Be good boy! Good bye!"

Owhhigh presented me, as a parting gift, his whip, which I had admired, a neat baton with a long hide lash and loop of otter fur for the wrist. I could by its aid modify, without altering, the system of education already pursued with my horses. Homeric studies had taught me that the gifts of heroes should be reciprocal. I therefore, for lack of more significant token, prayed Owhhigh to accept a piece of silver. We shook hands elaborately and parted. He was hung or shot last summer[28] in the late Indian wars of that region. I regret his martyrdom, and hope that in his present sphere his skill as a horse-thief is better directed.

I had also adieux to offer to Mr. H., and thanks for his kind energy in forwarding me. From him, as from all the gentlemen of the Hudson's Bay Company in the Northwest, I had received the most genuine hospitality, hearty entertainment, legendary and culinary.

And now for my long ride across the country! Here, Loolowcan, is Gubbins, thy steed,—drive thou Antipodes, clumsiest of cobs. I have mounted Klale,—let us gallop eastward.

Eastward I galloped with what eager joy! I flung myself again alone upon the torrent of adventure, with a lurking hope that I might prove new sensations of danger, new tests of manhood in its confident youth. I was going homeward across the breadth of the land, and with the excitement of this large thought there came a slight reactionary sinking of heart, and a dread lest I had exhausted onward life, and now, turning back from its foremost verge, should find myself dwindling into dull conservatism, and want of prophetic faith. I feared that I was retreating from the future into the past. Yet if one but knew it, his retreats are often his wisest and bravest advances.

I had, however, little time for meditation, morbid or healthy. Something always happens, in the go and the gallop of travel, demanding quick, instinctive action. Antipodes was in this case the agent to make me know my place. Antipodes, pointing his nose eastward toward his native valleys, had pounded along the trail for a couple of miles over the hillocks of a stony prairie, and on his back rattled my packs, for solace or annoyance, according to his own views. At a fork of the trail, Loolowcan urged Gubbins to the front, to indicate the route. Right-about went Antipodes. Back toward Squally bolted that stiff-legged steed,—stiff-legged no more, but far too limber,—and louder on his back rattled my pots and pans, a merry sound, could I have listened with no thought of the pottage and pancakes that depended upon the safety of my tin-ware. Still I could be amused at his grotesque gallop, for he had not discomfited me, and I could chuckle at the thought of another sound, when he was overtaken, and when upon a strawberry-roan surface fell the whip, the Owhhigh gift, now swinging at my wrist by its loop of otter-skin, for greater momentum of stroke. Clattering over the paved prairie we hied, the defaulter a little in advance and artfully dodging,—Loolowcan and I close upon him. Still more artfully at last he made show of finding the trail, and went pounding along, as if no traitorous stampede had happened. A total failure was this crafty sham, this too late repentance and acknowledgment of defeat. Vengeance will not thus be baffled. Men discover with bitterness that nature continues to use the scourge long after they have reformed, until relapse becomes impossible by the habit of virtue. So Antipodes experienced. Pendulum whips do not swing for nothing, and he never again attempted absolute revolt, but grumblingly acknowledged his duty to his master.

This was an evening of August, in a climate where summer is never scorching nor blasting. We breathe air as a matter of course,

unobservant usually of how fair a draught it is. But to-night the chalice of nature was brimming with a golden haze, which touched the
lips with luxurious winy flavor.[29]

So inhaling delicate gray-gold puffs of indolent summer-evening
air, and much tranquillized by such beverage, mild yet rich, I rode
on, now under the low oaks, now over a ripe prairie, and now beside
a lake fresh, pure, and feminine. And whenever a vista opened eastward, Tacoma appeared above the low-lying mists of the distance.
"Polikely, spose mika tikky, nesika mitlite copa Comcomli house;
to-night, if you please, we stop at Comcomli's house," said Loolowcan the taciturn.

Night was at hand, and where was the house? It is not wise to put
off choice of camping-ground till dark; foresight is as needful to a
campaigner as to any other mortal. But presently, in a pretty little
prairie, we reached the spot where a certain Montgomery, wedded
to a squaw, had squatted, and he should be our host. His name, too
articulate for Indian lips, they had softened to Comcomli. A similar corruption befell the name of the Scotticized chief of the Chinooks, whom Astor's people found at Astoria, and whom Mr. Irving
has given to history.[30]

Mr. Comcomli was absent, but his comely "mild-eyed, melancholy"[31] squaw received us hospitably. Her Squallyamish proportions were oddly involved in limp robes of calico, such as her sisters
from Pike County wear. She gave us a supper of fried pork, bread,
and tea. We encamped upon her floor, and were somewhat trodden
under foot by little half-breed Comcomlis, patrolling about during
the night-watches.

Loolowcan here began to show the white feather. His heart sank
when he contemplated the long leagues of the trail. He wanted to
return. He was solitary,—homesick for the congenial society of
other youths with matted hair, dusky skins, paint-daubed cheeks,

low brows, and distinguished frowziness of apparel. He wanted to squat by camp-fires, and mutter guttural gibberish to such as these. The old, undying feud of blackguard against gentleman seemed in danger of pronouncing itself. Besides, he feared hostile siwashes at the Dalles of the Columbia. In his superstitious soul of a savage he dreaded, or pretended to dread, some terrible magical influence in the gloomy forests of the mountains. Of evil omen to me, and worse than any demon spell in the craggy dells of the Cascades, was this vacillation of my guide. However, I argued somewhat, and somewhat wheedled and bullied the doubter. Loolowcan was harder to keep in line than Antipodes. One may tame Bucephalus, but several new elements of character are to be considered when the attempt is made to manage Pagan savages.

At last my guide seemed to waver over to the side of good faith, with a dishonest air and a pretence of wishing to oblige. Shaken confidence hardly returns, and from hour to hour, as the little Comcomlis pranced over my person, and trampled my upturned nose a temporary aquiline, I awoke and studied the dark spot where my dusky comrade lay. Each time I satisfied myself that he had not flitted. Nor did he. When morning came, his heart grew bigger. Difficulties portentous in the ghostly obscure of night vanished with cockcrowing. He contemplated his fair proportions, and felt that new clothes would become them. He rose, stalked about, and longed for the dignified drapery of a new blanket. How the other low-browed and squalid, from whom he had been selected for his knowledge as a linguist and his talents as a guide,—how they would scoff, and call him Kallapooya, meanest of Indians, if he sneaked back to camp bootless! He turned to me, and saw me a civilized man, in garb and guise to be envied. So for a time treachery was argued out of the heart of Loolowcan the frowzy.

5. Forests of the Cascades

To have started with dawn is a proud and exhilarating recollection all the day long. The most godlike impersonality men know is the sun. To him the body should pay its matinal devotions, its ardent, worshipful greetings, when he comes, the joy of the world; then is the soul elated to loftier energies, and nerved to sustain its own visions of glories transcending the spheres where the sun reigns sublime. Tame and inarticulate is the harmony of a day that has not known the delicious preludes of dawn. For the sun, the godlike, does not come hastily blundering in upon the scene. Nor does he bounce forth upon the arena of his action, like a circus clown. Much beautiful labor of love is done by earth and sky, preparing a pageant where their Lord shall enter. Slowly, like the growth of any feeling grand, deep, masterful, and abiding, nature's power of comprehending the coming blessing develops. First, up in the colorless ranges of night there is a feeling of quiver and life, broader than the narrow twinkle of stars,—a tender lucency, not light, but rather a

sense of the departing of darkness. Then a gray glimmer, like the
sheen of filed silver, trembles upward from the black horizon. Gray
deepens to violet. Clouds flush and blaze. The sky grows azure.
The pageant thickens. Beams dart up. The world shines golden.
The sun comes forth to cheer, to bless, to vivify.

For other reasons more obviously practical, needs must that campaigners stir with dawn, and start with sunrise. No daylight is long
enough for its possible work, as no life is long enough for its possible development in wisdom and love. In the beautiful, fresh hours
of early day vigorous influences are about. The sun is doing his
uphill work easily, climbing without a thought of toil to the breath-
ing-spot of high noon. Every flower of the world is boldly open;
there is no languid droop in any stem. Blades of grass have tossed
lightly off each its burden of a dew-drop, and now stand upright
and alert. Man rises from recumbency taller by fractions of an inch
than when he sank to repose, with a brain leagues higher up in the
regions of ability,—leagues above doubt and depression; and a man
on a march, with long wildness of mountain and plain to overpass,
is urged by necessity to convert power into achievement.[1]

Up, then, at earliest of light, I sprang from the ground. I roused
Loolowcan, and found him in healthier and braver mood, and ready
to lead on. While, after one sympathetic gaze at Aurora, I made up
my packs, my Klickatat untethered the horses from spots where
all night they had champed the succulent grasses. This control of
tethering was necessary on separating my steeds from their late
comrades. Indian nags, like Indian youths, are gregarious, and had
my ponies escaped, I should probably have seen them nevermore.
Even my graceful Adonis, the Spokan, would not have hesitated to
seclude a stray Antipodes, galloping back to the herd, and inno-

cently to offer me another and a sorrier, to be bought with fresh moneys.

The trail took us speedily into a forest-temple. Long years of labor by artists the most unconscious of their skill had been given to modelling these columnar firs.[2] Unlike the pillars of human architecture, chipped and chiselled in bustling, dusty quarries, and hoisted to their site by sweat of brow and creak of pulley, these rose to fairest proportion by the life that was in them,—and blossomed into foliated capitals three hundred feet overhead.

Riding steadily on, I found no thinning of this mighty array, no change in the monotony of this monstrous vegetation. These giants with their rough plate-armor were masters here; one of human stature was unmeaning and incapable. With an axe, a man of muscle might succeed in smiting off a flake or a chip, but his slight fibres seemed naught to battle, with any chance of victory, with the time-hardened sinews of these Goliaths. It grew somewhat dreary to follow down the vistas of this ungentle woodland, passing forever between rows of rough-hewn pillars, and never penetrating to any shrine where sunshine entered and dwelt, and garlands grew for the gods of the forest. Wherever I rode into the sombre vista, and turned by chance to trace the trail behind me, the dark-purple trunks drew together, like a circuit of palisades, and closed after, crowding me forward down the narrow inevitable way, as ugly sins, co-operating only to evolve an uglier remorse, forbid the soul to turn back to purity, and crowd it, shrinking, on into blacker falseness to itself.

Before my courage was quelled by a superstitious dread that from this austere wood was no escape, I came upon a river, cleaving the darkness with a broad belt of sunshine. A river signifies much on the earth. It signifies something to mix with proper drinkables; it signifies navigation, in birch-canoe, seventy-four,[3] floating palace, dug-out, or lumber ark; it signifies motion, less transitory than the tremble of leaves, and shadows. This particular river, the Puyallop, had another distinct significance to me,—it was certain to supply provisions, fish, salmon. As I expected, some fishing Indians were here to sell me their silver beauty, a noble fellow who this morning had tasted the pickle of Whulge, and had the cosmopolitan look of a fish but now from ocean palace and grot, where he was a welcome guest and a regretted absentee. It was truly to be deplored that he could never reappear in those Neptunian realms with tales of wild adventure; yet if to this most brilliant of fish his hour of destiny had come, how much better than feeding foul Indians it was to belong to me, who would treat his proportions with respect, feel the exquisiteness of his coloring, grill him delicately, and eat him daintily!

Potatoes, also, I bought of the Indians, and bagged them till my bags were knobby withal,—potatoes with skins of smooth and refined texture, like the cheeks of a brunette, and like them showing fair rosiness through the transparent brown. For these peaceful products I paid in munitions of war. Four charges of powder and shot were deemed by the Nestor[4] of the siwash family a liberal, even a lavishly bounteous price, for twoscore of tubers and a fifteen-pound salmon; and in two corners of the flap of his sole inner and outer garment that tranquil sage tied up his hazardous property. Such barter dignifies marketing. Usually what a man pays for his dinner does not interest the race; but here I was giving destruction for provender, death for life. Perhaps Nestor shot the next traveler with my ammunition, and the juices of that salmon were really my brother Yankee's blood. Avaunt, horrid thought! and may it be that the powder and the shot went for killing porcupines, or that their treasurer stumbled in the stream, and drowned his deadly stores!

Well satisfied with my new possessions, I said adieu to the monotonous mumblers of Puyallop,—a singularly fishy old gentleman, his wife an oleaginous hag, an emotionless youth of the Loolowcan type, and a flat-faced young damsel with a circle of vermilion on each broad cheek and a red blanket for all raiment. I waded the milky stream, scuffled across its pebbly bed, and plunged again among the phalanxes of firs. These opened a narrow trail, wide enough to wind rapidly along, and my little cortege dashed on deeper into the wilderness. I had not yet entirely escaped from civilization, so much as Yankee pioneers carry with them, namely, blue blankets and the smell of fried pork. In a prairie about noon to-day I saw a smoke, near that smoke a tent, and at that smoke two men in ex-soldier garb. Frying pork were these two braves, as at most habitations, up and down and athwart this continent, cooking braves or their wives are doing three times a day, incensing dawn, noon, and sunset. These two had taken this pretty prairie as their "claim," hoping to become the vanguard of colonization. They became its forlorn hope. The point of civilization's entering wedge into barbarism is easily knocked off. These squatters were knocked off, as some of the earliest victims of the Indian war three summers after my visit. It is odd how much more interest I take in these two settlers since I heard that they were scalped. More fair prairies strung themselves along the trail, possibly less fair in seeming to me then, could I have known that murder would soon disfigure them; that savages, and perhaps among them the low-browed Loolowcan, would lurk behind the purple trunks of these colossal firs, watching not in vain for the safe moment to slay. For so it was, and the war in that territory began three years after, by massacres in these outlying spots.

I was now to be greeted by a nearer vision of an old love. A great bliss, or a sublime object, or a giant aspiration of our souls, lifts first upon our horizon, and swelling fills our sphere, and stoops forward with winsome condescension. And taking our clew, we approach through the labyrinths. Glimpses are never wanting to sustain us, lest we faint and fail along the lacerating ways. Such a glimpse I was now to have of Tacoma. I had long been obstructedly nearing it, first in the leaky Bucentaur, propelled over strong-flowing Whulge by Klalams, drunken, crapulous, unsteady, timid,—such agents progress finds; next by alliance of Owhhigh, the horse-thief, and aid from the Hudson's Bay Company; then between the files of veteran evergreens in plate-armor, tempered purple by the fiery sun, and across prairies where might have hung an ominous mist of blood. Now suddenly, as Klale the untiring disentangled us from the black forest, and galloped out upon a little prairie, delighted to comb his fetlocks in the long yellow grass, I beheld Tacoma at hand, still undwarfed by any underlift of lower ridges, and only its snows above the pines. Over the pines, the snow peak against the sky presented the quiet fraternal tricolor of nature, who always, where there is default of uppermost peaks to be white with clouds fallen in the form of snow, brings the clouds themselves, so changefully fair that we hardly wish them more sublimely permanent, and heaps them above the green against the blue. Here, then, against the unapproachable glory of an Oregon summer sky stood Tacoma, less dreamy than when I floated over its shadow, but not less divine,— no divine thing dwindles as one with spark of divineness in his mind approaches.

Yet I could not dally here to watch Tacoma bloom at sunset against a violet sky. Alas that life with an object cannot linger among its own sweet episodes! My camp was farther on, but the revolutionary member of the party, Antipodes, hinted that we would do wisely to set up our tabernacle here. His view of such a hint was to bolt off where grass grew highest, and standing there interpose a mobile battery of heels between his flanks and their castigators. This plan failed; a horse cannot balance on his fore legs and take hasty bites of long, luxurious fodder, while he brandishes his hind legs in the air. Some sweeter morsel will divert his mind from self-defence; his assailants will get within his guard. Penance follows, and Antipodes must again hammer elephantine along the trail.

What now? What is this strange object in the utterly lonely woods,—a furry object hanging on a bush by our faint and obstructed trail? A cap of fox-skin, fantastic with tails. And what, O Loolowcan the mysterious, means this tailful head-gear, hung carefully, as if a signal? "It is," replied Loolowcan, depositing it upon his capless mop of hair, "my brother's cap, and he must be hereabouts; he informs me of his neighborhood, and will meet us presently." "Son of Owhhigh, what doth thy brother skulking along our trail?" "How should I know, my chief? Indian come, Indian go; he somewhere, he nowhere. Perhaps my brother go to mountains see Tamanous,— want to be big medicine."

Presently, appearing from nowhere, there stood in the trail a little, shabby, capless Indian, armed with a bow and arrows,—a personage not at all like the pompous, white-cravatted, typical big-medicine man of civilization, armed with gold-headed cane. Where this M. D. had been prowling, or from what lair he discovered our approach, or by what dodging he evaded us along the circuits of the trail, was a mystery of which he offered no explanation. The presence of this disciple of Tamanous, this tyro magician, this culler of simples, this amateur spy, or whatever else he might be, was unaccountable. He was the counterpart of Loolowcan, but evidently an inferior spirit to that youth of promise. He offered me his hand, not without Indian courtesy, and he and his compatriot, if not brother, plunged together into a splutter of confidential talk.

The Doctor, for he did not introduce himself by name, trotted along by the side of the ambling Gubbins, and soon, just before sunset, we emerged upon a little circle of ferny prairie, our camp, already known to me by the description of Owhhigh. The White River, the S'Kamish flowed hard by, behind a belt of luxuriant arbor-vitae. With the Doctor's aid, we took down pot and pan, blanket and bread-bag, from the galled back of the much-enduring Antipodes, and gave to him and his two comrades full license to bury themselves among the tall, fragrant ferns, and nibble, without stooping, top bits from the gigantic grass. It was a perfect spot for a bivouac, a fairy ring of ferns beneath the tall, dark shelter of the firs. Tacoma was near, an invisible guardian, hidden by the forest. Beside us the rushing river sounded lulling music, making rest sweeter by its contrast of tireless toil. And thus under favorable auspices we set ourselves to prepare for the great event of supper,—the Doctor slipping quietly into the position of a welcome guest without invitation.

I lifted the salmon to view. Loolowcan's murky brow expanded. A look became decipherable upon that mysterious phiz, and that look meant gluttony. The delicate substance of my aristocratic fish was presently to be devoured by frowzy Klickatat. At least, O pair of bush-boys, you shall have cleanlier ideas of cookery than heretofore in your gypsy life, and be taught that civilization in me, its representative for want of a better, does not disdain accepting the captaincy of a kitchen battery. First, then, my marmitons,[5] clear ye a space carefully of herbage, and trample down the ferns about, lest the flame of our fire show affinity to this natural hay, and our fair paddock become a charred and desolate waste. We will have salmon in three courses on this festive occasion, when I, for the first time, entertain two young Klickatats of distinction. Do thou, Loolowcan, seek by the river-side tenacious twigs of alder and maple, wherewith to construct an upright gridiron. One blushing half of that swimmer of the Puyallop shall stand and toast on this slight scaffolding. Portions from the other half shall be fried in this pan, and other portions, from the thicker part, shall be neatly wrapped in green leaves, and bake beneath the ashes.

So it was done, and well done. The colors that are encased within a salmon, awaiting fire that they may bloom, came forth artistically. On the toasted surface brightened warm yellows, and ruddy orange; and delicate pinkness, softened with downy gray, suffused the separating flakes. Potatoes, too, roasted beneath aromatic ashes by the side of roasting blocks of salmon,—potatoes hardened their crusts against too ardent heat, that slowly ripeness might penetrate to their heart of hearts. Unworthy the cook that does not feel the poetry of his trade!

The two Klickatats, whether brothers or fellow-clansmen, feasted enormously. Rasher after rasher of the fried, block after block of the roasted, flake after flake of the toasted salmon vanished. I should have supposed that the Doctor was suffering with a bulimy,[6] after short commons in his worship of Tamanous, the mountain demon, had not the appetite of Loolowcan, although well fed at three meals in my service, been equal or greater. Before they were quite gorged, I made them a pot of tea, well boiled and sticky with sugar, and then retired to my dhudeen. The summer evening air enfolded me sweetly, and down from the cliffs and snowy mounds of Tacoma a cool breeze fell like the spray of a cascade.

After their banquet, the Indians were in merry mood, and fell to chaffing one another. With me Loolowcan was taciturn. I could not tell whether he was dull, sulky, or suspicious. When I smote him with the tempered steel of a keen query, meaning to elicit sparks of information on Indian topics, no illumination came. He acted judiciously his part, and talked little. Nor did he bore me with hints, as bystanders do in Christendom, but believed that I knew also my part. With his comrade he was communicative and jolly, even to uproariousness. They laughed sunset out and twilight in, finding entertainment in everything that was or that happened,—in their raggedness, in the holes in their moccasins, in their overstuffed proportions after dinner, in the little skirmishes of the horses, when a grasshopper chirped or a cricket sang, when either of them found a sequence of blackberries or pricked himself with a thorn,—in every fact of our little world these children of nature found wonderment and fun. They laughed themselves sleepy, and then dropped into slumber in the ferny covert.

As night drew on, heaven overhead, seen as from the bottom of a well, was so starry clear and intelligible, and the circuit of forest so dreamy mysterious by contrast, that I found restful delight, better than sleep, in studying the clearness above the mystery. But twilight drifted away after the sun, and darkness blackened my green blankets. I mummied myself in their folds, and rolled in among the tall, elastic, fragrant ferns.

My last vision, as sleep came upon me, was the eyes of Loolowcan staring at me, and glowing serpent-like. At midnight, when I stirred, the same look watched me by the dim light of our embers. And when gray dawn drew over our bivouac, and my blankets from black to green began to turn, the same dusky, unvariegated eyeballs were inspecting me still. As to the little medicine-man, he had no responsibility at present; a pleasant episode had befallen him, and he made the most of it, sleeping unwatchfully.

Seediness of a morning is not the meed of him who has slept near Tacoma with naught but a green blanket and miles of elastic atmosphere between him and the stars. When I woke, sleep fell from me suddenly, as a lowly disguise falls from a prince in a pantomime. I sprang up, myself, fresh, clear-eyed, and with never a regretful yawn. Nothing was astir in nature save the river, rushing nigh at hand, and rousing me to my day's career by its tale of travel and urgency.

It was a joy to behold three horses so well fed as my stud appeared. Klale looked toward me and whinnied gratefully for the juicy grasses and ferny bed of his sheltered paddock, and also for the remembrance of a new sensation he had had the day before,—he had carried a biped through a day of travel, and the biped had not massacred him with his whip. Klale thought better and more hopefully of humanity. Tougher Gubbins, who, with Loolowcan on his back, had had no such experience, sung no paeans, but stood doltishly awaiting a continuance of the inevitable discomforts of life.

After breakfast, the Doctor hinted that he liked my cheer and my society, and would gladly volunteer to accompany me if I would mount him upon Antipodes. I pointed out to him that it would be weak to follow with us along flowery paths of pleasure, when stern virtue called him to the mountain-tops; that Tamanous would not pardon backsliding. I suggested that I was prepared for the appetite of only one Klickatat gourmand, and that my tacit bargain with Antipodes did not include his carrying an eater as well as provisions. The youth received my refusal impassively; to ask for everything, and never be disappointed at getting nothing, is Indian manners. We left him standing among the ferns, gazing vacantly upon the world, and devouring a present of hardtack I had given him,— he was ridding himself at once of that memorial of civilization, that, with bow and arrows in hand, he might relapse into barbarism, in pathless wilds along the flanks of Tacoma.

Soon the trail took a dip in the river,—a morning bath in S'Kamish. Rapid, turbulent, and deep was the S'Kamish, white with powder of the boulders it had been churning above, and so turbid that boulders here were invisible. We must ford with our noses pointing up stream, lest the urgent water, bearing against the broadsides of our unsteady horses, should dowse, if not drown us. Klale, floundering sometimes, but always recovering himself, took me over stoutly. My moccasins and scarlet leggins were wet, but I had not become dazed in the whirr and fallen, as it is easy to do. Lubberly Antipodes flinched. He had some stupid theory that the spot we had chosen, just at the break above of a rapid, was a less commodious ford than the smooth whirlpools below. He turned aside from honest roughness to deluding smoothness. He stepped into the treacherous pool, and the waters washed over him. There was bread in the bags he bore. In an instant he scrambled out, trying to look meritorious, as dolts do when they have done doltishly and yet escaped. And there was pulp in the bags he bore. Pulp of hardtack was now oozing through the seams. I was possessor of two bag puddings. My cakes were dough. Downright and desiccating may be the sunshine of Oregon August, but pilot-bread converted into wet sponge resists a sunbeam as a cotton-bale resists a cannon-ball. Only a few inner layers of the bread were untouched; as to the outer strata, mouldiness pervaded them. Yet some one profited by this disaster; Loolowcan henceforth had mouldy biscuit at discretion. His discretion would not have rejected even a fungous article. To him my damp and crumbling crackers were a delicacy, the better for their earthy fragrance and partial fermentation.

We struck the trail again after this slight misadventure, and went on through forests nobler and denser than those of the dry levels near Whulge. The same S'Kamish floods that spoiled my farinaceous stores nourished to greater growth the mighty vegetables of this valley. The arbor-vitae here gained grander arborescence and fresher vitality. This shrub of our gardens in the Middle States, and gnarled tree of the Northeast, becomes in the Northwest a giant pyramid, with rich plates of foliage drooping massively about a massive trunk. Its full, juicy verdure, sweeping to the ground, is a relief after the monotony of the stark stems of fir forests. There was no lack of luxuriant undergrowth along these lowlands by the river. The narrow trail plunged into thickets impenetrable but for its aid. Wherever ancient trunks had fallen, there they lay; some in old decay had become green, mossy mounds, the long graves of prostrate giants, so carefully draped with their velvet covering, that all sense of ruin was gone. And some, that fell from uprightness but a few seasons ago, showed still their purple bark deepening in hue and dotted with tufts of moss; or where a crack had opened and revealed their inner structure rotting slowly away, there was such warm coloring as nature loves to shed, that even decay may not be unlovely, and the powdery wood, fractured into flaky cubes, showed browns deep as the tones of old Flemish pictures, or changeful agate-like crimsons and solid yellows. Not always had the ancient stem fallen to lie prone and bidden by younger growths, whose life was sucked from the corpse of their ancestor. Sometimes, as the antiquated arbor-vitae, worn away at its base, swayed, bent, and went crashing downward, it had been arrested among the close ranks of upstart trunks, and hung there still, with long gray moss floating from it, like the torn banners in a baronial chapel,—hung there until its heart should rot and crumble, and then, its shell of bark breaking, it should give way, and shower down in scales and dust.

In this Northern forest there was no feverish apprehension, such as we feel in a jungle of the tropics, that every breath may be poison,—that centipede in boot and scorpion in pocket, mere external perils, will be far less fatal than the inhaling of dense miasmas, stirred from villainous ambushes beneath mounds of flowery verdure. Here no black and yellow serpent defended the way, lifting above its ugly coil a mobile head, with jaws that quiver and fangs that play. It was a forest without poison,—without miasma, and without venom.

It was a forest just not impassable for a train like mine, and the trail was but a faint indication of a way, suggesting nothing except to the trained eye of an Indian. Into the pleached[7] thickets Klale could plunge and crash through, while his cavalier fought against buffeting branches, and bent to saddle-horn to avoid the fate of Absalom.[8] But when new-fallen trunks of the sylvan giants, or great mossy mounds, built barricades across the path, tall as the quadruped whose duty it was to leap over them—how in such case Klale the sprightly? how here Antipodes the flounderer? how Gubbins, stiff in the joints?

Thus, by act answered Klale,—thus; by a leap, by a scramble, by a jerking plunge, by a somerset; like a cat, like a squirrel, like a monkey, like an acrobat, like a mustang. To overpass these obstacles is my business; be it yours to pass with me. You must prove to me, a nag of the Klickatats, that Boston strangers are as sticky as siwashes. Centaurs have somewhat gone out. I have been a party and an actor when the mustang sprang lightly over the barricade, and his rider stayed upon the other side supine, and gazing still where he had just seen a disappearance of horse-heels.

Not wishing to lose the respect of so near a comrade as my horse, I did not allow our union to be dissolved. We clung together like voluntary Siamese twins, dashing between fir-trunks, where my nigh leg or my off leg must whisk away to avoid amputation, thrusting ourselves beneath the aromatic denseness of the drooping arborvitae, smothered together in punk when a moss mound gave way and we sank down into the dusty grave of a buried monarch of his dell, or caught and balanced half-way over as we essayed to leap the broad back of a fir fifteen feet in the girth. Whether Klale, in our frantic scrambles, became a biped, gesticulating and clutching the air with two hoofed arms,—or whether a monopod, alighted on his nose and lifting on high a quintette of terminations, four legs and a tail,—still Klale and I remained inseparable.

Assuredly the world has no path worse than that,—not even South American muds or damaged corduroys in tropic swamps. But men must pay their footing by labor, and we urged on, with horses educated to their task, often fording the S'Kamish, and careless now of wetting, clambering up ridges black with sunless woods, and penetrating steadily on through imperviousness. Indian trails aim at the open hill-sides and avoid the thickset valleys; but in this most primeval of forests the obstacles on the rugged buttresses of the Cascade chain were impracticable as the dense growth below.

"Ancoti nesika nanitch Boston hooihut; presently we see the Boston road," said Loolowcan. A glad sight whenever it comes, should "Boston road" here imply neat Macadam, well-kept sidewalks, and files of pretty cottages, behind screens of disciplined shrubbery. I had heard indefinitely that a party of "Boston" men—for so all Americans are called in the Chinook jargon—were out from the settlements of Whulge, viewing, or possibly opening, a way across the Cascades, that emigrants of this summer might find their way

into Washington Territory direct, leaving the great overland cara-
van route near the junction of the two forks of the Columbia. Such
an enterprise was an epoch in progress. It was the first effort of an
infant community to assert its individuality and emancipate itself
from the tutelage of Oregon.

Very soon the Boston hooihut became apparent. An Indian's trail
came into competition with a civilized man's rude beginnings of
a road. Wood-choppers had passed through the forest, like a tor-
nado, making a broad belt of confusion. Trim Boston neighbor-
hoods would have scoffed at this rough-and-tumble cleft of the wild
wood, and declined being responsible for its title. And yet two centuries before this tramp of mine, my progenitors were cutting just
such paths near Boston, and then Canonicus, Chickatabot, and
Passaconomy,[9] sagamores of that region, were regarding the work
very much as Owhhigh, Skloo, and Kamaiakan, the "tyees" hereabouts, might contrast this path with theirs. At present this trium-
virate of chieftainly siwashes would have rightly deemed the Boston road far inferior to their own. So the unenlightened generally
deem, when they inspect the destruction that precedes reconstruction. This was a transition period. In the Cascades, Klickatat institutions were toppling, Boston notions coming in. It was the fullness of time. Owhhigh and his piratical band, slaves of Time and
Space, might go dodging with lazy detours about downcast trunks,
about tangles of shrubs and brambles, about zones of morass; but
Boston clans were now, in the latter day, on the march, intending
to be masters of Time and Space, and straightforwardness was to
be the law of motion here.

It was a transition state of things on the Boston hooihut, with all
the incommodities of that condition. The barricades of destructive

disorder were in place, not yet displaced by constructive order. Passage by this road of the future was monstrous hard.

There is really no such thing as a conservative. Joshua is the only one on record who ever accomplished anything, and he only kept things quiet for one day.[10] We must either move forward with Hope and Faith, or backward to decay and death of the soul. But though no man, not even himself, has any real faith in a conservative, for this one occasion I was compelled to violate the law of my nature,—to identify myself with conservatism, and take the ancient trail instead of the modern highway. Stiff as the obstacles in the trail might be, the obstacles of the road were still stiffer; stumps were in it, fresh cut and upstanding with sharp or splintered edges; felled trunks were in it, with wedge-shaped butts and untrimmed branches, forming impregnable abattis.[11] One might enter those green bowers as a lobster enters the pot; extrication was another and a tougher task. Every inch of the surface was planted with laming caltrops, and the saplings and briers that once grew there elastic were now thrown together, a bristling hedge. A belt of forest had been unmade and nothing made. Patriotic sympathy did indeed influence me to stumble a little way along this shaggy waste. I launched my train into this complexity, floundered awhile in one of its unbridged bogs, and wrestled in its thorny labyrinths, until so much of my patience as was not bemired was flagellated to death by scorpion scourges of briers. I trod these mazes until even Klale showed signs of disgust, and Antipodes, ungainly plodder, could only be propelled by steady discipline of thwacks. Then I gave up my attempt to be a consistent radical. I shook off the shavings and splinters of a pioneer chaos, and fell back into primeval ways. In the siwash hooihut there was nothing to be expected, and therefore no acrid pang of disappointment pierced my prophetic soul when I found that path

no better than it should be. Pride fired those dusky tunnels, the
eyes of Loolowcan, when we alighted again upon his national road.
The Boston hooihut was a failure, a miserable muddle. Loolowcan leaped Gubbins over the first barricade, and, pointing where
Antipodes trotted to the sound of rattling packs along the serpentine way, said calmly, and without too ungenerous scorn, "Closche
ocook; beautiful this."

Though I had abandoned their undone road, I was cheered to
have met fresh traces of my countrymen. Their tree surgery was
skilful. No clumsy, tremulous hand had done butchery here with
haggling axe. The chopping was handiwork of artists, men worthy
to be regicide headsmen of forest monarchs. By their cleavage light
first shone into this gloaming; the selfish grandeurs of this incog-
nito earth were opened to-day. I flung myself forward two centuries, and thanked these pioneers in the persons of posterity dwelling
peacefully in this noble region. He who strikes the first blow merits
all thanks. May my descendants be as grateful to these Boston men
as I am now to the Boston men of two centuries ago. And may they
remember ancestral perils and difficulties kindly, as I now recall
how godly Puritans once brandished ruder axes and bill-hooks,
opening paths of future peace on the shores of Massachusetts.

Our ascent was steady along the gorge of the S'Kamish, ever in
this same dense forest. We had, however, escaped from the monotony of the bare fir-trunks. Columns, even such as those graceful-
lest relics of Olympian Jove's temple by the Cephissus, would weary
were they planted in ranks for leagues. The magnificent pyramids of
arbor-vitae filled the wood with sheen from their bright, varnished
leafage. It was an untenanted, silent forest, but silence here in this
sunshiny morning I found not awful, hardly even solemn. Solitude
became to me personal, and pregnant with possible emanations, as

if I were a faithful pagan in those early days when gods were seen
of men, and when, under Grecian skies, Pan and the Naiads whispered their secrets to the lover of Nature.

There was rough vigor in these scenes, which banished the half-
formed dread that forest loneliness and silence without a buzz or
a song, and dim vistas where sunlight falls in ghostly shapes, and
leaves shivering as if a sprite had passed, may inspire. Pan here
would have come in the form of a rough, jolly giant, typifying the
big, beneficent forces of Nature in her rugged moods. Instead of
dreading such a comrade, his presence seemed a fitting culmina-
tion to the influences of the spot, and, yielding to a wild exhilaration, I roused the stillness with appealing shouts.

"Mika wah wah copa Tamanous? you talk with demons?" inquired
Loolowcan with something of mysterious awe in his tone.

I called unto the gods of the forest, but none answered. No sound
came back to me save some chance shots of echo where my voice
struck a gray, sinewy cedar-trunk, that rang again, or the gentle
murmur of solitude disturbed deep in the grove, as the circles of agitated air vibrated again to calmness. No answer from Pan or Pan's
unruly rout,—no sound from Satyr, Nymph, or Faun,—though I
shouted and sang ever so loudly to them upon my way.

Through this broad belt of woodland, utterly lifeless and lonely,
I rode steadily, never dallying. In the early afternoon I came upon
a little bushy level near the S'Kamish. We whisked along the bends
of the trail, when, suddenly whisking, I pounced upon a biped,—
a man,—a Caucasian man,—a Celtic soldier,—a wayworn U. S.
Fourth Infantry sergeant,—a meditative smoker, apart from the little army encamped within hail.

I followed him toward the tent of his fellows. They were not rev-
elling in the mad indulgence of camp-life. Nor were their pranc-

ing steeds champing angry bits and neighing defiance at the foe.
Few of those steeds were in marching, much less in prancing order.
If they champed their iron bits, it was because they had no other
nutriment to nibble at in that adust halting-place. As to camp revelry, the American army has revelled but once,—in the Halls of the
Montezumas,[12]—a very moderate allowance of revelry for a space
of threescore and ten years. Since that time they have fortunately
escaped the ugly business of butchery, antecedent to revelry. Their
better duty has been to act as the educated pioneers and protectors
of Western progress.

Such was the office of this detachment. They were of Capt.
McClellan's expedition for flushing a Pacific Railroad in the brakes
and bosks and tangled forests of the Cascades.[13] I, taking casual
glimpses through intricacy, had flushed or scared up only an
unfledged Boston hooihut. Their success had been no greater, and
while the main body continued the hunt, this smaller party was on
commissariat service, going across to Squally and Steilacoom for
other bags of pork and hardtack, lest dinnerlessness should befall
the Hunters of Railroads, and there should be aching voids among
them that no tightening of belt-buckles could relieve.

I found an old acquaintance, Lieut. H., in command of these for-
agers. Three months before we had descended the terrace where
Columbia Barracks behold the magnificent sweeps of the Columbia, and, far beyond, across a realm of forest, Mt. Hood, sublime
pyramid of snows,—we had strolled down together to the river-bank
to take our stirrup-cup with Governor Ogden,[14] kindliest of hosts,
at the Hudson's Bay Company's post of Fort Vancouver. Now, after
wanderings hither and yon, we suddenly confronted each other in
the wilderness, and exchanged hearty greetings. I was the enviable man, with my compact party and horses in tolerable condi-

tion. He officered a squadron of Rosinantes, a very wayworn set, and the obstacles on the trail that I could lightly skip over he must painfully beleaguer. He informed me that the road-makers were at work somewhere this side of the summit of the Pass. I might overtake them before night.

While we sympathized and gossiped, Loolowcan slunk forward to say, "Sia-a-ah mitlite ocook tipsoo, car nesika moo sum; far, far is that grass spot where we sleep;—pe wake siah chaco polikely; and not far comes night."

So I turned from the tents of the busy camp, busy even in repose. H. walked with me to the S'Kamish to show me the ford. If from the scanty relics of his stores he could not offer hospitality, he would give me a fact from his experience of crossing the river, so that I need not dip involuntarily in the deeps, and swallow cold comfort. On the bank some whittlers of his squad had amused themselves with whittling down a taper fir-tree, a slender wand, three hundred feet in length from where its butt lay among the chips, to the tip of its pompon,[15] where it had fallen across the stream.

H. looked suspiciously upon the low-browed and frowzy Loolowcan, and doubted the safety and certainty of journeying with such a guide in such a region,—as, indeed, I did myself. I forded unducked in the ripples, turned to wave him adieu, and blotted myself out of his sphere behind the sky-scraper firs. We met next in the *foyer* of the opera, between acts of Traviata.

Loneliness no longer lay heavy in the woods. It was shattered and trampled out where that little army had marched. Presently in their trail a ghostly object appeared,—not a ghost, but something tending fast toward the ghostly state; a poor, wasted, dreary white horse, standing in the trail, abandoned, too stiff to fall, too weary to stir. Every winged phlebotomizer of the Oregon woods seemed to have hastened hither to blacken that pale horse, soon to be Death's, and, though he trembled feebly, he had not power to scatter the nipping insects with a convulsive shake. I approached, and whisked away his tormentors by the aid of a maple-bush. They fought me for a while, but finding me resolute, confident in their long-enduring patience, they retired with a loud and angry buzz. I could find no morsel of refreshment for him in the bitter woods. At mouldy hardtack he shook a despairing head. In fact, it was too late. There comes a time to horses when they cannot prance with the prancers, or plod with the plodders, or trail weary hoofs after the march of their comrades. Yet it was more chivalric for this worn-out estray[16] to die here in the aromatic forest, than to lose life in the vile ooze of a Broadway.

Poor, lean mustang, victim of progress! Nothing to do but let him die, since I could not bring myself to a merciful assassination. So I went on disconsolate after the sight of suffering, until my own difficulties along that savage trail compelled my thought away from dwelling on another's pain.

L'Quoit, as his name appeared on the rolls of the Spokane Tribe, in 1899. Born a Yakama, he enrolled in the Spokane Tribe ca. 1899. Courtesy of the Spokane Tribe of Indians Cultural Preservation Office.

Winthrop's overland guide Loolowcan, known more commonly as Lo-kout or LaQuoit, as photographed in 1910 by Edward S. Curtis and there named Luquaiot. Courtesy of Smithsonian Institution Libraries, Washington DC.

Lo-kout or Loolowcan with an Indian police officer ca. 1912. Note the gouge in his forehead gotten from a rifle butt on a battlefield ca. 1856. Courtesy of Washington State University Libraries.

The Duke of York, as Winthrop knew him, actually Chits-a-mah-han or Chet-ze-moka (ca. 1808–1883), later chief of the S'Klallam Tribe. Courtesy of the Jefferson County Historical Society, Port Townsend, Washington.

Theodore Winthrop, 1861. Courtesy of the author's family.

6. "Boston Tilicum"

Night was now coming,—twilight, dearest and tenderest of all the beautiful changes of circling day was upon us. But twilight, the period of repose, and night, of restful slumbers, are not welcome to campaigners, unless a camp, with water, fodder, and fuel, the three requisites of a camp, are provided. We saw our day waning without having revealed to us a spot where these three were coincident. Fuel, indeed, there was anywhere without stint, and water might be found without much searching. But in this primeval wood there were no beds of verdant herbage where Klale and his companions might solace themselves for clambering and plunging and leaping all day. Verdancy enough there was under foot, but it was the green velvet of earthy moss. In some dusty, pebbly openings where the river overflows in spring, the horses had had a noon nibble at spears of grass, juiceless, scanty, and unattractive. My trio of hungry horses flagged sadly.

It was darkening fast when we reached an open spot where Loolowcan had hoped to find grass. Arid starvation alone was visible. Even such wiry attempts at verdure as the stagnant blood of this petty desert had been able to force up through its harsh pores were long ago shaved away by drought. The last nibbles had been taken to-day by the sorry steeds of the exploring party.

There was nothing for it but to go on. Whither? To the next crossing of the river, where the horses might make what they could out of water, and entertain themselves with browsing at alder and maple.

We hurried on, for it was now dark. The Boston hooihut suddenly came charging out of the gloaming, and crossed the trail. Misunderstanding the advice of my taciturn and monosyllabic guide, I left the Indian way, and followed the white man's. Presently it ended, but the trees were blazed where it should pass. Blazes were but faint signals of guidance by twilight. Dimmer grew the woods. Stars were visible overhead, and the black circles of the forest shut off the last gleams of the west. Every obstacle of fallen tree, bramble, and quagmire now loomed large and formidable. And then in the darkness, now fully possessor of the woods, the blazes suddenly disappeared, went out, and ceased, like a deluding will-o'-the-wisp. Here was a crisis. Had the hooihut actually given out here in an invisible blaze, high up a stump? Road that dared so much and did so much, were its energies effete, its purpose broken down? And the pioneers, had they shrunk away from leadership of civilization and slunk homeward?

However that might be, we were at present lost. Ride thou on, Loolowcan, and see if Somewhere is hereabouts; we cannot make a night of it in Nowhere.

Loolowcan dashed Gubbins at darkness; it opened and closed upon him. For a moment I could hear him crashing through the wood; then there was silence. I was quite alone.

Prying into silence for sight or sound, I discerned a rumble, as if of water over a pebbly path. I fastened Klale and Antipodes, as beacons of return, and, laying hold of the pleasant noise of flowing, went with it. Somewhere was actually in my near neighborhood. Sound guided me to sight. Suddenly behind the fir-trunks I caught the gleam of fire. At the same moment, Loolowcan, cautiously stealing back, encountered me.

"Hin pasaiooks copa pire, nika nanitch-pose wake siks; many blanketeers, by a fire, I behold," he whispered, "perhaps not friends."

"Conoway pasaiooks siks copa pasaiooks; all blanketeers friends to blanketeers," I boldly asseverated without regard to history; "wake quash,—ocook Boston tilicum, mamook hooihut; fear not,— these are Boston folk, road-makers."

I led the way confidently toward their beacon-fire. Friends or not, the pasaiooks were better company than black tree-trunks. The flame, at first but a cloudy glimmer, then a flicker, now gave broad and welcome light. It could not conquer darkness with its bold illumination, for darkness is large and strong; but it showed a path out of it. As we worked our way slowly forward, the great trees closed dimly after us,—giants attending out of their domain intruders very willing to be thus sped into realms of better omen.

Beating through a flagellant thicket, we emerged upon the bank of my rumbling stream. Across it a great camp-fire blazed. A belt of reflected crimson lay upon the clear water. Every ripple and breaker of the hostile element tore at this shadow of light, riving it into rags and streamers, and drowning them away down the dell. Still the shattered girdle was there undestroyed, lashing every coming gush of waves, and smiting the stream as if to open a pathway for us, newcomers forth from the darksome wood.

A score of men were grouped about the fire. Several had sprung up alert at the crashing of our approach. Others reposed untroubled. Others tended viands odoriferous and fizzing. Others stirred the flame. Around, the forest rose, black as Erebus,[1] and the men moved in the glare against the gloom like pitmen in the blackest of coal-mines.

I must not dally on the brink, half hid in the obscure thicket, lest the alert ones below should suspect an ambush, and point towards me open-mouthed rifles from their stack near at hand. I was enough out of the woods to halloo, as I did heartily. Klale sprang forward at shout and spur. Antipodes obeyed a comprehensible hint from the whip of Loolowcan. We dashed down into the crimson pathway, and across among the astonished road-makers,—astonished at the sudden alighting down from Nowhere of a pair of cavaliers, pasaiook and siwash. What meant this incursion of a strange couple? I became at once the centre of a red-flannel-shirted circle. The recumbents stood on end. The cooks let their frying-pans bubble over, while, in response to looks of expectation, I hung out my handbill, and told the society my brief and simple tale. I was not running away from any fact in my history. A harmless person, asking no favors, with plenty of pork and spongy biscuit in his bags,— only going home across the continent, if may be, and glad, gentlemen pioneers, of this unexpected pleasure.

My quality thus announced, the boss of the road-makers, without any dissenting voice, offered me the freedom of their fireside. He called for the fatted pork, that I might be entertained right republicanly. Every cook proclaimed supper ready. I followed my representative host to the windward side of the greenwood pyre, lest smoke wafting toward my eyes should compel me to disfigure the banquet with lachrymose countenance.

Fronting the coals, and basking in their embrowning beams, were certain diminutive targets, well known to me as defensive armor against darts of cruel hunger,—cakes of unleavened bread, hight flapjacks in the vernacular, confected of flour and the saline juices of fire-ripened pork, and kneaded well with drops of the living stream. Baked then in frying-pan, they stood now, each nodding forward, and resting its edge upon a planted twig, toasting crustily till crunching-time should come. And now to every man his target! Let supper assail us! No dastards with trencher are we.

In such a Platonic republic as this, a man found his place according to his powers. The cooks were no base scullions; they were brethren, whom conscious ability, sustained by universal suffrage, had endowed with the frying-pan. Each man's target flapjack served him for platter and edible-table. Coffee, also, for beverage, the fraternal cooks set before us in infrangible tin pots,—coffee ripened in its red husk by Brazilian suns thousands of leagues away, that we, in cool Northern forests, might feel the restorative power of its concentrated sunshine, feeding vitality with fresh fuel.

But for my graminivorous steeds, gallopers all day long in rough, unflinching steeple-chase, what had nature done here in the way of provender? Alas! little or naught. This camp of plenty for me was a starvation camp for them. Water, indeed, was turned on liberally; water was flowing in full sluices from the neighbor snows of Tacoma; but more than water was their need, while they feverishly browsed on maple-leaves, to imbitter away their appetites. Only a modicum of my soaked and fungous hardtack could be spared to each. They turned upon me melancholy, reproachful looks; they suffered, and I could only suffer sympathetically. Poor preparation this for toil ahead! But fat prairies also are ahead; have patience, empty mustangs!

My hosts were a stalwart gang. I had truly divined them from
their cleavage on the hooihut. It was but play to anyone of these
to whittle down a cedar five feet in diameter; in the morning, this
compact knot of comrades would explode into a *mitraille*[2] of men
wielding keen axes, and down would go the dumb, stolid files of
the forest. Their talk was as muscular as their arms. When these
laughed, as only men fresh and hearty and in the open air can
laugh, the world became mainly grotesque: it seemed at once a
comic thing to live,—a subject for chuckling, that we were bipeds,
with noses,—a thing to roar at, that we had all met there from the
wide world, to hobnob by a frolicsome fire with tin pots of coffee,
and partake of crisped bacon and toasted doughboys in ridiculous abundance. Easy laughter infected the atmosphere. Echoes
ceased to be pensive, and became jocose. A rattling humor pervaded the forest, and Green River rippled with noise of fantastic
jollity. Civilization and its *dilettante* diners-out sneer when Clodpole at Dives's table[3] doubles his soup, knifes his fish, tilts his plate
into his lap, puts muscle into the crushing of his meringue, and
tosses off the warm beaker in his finger-bowl. Camps by Tacoma
sneer not at all, but candidly roar, at parallel accidents. Gawky
makes a cushion of his flapjack. Butterfingers drops his red-hot
rasher into his bosom, or lets slip his mug of coffee into his boot
drying at the fire,—a boot henceforth saccharine. A mule, slipping
his halter, steps forward unnoticed, puts his nose into the circle,
and brays resonant. These are the jocular boons of life, and at these
the woodsmen guffaw with lusty good-nature. Coarse and rude the
jokes may be, but not nasty, like the innuendoes of pseudo-refined
cockneys. If the woods-men are guilty of uncleanly wit, it differs
from the uncleanly wit of cities as the mud of a road differs from
the sticky slime of slums.

It is a stout sensation to meet masculine, muscular men at the brave point of a penetrating Boston hooihut,—men who are mates,—men to whom technical culture means naught,—men to whom myself am naught, unless I can saddle, lasso, cook, sing, and chop; unless I am a man of nerve and pluck, and a brother in generosity and heartiness. It is restoration to play at cudgels of jocoseness with a circle of friendly roughs, not one of whom ever heard the word bore,—with pioneers, who must think and act, and wrench their living from the closed hand of Nature.

Men who slash with axes in Oregon woods need not be chary of fuel. They fling together boles and branches enough to keep any man's domestic Lares[4] warm for a winter. And over this vast pyre flame takes its splendid pleasure with corybantic dances and roaring paeans of victory.[5] Fire, encouraged to do its work fully, leaves no unsightly grim corses[6] on the field. The glow of embers wastes into the pallor of thin ashes; and winds may clear the spot, drifting away and sprinkling upon brother trees faint, filmy relics of their departed brethren.

While fantastic flashes were still leaping up and illumining the black circuit of forest, every man made his bed, laid down his blankets in starry bivouac, and slept like a mummy. The camp became vocal with snores; nasal with snores of various calibre was the forest. Some in triumphant tones announced that dreams of conflict and victory were theirs; some sighed in dulcet strains that told of lover dreams; some drew shrill whistles through cavernous straits; some wheezed grotesquely, and gasped piteously; and from some who lay supine, snoring up at the fretted roof of forest, sound gushed in spasms, leaked in snorts, bubbled in puffs, as steam gushes, leaks, and bubbles from yawning valves in degraded steamboats. They died away into the music of my dreams, a few moments seemed to pass, and it was day.

As the erect lily droops when the subterranean worm has taken a gnaw at its stalk,—as the dahlia desponds from blossom to tuber when September frosts nip shrewdly,—so at breakfastless morn, after supperless eve, drooped Klale, feebly drooped Gubbins, flabbily drooped Antipodes. A sorry sight! Starvation, coming on the heels of weariness, was fast reducing my stud to the condition of the ghostly estray from the exploring party. But prosperity is not many leagues away from this adversity. Have courage, my trio, if such a passion is possible to the unfed!

If horses were breakfastless, not so was their master. The road-makers had insisted that I should be their guest, partaking not only of the fire, air, earth, and water of their bivouac, but of an honorable share at their feast. Hardly had the snoring of the snorers ceased, when the frying of the fryers began. In the pearly-gray mists of dawn, purple shirts were seen busy about the kindling pile; in the golden haze of sunrise, cooks brandished pans over fierce coals raked from the red-hot jaws of flame that champed their breakfast of fir logs. Rashers, doughboys not without molasses, and coffee—a bill of fare identical with last night's—were our morning meal; but there was absolute change of circumstance to prevent monotony. We had daylight instead of firelight, freshness instead of fatigue, and every man flaunted a motto of "Up and doing!" upon his oriflamme, instead of trailing a drooping flag, inscribed "Done up!"

And so adieu, gentlemen pioneers, and thanks for your frank, manly hospitality! Adieu, "Boston tilicum," far better types of robust Americanism than some of those selected as its representatives by Boston of the Orient, where is too much worship of what is, and not too much uplifting of hopeful looks toward what ought to be!

As I started, the woodsmen gave me a salute. Down, to echo my shout of farewell, went a fir of fifty years' standing. It cracked sharp, like the report of a howitzer, and crashed downward, filling the woods with shattered branches. Under cover of this first shot, I dashed at the woods. I could ride more boldly forward into savageness, knowing that the front ranks of my nation were following close behind.

7. Tacoma

Up and down go the fortunes of men, now benignant, now malignant. *Ante meridiem*[1] of our lives, we are rising characters. Our full noon comes, and we are borne with plaudits on the shoulders of a grateful populace. *Post meridiem*, we are ostracized, if not more rudely mobbed. At twilight, we are perhaps recalled, and set on the throne of Nestor.[2]

Such slow changes in esteem are for men of some import and of settled character. Loolowcan suffered under a more rapidly fluctuating public opinion. At the camp of the road-makers, he had passed through a period of neglect,—almost of ignominy. My hosts had prejudices against red-skins; they treated the son of Owhhigh with no consideration; and he became depressed and slinking in manner under the influence of their ostracism. No sooner had we disappeared from the range of Boston eyes than Loolowcan resumed his leadership and his control. I was very secondary now, and followed him humbly enough up the heights we had reached. Here were all the old difficulties increased, because they were no longer met on a level. We were to climb the main ridge,—the mountain of La Tete,—abandoning the valley, assaulting the summits. And here, as Owhhigh had prophesied in his harangue at Nisqually, the horse's mane must be firmly grasped by the climber. Poor, panting, weary nags! may it be true, the promise of Loolowcan, that not far away is abundant fodder! But where can aught, save firs with ostrich digestion, grow on these rough, forest-clad shoulders?

So I clambered on till near noon.

I had been following thus for many hours the blind path, harsh, darksome, and utterly lonely, urging on with no outlook, encountering no landmark,—at last, as I stormed a ragged crest, gaining a height that overtopped the firs, and, halting there for panting moments, glanced to see if I had achieved mastery as well as position,—as I looked somewhat wearily and drearily across the solemn surges of forest, suddenly above their sombre green appeared Tacoma. Large and neighbor it stood, so near that every jewel of its snow-fields seemed to send me a separate ray; yet not so near but that I could with one look take in its whole image, from clear-cut edge to edge.

All around it the dark evergreens rose like a ruff; above them the mountain splendors swelled statelier for the contrast. Sunlight of noon was so refulgent upon the crown, and lay so thick and dazzling in nooks and chasms, that the eye sought repose of gentler lights, and found it in shadowed nooks and clefts, where, sunlight entering not, delicate mist, an emanation from the blue sky, had fallen, and lay sheltered and tremulous, a mild substitute for the stronger glory. The blue haze so wavered and trembled into sun-light, and sunbeams shot glimmering over snowy brinks so like a constant avalanche, that I might doubt whether this movement and waver and glimmer, this blending of mist with noontide flame, were not a drifting smoke and cloud of yellow sulphurous vapor floating over some slowly chilling crater far down in the red crevices.

But if the giant fires had ever burned under that cold summit, they had long since gone out. The dome that swelled up passionately had crusted over and then fallen in upon itself, not vigorous enough with internal life to bear up in smooth proportion. Where it broke into ruin was no doubt a desolate waste, stern, craggy, and riven, but such drear results of Titanic convulsion the gentle snows hid from view.

No foot of man had ever trampled those pure snows. It was a virginal mountain, distant from the possibility of human approach and human inquisitiveness as a marble goddess is from human loves. Yet there was nothing unsympathetic in its isolation, or despotic in its distant majesty. But this serene loftiness was no home for any deity of those that men create. Only the thought of eternal peace arose from this heaven-upbearing monument like incense, and, overflowing, filled the world with deep and holy calm.

Wherever the mountain turned its cheek toward the sun, many fair and smiling dimples appeared, and along soft curves of snow, lines of shadow drew tracery, fair as the blue veins on a child's temple. Without the infinite sweetness and charm of this kindly changefulness of form and color, there might have been oppressive awe in the presence of this transcendent glory against the solemn blue of noon. Grace played over the surface of majesty, as a drift of rose-leaves wavers in the air before a summer shower, or as a wreath of rosy mist flits before the grandeur of a storm. Loveliness was sprinkled like a boon of blossoms upon sublimity.

Our lives forever demand and need visual images that can be symbols to us of the grandeur or the sweetness of repose. There are some faces that arise dreamy in our memories, and look us into calmness in our frantic moods. Fair and happy is a life that need not call upon its vague memorial dreams for such attuning influence, but can turn to a present reality, and ask tranquillity at the shrine of a household goddess. The noble works of nature, and mountains most of all,

> *"have power to make*
> *Our noisy years seem moments in the being*
> *Of the eternal silence."*[3]

And, studying the light and the majesty of Tacoma, there passed from it and entered into my being, to dwell there evermore by the side of many such, a thought and an image of solemn beauty, which I could thenceforth evoke whenever in the world I must have peace or die. For such emotion years of pilgrimage were worthily spent. If mortal can gain the thoughts of immortality, is not his earthly destiny achieved? For, when we have so studied the visible poem, and so fixed it deep in the very substance of our minds, there is forever with us not merely a perpetual possession of delight, but a watchful monitor that will not let our thoughts be long unfit for the pure companionship of beauty. For whenever a man is false to the light that is in him, and accepts meaner joys, or chooses the easy indulgence that meaner passions give, then every fair landscape in all his horizon dims, and all its grandeurs fade and dwindle away, the glory vanishes, and he looks, like one lost, upon his world, late so lovely and sinless.

While I was studying Tacoma, and learning its fine lesson, it in turn might contemplate its own image far away on the waters of Whulge, where streams from its own snows, gushing seaward to buffet in the boundless deep, might rejoice in a last look at their

parent ere they swept out of Puyallop Bay. Other large privilege of
view it had. It could see what I could not,—Tacoma the Less, Mt.
Adams, meritorious but clumsy; it could reflect sunbeams gracefully across a breadth of forest to St. Helen's, the vestal virgin,[4] who
still kept her flame kindled, and proved her watchfulness ever and
anon. Continuing its panoramic studies, Tacoma could trace the
chasm of the Columbia by silver circles here and there,—could see
every peak, chimney, or unopened vent, from Kulshan to Shasta
Butte. The Blue Mountains eastward were within its scope, and
westward the faint-blue levels of the Pacific. Another region, worthy of any mountain's beholding, Tacoma sees, somewhat vague
and dim in distance: it sees the sweet Arcadian valley of the Willamette, charming with meadow, park, and grove. In no older world
where men have, in all their happiest moods, recreated themselves
for generations in taming earth to orderly beauty, have they achieved
a fairer garden than Nature's simple labor of love has made there,
giving to rough pioneers the blessings and the possible education of
refined and finished landscape, in the presence of landscape strong,
savage, and majestic.

All this Tacoma beholds, as I can but briefly hint; and as one who
is a seer himself becomes a tower of light and illumination to the
world, so Tacoma, so every brother seer of his among the lofty snow-
peaks, stands to educate, by his inevitable presence, every dweller
thereabouts. Our race has never yet come into contact with great
mountains as companions of daily life, nor felt that daily development of the finer and more comprehensive senses which these signal
facts of nature compel. That is an influence of the future. The Oregon people, in a climate where being is bliss,—where every breath
is a draught of vivid life,—these Oregon people, carrying to a new
and grander New England of the West a fuller growth of the Amer-

ican Idea, under whose teaching the man of lowest ambitions must still have some little indestructible respect for himself, and the brute of most tyrannical aspirations some little respect for others; carrying there a religion two centuries farther on than the crude and cruel Hebraism of the Puritans; carrying the civilization of history where it will not suffer by the example of Europe,—with such material, that Western society, when it crystallizes, will elaborate new systems of thought and life. It is unphilosophical to suppose that a strong race, developing under the best, largest, and calmest conditions of nature, will not achieve a destiny.

Up to Tacoma, or into some such solitude of nature, imaginative men must go, as Moses went up to Sinai, that the divine afflatus may stir within them. The siwashes appreciate, according to their capacity, the inspiration of lonely grandeur, and go upon the mountains, starving and alone, that they may become seers, enchanters, magicians, diviners,—what in conventional lingo is called "big medicine." For though the Indians here have not peopled these thrones of their world with the creatures of an anthropomorphic mythology, they yet deem them the abode of Tamanous. Tamanous is a vague and half-personified type of the unknown, of the mysterious forces of nature; and there is also an indefinite multitude of undefined emanations, each one a tamanous with a small t, which are busy and impish in complicating existence, or equally active and spritely in unravelling it. Each Indian of this region patronizes his own personal tamanous, as men of the more eastern tribes keep a private manitto, and as Socrates kept a daimon.[5] To supply this want, Tamanous with a big T undergoes an avatar, and incarnates himself into a salmon, a beaver, a clam, or into some inanimate object, such as a canoe, a paddle, a fir-tree, a flint; or into some elemental essence, as fire, water, sun, mist; and tamanous thus individualized becomes the "guide, philosopher, and friend" of every siwash, conscious that otherwise he might stray and be lost in the unknown realms of Tamanous.

Hamitchou, a frowzy ancient of the Squallyamish, told to Dr. Tolmie and me, at Nisqually, a legend of Tamanous and Tacoma, which, being interpreted, runs as fellows:—

HAMITCHOU'S LEGEND

"Avarice, O Boston tyee," quoth Hamitchou, studying me with dusky eyes, "is a mighty passion. Now, be it known unto thee that we Indians anciently used not metals nor the money of you blanketeers. Our circulating medium was shells,—wampum you would name it. Of all wampum, the most precious is Hiaqua.[6] Hiaqua comes from the far north. It is a small, perforated shell, not unlike a very opaque quill toothpick, tapering from the middle, and cut square at both ends. We string it in many strands, and hang it around the neck of one we love,—namely, each man his own neck. We also buy with it what our hearts desire. He who has most hiaqua is best and wisest and happiest of all the northern Haida and of all the people of Whulge. The mountain horsemen value it; and braves of the terrible Blackfeet have been known, in the good old days, to come over and offer a horse or a wife for a bunch of fifty hiaqua.

"Now, once upon a time there dwelt where this fort of Nisqually now stands a wise old man of the Squallyamish. He was a great fisherman and a great hunter; and the wiser he grew, much the wiser he thought himself. When he had grown very wise, he used to stay apart from every other siwash. Companionable salmon-boilings round a common pot had no charms for him. 'Feasting was wasteful,' he said, 'and revellers would come to want.' And when they verified his prophecy, and were full of hunger and empty of salmon, he came out of his hermitage, and had salmon to sell.

"Hiaqua was the pay he always demanded; and as he was a very wise old man, and knew all the tideways of Whulge, and all the enticing ripples and placid spots of repose in every river where fish might dash or delay, he was sure to have salmon when others wanted, and thus bagged largely of its precious equivalent, hiaqua.

"Not only a mighty fisher was the sage, but a mighty hunter, and elk, the greatest animal of the woods, was the game he loved. Well had he studied every trail where elk leave the print of their hoofs, and where, tossing their heads, they bend the tender twigs. Well had he searched through the broad forest, and found the longhaired prairies where elk feed luxuriously; and there, from behind palisade fir-trees, he had launched the fatal arrow. Sometimes, also, he lay beside a pool of sweetest water, revealed to him by gemmy reflections of sunshine gleaming through the woods, until at noon the elk came down, to find death awaiting him as he stooped and drank. Or beside the same fountain the old man watched at night, drowsily starting at every crackling branch, until, when the moon was high, and her illumination declared the pearly water, elk dashed forth incautious into the glade, and met their midnight destiny.

"Elk-meat, too, he sold to his tribe. This brought him pelf, but, alas for his greed, the pelf came slowly. Waters and woods were rich in game. All the Squallyamish were hunters and fishers, though none so skilled as he. They were rarely in absolute want, and, when they came to him for supplies, they were far too poor in hiaqua.

"So the old man thought deeply, and communed with his wisdom, and, while he waited for fish or beast, he took advice within himself from his demon,—he talked with Tamanous. And always the question was, 'How may I put hiaqua in my purse?'

"Tamanous never revealed to him that far to the north, beyond the waters of Whulge, are tribes with their under lip pierced with a fishbone, among whom hiaqua is plenty as salmon-berries are in the woods what time in mid-summer salmon fin it along the reaches of Whulge.

"But the more Tamanous did not reveal to him these mysteries of nature, the more he kept dreamily prying into his own mind, endeavoring to devise some scheme by which he might discover a treasure-trove of the beloved shell. His life seemed wasted in the patient, frugal industry, which only brought slow, meagre gains. He wanted the splendid elation of vast wealth and the excitement of sudden wealth. His own peculiar tamanous was the elk. Elk was also his totem, the cognizance of his freemasonry with those of his own family, and their family friends in other tribes. Elk, therefore, were every way identified with his life; and he hunted them farther and farther up through the forests on the flanks of Tacoma, hoping that some day his tamanous would speak in the dying groan of one of them, and gasp out the secret of the mines of hiaqua, his heart's desire.

"Tacoma was so white and glittering, that it seemed to stare at him very terribly and mockingly, and to know his shameful avarice, and how it led him to take from starving women their cherished lip and nose jewels of hiaqua, and to give them in return only tough scraps of dried elk-meat and salmon. When men are shabby, mean, and grasping, they feel reproached for their grovelling lives by the unearthliness of nature's beautiful objects, and they hate flowers, and sunsets, mountains, and the quiet stars of heaven.

"Nevertheless," continued Hamitchou, "this wise old fool of my legend went on stalking elk along the sides of Tacoma, ever dreaming of wealth. And at last, as he was hunting near the snows one day, one very clear and beautiful day of late summer, when sunlight was magically disclosing far distances, and making all nature supernaturally visible and proximate, Tamanous began to work in the soul of the miser.

"'Are you brave,' whispered Tamanous in the strange, ringing, dull, silent thunder-tones of a demon voice. 'Dare you go to the caves where my treasures are hid?'

"'I dare,' said the miser.

"He did not know that his lips had syllabled a reply. He did not even hear his own words. But all the place had become suddenly vocal with echoes. The great rock against which he leaned crashed forth, 'I dare.' Then all along through the forest, dashing from tree to tree and lost at last among the murmuring of breeze-shaken leaves, went careering his answer, taken up and repeated scornfully, 'I dare.' And after a silence, while the daring one trembled and would gladly have ventured to shout, for the companionship of his own voice, there came across from the vast snow wall of Tacoma a tone like the muffled, threatening plunge of an avalanche into a chasm, 'I dare.'

"'You dare,' said Tamanous, enveloping him with a dread sense of an unseen, supernatural presence; 'you pray for wealth of hiaqua. Listen!'

"This injunction was hardly needed; the miser was listening with dull eyes kindled and starting. He was listening with every rusty hair separating from its unkempt mattedness, and outstanding upright, a caricature of an aureole.

"'Listen,' said Tamanous, in the noonday hush. And then Tamanous vouchsafed at last the great secret of the hiaqua mines, while in terror near to death the miser heard, and every word of guidance toward the hidden treasure of the mountains seared itself into his soul ineffaceably.

"Silence came again more terrible now than the voice of Tamanous,—silence under the shadow of the great cliff,—silence deepening down the forest vistas,—silence filling the void up to the snows of Tacoma. All life and motion seemed paralyzed. At last Skai-ki, the Blue-Jay, the wise bird, foe to magic, sang cheerily overhead. Her song seemed to refresh again the honest laws of nature. The buzz of life stirred everywhere again, and the inspired miser rose and hastened home to prepare for his work.

"When Tamanous has put a great thought in a man's brain, has whispered him a great discovery within his power, or hinted at a great crime, that spiteful demon does not likewise suggest the means of accomplishment.

"The miser, therefore, must call upon his own skill to devise proper tools, and upon his own judgment to fix upon the most fitting time for carrying out his quest. Sending his squaw out to the kamas prairie, under pretence that now was the season for her to gather their winter store of that sickish-sweet esculent root, and that she might not have her squaw's curiosity aroused by seeing him at strange work, he began his preparations. He took a pair of enormous elk-horns, and fashioned from each horn a two-pronged pick or spade, by removing all the antlers except the two topmost. He packed a good supply of kippered salmon, and filled his pouch with kinnikinnick[7] for smoking in his black stone pipe. With his bow and arrows and his two elk-horn picks wrapped in buckskin hung at his back, he started just before sunset, as if for a long hunt. His old, faithful, maltreated, blanketless, vermilionless squaw, returning with baskets full of kamas, saw him disappearing moodily down the trail.

"All that night, all the day following, he moved on noiselessly by paths he knew. He hastened on, unnoticing outward objects, as one with a controlling purpose hastens. Elk and deer, bounding through the trees, passed him, but he tarried not. At night he camped just below the snows of Tacoma. He was weary, weary, and chill night-airs blowing down from the summit almost froze him. He dared not take his fire-sticks, and, placing one perpendicular upon a little hollow on the flat side of the other, twirl the upright stick rapidly between his palms until the charred spot kindled and lighted his 'tipsoo,' his dry, tindery wool of inner bark. A fire, gleaming high upon the mountain-side, might be a beacon to draw thither any night-wandering savage to watch in ambush, and learn the path toward the mines of hiaqua. So he drowsed chilly and fireless, awakened often by dread sounds of crashing and rumbling among the chasms of Tacoma. He desponded bitterly, almost ready to abandon his quest, almost doubting whether he had in truth received a revelation, whether his interview with Tamanous had not been a dream, and finally whether all the hiaqua in the world was worth this toil and anxiety. Fortunate is the sage who at such a point turns back and buys his experience without worse befalling him.

"Past midnight he suddenly was startled from his drowse, and sat bolt upright in terror. A light! Was there another searcher in the forest, and a bolder than he? That flame just glimmering over the tree-tops, was it a camp-fire of friend or foe? Had Tamanous been revealing to another the great secret? No, smiled the miser, his eyes fairly open, and discovering that the new light was the moon. He had been waiting for her illumination on paths heretofore untrodden by mortal. She did not show her full, round, jolly face, but turned it askance as if she hardly liked to be implicated this night's transactions.

"However, it was light he wanted, not sympathy, and he started up at once to climb over the dim snows. The surface was packed by the night's frost, and his moccasins gave him firm hold; yet he traveled but slowly, and could not always save himself from a *glissade* backwards, and a bruise upon some projecting knob or crag.

Sometimes, upright fronts of ice diverted him for long circuits, or a broken wall of cold cliff arose, which he must surmount painfully. Once or twice he stuck fast in a crevice, and hardly drew himself out by placing his bundle of picks across the crack. As he plodded and floundered thus deviously and toilsomely upward, at last the wasted moon gan pale overhead, and under foot the snow grew rosy with coming dawn. The dim world about the mountain's base displayed something of its vast detail. He could see, more positively than by moonlight, the far-reaching arteries of mist marking the organism of Whulge beneath; and what had been but a black chaos now resolved itself into the Alpine forest whence he had come.

"But he troubled himself little with staring about; up he looked, for the summit was at hand. To win that summit was wellnigh the attainment of his hopes, if Tamanous were true; and that, with the flush of morning ardor upon him, he could not doubt. There, in a spot Tamanous had revealed to him, was hiaqua,—hiaqua that should make him the richest and greatest of all the Squallyamish.

"The chill before sunrise was upon him as he reached the last curve of the dome. Sunrise and he struck the summit together. Together sunrise and he looked over the glacis.[8] They saw within a great hollow all covered with the whitest of snow, save at the centre, where a black lake lay deep in a well of purple rock.

"At the eastern end of this lake was a small, irregular plain of snow, marked by three stones like monuments. Toward these the miser sprang rapidly, with full sunshine streaming after him over the snows.

"The first monument he examined with keen looks. It was tall as a giant man, and its top was fashioned into the grotesque likeness of a salmon's head. He turned from this to inspect the second. It was of similar height, but bore at its apex an object in shape like the regular flame of a torch. As he approached, he presently discovered that this was an image of the kamas-bulb in stone. These two semblances of prime necessities of Indian life delayed him but an instant, and he hastened on to the third monument, which stood apart on a perfect level. The third stone was capped by something he almost feared to behold, lest it should prove other than his hopes. Every word of Tamanous had thus far proved veritable; but might there not be a bitter deceit at the last? The miser trembled.

"Yes, Tamanous was trustworthy. The third monument was as the old man anticipated. It was a stone elk's-head, such as it appears in earliest summer, when the antlers are sprouting lustily under their rough jacket of velvet.

"You remember, Boston tyee," continued Hamitchou, "that Elk was the old man's tamanous, the incarnation for him of the universal Tamanous. He therefore was right joyous at this good omen of protection; and his heart grew big and swollen with hope, as the black salmon-berry swells in a swamp in June. He threw down his 'ikta'; every impediment he laid down upon the snow; and, unwrapping his two picks of elk-horn, he took the stoutest, and began to dig in the frozen snow at the foot of the elk-head monument.

"No sooner had he struck the first blow than he heard behind him a sudden puff, such as a seal makes when it comes to the surface to breathe. Turning round much startled, he saw a huge otter just clambering up over the edge of the lake. The otter paused, and struck on the snow with his tail, whereupon another otter and another appeared, until, following their leader in slow and solemn file, were twelve other otters, marching toward the miser. The twelve approached, and drew up in a circle around him. Each was twice as large as any otter ever seen. Their chief was four times as large as the most gigantic otter ever seen in the regions of Whulge, and certainly was as great as a seal. When the twelve were arranged, their leader skipped to the top of the elk-head stone, and sat there between the horns. Then the whole thirteen gave a mighty puff in chorus.

"The hunter of hiaqua was for a moment abashed at his uninvited ring of spectators. But he had seen otter before, and bagged them. These he could not waste time to shoot, even if a phalanx so numerous were not formidable. Besides, they might be tamanous. He took to his pick, and began digging stoutly.

"He soon made way in the snow, and came to solid rock beneath. At every thirteenth stroke of his pick, the fugleman otter tapped with his tail on the monument. Then the choir of lesser otters tapped together with theirs on the snow. This caudal action produced a dull, muffled sound, as if there were a vast hollow below.

"Digging with all his force, by and by the seeker for treasure began to tire, and laid down his elk-horn spade to wipe the sweat from his brow. Straightway the fugleman otter turned, and, swinging his tail, gave the weary man a mighty thump on the shoulder; and the whole band, imitating, turned, and backing inward, smote him with centripetal tails, until he resumed his labors, much bruised.

"The rock lay first in plates, then in scales. These it was easy to remove. Presently, however, as the miser pried carelessly at a larger mass, he broke his elkhorn tool. Fugleman otter leaped down, and, seizing the supplemental pick between his teeth, mouthed it over to the digger. Then the amphibious monster took in the same manner the broken pick, and bore it round the circle of his suite, who inspected it gravely with puffs.

"These strange, magical proceedings disconcerted and somewhat baffled the miser; but he plucked up heart, for the prize was priceless, and worked on more cautiously with his second pick. At last its blows and the regular thumps of the otters' tails called forth a sound hollower and hollower. His circle of spectators narrowed so that he could feel their panting breath as they bent curiously over the little pit he had dug.

"The crisis was evidently at hand.

"He lifted each scale of rock more delicately. Finally he raised a scale so thin that it cracked into flakes as he turned it over. Beneath was a large square cavity.

"It was filled to the brim with hiaqua.

"He was a millionnaire.

"The otters recognized him as the favorite of Tamanous, and retired to a respectful distance.

"For some moments he gazed on his treasure, taking thought of his future proud grandeur among the dwellers by Whulge. He plunged his arm deep as he could go; there was still nothing but the precious shells. He smiled to himself in triumph; he had wrung the secret from Tamanous. Then, as he withdrew his arm, the rattle of the hiaqua recalled him to the present. He saw that noon was long past, and he must proceed to reduce his property to possession.

"The hiaqua was strung upon long, stout sinews of elk, in bunches of fifty shells on each side. Four of these he wound about his waist; three he hung across each shoulder; five he took in each hand;— twenty strings of pure white hiaqua, every shell large, smooth, unbroken, beautiful. He could carry no more; hardly even with this could he stagger along. He put down his burden for a moment, while he covered up the seemingly untouched wealth of the deposit carefully with the scale stones, and brushed snow over the whole.

"The miser never dreamed of gratitude, never thought to hang a string from the buried treasure about the salmon and kamas tamanous stones, and two strings around the elk's head; no, all must be his own, all he could carry now, and the rest for the future.

"He turned, and began his climb toward the crater's edge. At once the otters, with a mighty puff in concert, took up their line of procession, and, plunging into the black lake, began to beat the water with their tails.

"The miser could hear the sound of splashing water as he struggled upward through the snow, now melted and yielding. It was a long hour of harsh toil and much backsliding before he reached the rim, and turned to take one more view of this valley of good fortune.

"As he looked, a thick mist began to rise from the lake centre, where the otters were splashing. Under the mist grew a cylinder of black cloud, utterly hiding the water.

"Terrible are storms in the mountains; but in this looming mass was a terror more dread than any hurricane of ruin ever bore within its wild vortexes. Tamanous was in that black cylinder, and as it strode forward, chasing in the very path of the miser, he shuddered, for his wealth and his life were in danger.

"However, it might be but a common storm. Sunlight was bright as ever overhead in heaven, and all the lovely world below lay dreamily fair, in that afternoon of summer, at the feet of the rich man, who now was hastening to be its king. He stepped from the crater edge and began his descent.

"Instantly the storm overtook him. He was thrown down by its first assault, flung over a rough bank of iciness, and lay at the foot torn and bleeding, but clinging still to his precious burden. Each hand still held its five strings of hiaqua. In each hand he bore a nation's ransom. He staggered to his feet against the blast. Utter night was around him,—night as if daylight had forever perished, had never come into being from chaos. The roaring of the storm had also deafened and bewildered him with its wild uproar.

"Present in every crash and thunder of the gale was a growing undertone, which the miser well knew to be the voice of Tamanous. A deadly shuddering shook him. Heretofore that potent Unseen had been his friend and guide; there had been awe, but no terror, in his words. Now the voice of Tamanous was inarticulate, but the miser could divine in that sound an unspeakable threat of wrath and vengeance. Floating upon this undertone were sharper tamanous voices, shouting and screaming always sneeringly, 'Ha ha, hiaqua!—ha, ha, ha!'

"Whenever the miser essayed to move and continue his descent, a whirlwind caught him, and with much ado tossed him hither and thither, leaving him at last flung and imprisoned in a pinching crevice, or buried to the eyes in a snowdrift, or bedded upside down on a shaggy boulder, or gnawed by lacerating lava jaws. Sharp torture the old man was encountering, but he held fast to his hiaqua.

"The blackness grew ever deeper and more crowded with perdition; the din more impish, demoniac, and devilish; the laughter more appalling; and the miser more and more exhausted with vain buffeting. He determined to propitiate exasperated Tamanous with a sacrifice. He threw into the black cylinder storm his left-handful, five strings of precious hiaqua."

"Somewhat long-winded is thy legend, Hamitchou, Great Medicine-Man of the Squallyamish," quoth I. "Why didn't the old fool drop his wampum,—shell out, as one might say,—and make tracks?"

"Well, well!" continued Hamitchou; "when the miser had thrown away his first handful of hiaqua, there was a momentary lull in elemental war, and he heard the otters puffing around him invisible. Then the storm renewed, blacker, louder, harsher, crueller than before, and over the dread undertone of the voice of Tamanous, tamanous voices again screamed, 'Ha, ha, ha, hiaqua!' and it seemed as if tamanous hands, or the paws of the demon otters, clutched at the miser's right-handful and tore at his shoulder and waist belts.

"So, while darkness and tempest still buffeted the hapless old man, and thrust him away from his path, and while the roaring was wickeder than the roars of tens and tens of tens of bears when ahungered they pounce upon a plain of kamas, gradually wounded and terrified, he flung away string after string of hiaqua, gaining never any notice of such sacrifice, except an instant's lull of the cyclon and a puff from the invisible otters.

"The last string he clung to long, and before he threw it to be caught and whirled after its fellows, he tore off a single bunch of fifty shells. But upon this, too, the storm laid its clutches. In the final desperate struggle the old man was wounded so sternly that, when he had given up his last relic of the mighty treasure, when he had thrown into the formless chaos, instinct with Tamanous, his last propitiatory offering, he sank and became insensible.

"It seemed a long slumber to him, but at last he awoke. The jagged moon was just paling overhead, and he heard Skai-ki, the Blue-Jay, foe to magic, singing welcome to sunrise. It was the very spot whence he started at morning.

"He was hungry, and felt for his bag of kamas and pouch of smoke-leaves. There, indeed, by his side were the elk-sinew strings of the bag, and the black stone pipe-bowl,—but no bag, no kamas, no kinnikinnick. The whole spot was thick with kamas plants, strangely out of place on the mountain-side, and overhead grew a large arbutus-tree, with glistening leaves, ripe for smoking. The old man found his hard-wood fire-sticks safe under the herbage, and soon twirled a light, and, nurturing it in dry grass, kindled a cheery fire. He plucked up kamas, set it to roast, and laid a store of the arbutus-leaves to dry on a flat stone.

"After he had made a hearty breakfast on the chestnut-like kamas-bulbs, and, smoking the thoughtful pipe, was reflecting on the events of yesterday, he became aware of an odd change in his condition. He was not bruised and wounded from head to foot, as he expected, but very stiff only, and as he stirred, his joints creaked like the creak of a lazy paddle upon the rim of a canoe. Skai-ki, the Blue-Jay, was singularly familiar with him, hopping from her perch in the arbutus, and alighting on his head. As he put his hand to dislodge her, he touched his scratching-stick of bone, and attempted to pass it, as usual, through his hair. The hair was matted and interlaced into a network reaching fully two ells down his back. 'Tamanous,' thought the old man.

"Chiefly he was conscious of a mental change. He was calm and content. Hiaqua and wealth seemed to have lost their charms for him. Tacoma, shining like gold and silver and precious stones of gayest lustre, seemed a benign comrade and friend. All the outer world was cheerful and satisfying. He thought he had never awakened to a fresher morning. He was a young man again, except for that unusual stiffness and unmelodious creaking in his joints. He felt no apprehension of any presence of a deputy tamanous, sent by Tamanous to do malignities upon him in the lonely wood. Great Nature had a kindly aspect, and made its divinity perceived only by the sweet notes of birds and the hum of forest life, and by a joy that clothed his being. And now he found in his heart a sympathy for man, and a longing to meet his old acquaintances down by the shores of Whulge.

"He rose, and started on the downward way, smiling, and sometimes laughing heartily at the strange croaking, moaning, cracking, and rasping of his joints. But soon motion set the lubricating valves at work, and the sockets grew slippery again. He marched rapidly, hastening out of loneliness into society. The world of wood, glade, and stream seemed to him strangely altered. Old colossal trees, firs behind which he had hidden when on the hunt, cedars under whose drooping shade he had lurked, were down, and lay athwart his path, transformed into immense mossy mounds, like barrows of giants, over which he must clamber warily, lest he sink and be half stifled in the dust of rotten wood. Had Tamanous been widely at work in that eventful night?—or had the spiritual change the old man felt affected his views of the outer world?

"Travelling downward, he advanced rapidly, and just before sunset came to the prairies where his lodge should be. Everything had seemed to him so totally altered, that he tarried a moment in the edge of the woods to take an observation before approaching his home. There was a lodge, indeed, in the old spot, but a newer and far handsomer one than he had left on the fourth evening before.

"A very decrepit old squaw, ablaze with vermilion and decked with countless strings of hiaqua and costly beads, was seated on the ground near the door, tending a kettle of salmon, whose blue and fragrant steam mingled pleasantly with the golden haze of sunset. She resembled his own squaw in countenance, as an ancient smoked salmon is like a newly-dried salmon. If she was indeed his spouse, she was many years older than when he saw her last, and much better dressed than the respectable lady had ever been during his miserly days.

"He drew near quietly. The bedizened dame was crooning a chant, very dolorous,—like this:

'My old man has gone, gone, gone,—
My old man to Tacoma has gone.
To hunt the elk, he went long ago.
When will he come down, down, down,
Down to the salmon-pot and me?'

'He has come from Tacoma down, down, down,—
Down to the salmon-pot and thee,'

shouted the reformed miser, rushing forward to supper and his faithful wife."

"And how did Penelope explain the mystery?" I asked.[9]

"If you mean the old lady," replied Hamitchou, "she was my grandmother, and I'd thank you not to call names. She told my grandfather that he had been gone many years;—she could not tell how many, having dropped her tally-stick in the fire by accident that very day. She also told him how, in despite of the entreaties of many a chief who knew her economic virtues, and prayed her to become mistress of his household, she had remained constant to the Absent, and forever kept the hopeful salmon-pot boiling for his return. She had distracted her mind from the bitterness of sorrow by trading in kamas and magic herbs, and had thus acquired a genteel competence. The excellent dame then exhibited with great complacency her gains, most of which she had put in the portable and secure form of personal ornament, making herself a resplendent magazine of valuable frippery.

"Little cared the repentant sage for such things. But he was rejoiced to be again at home and at peace, and near his own early gains of hiaqua and treasure, buried in a place of security. These, however, he no longer overesteemed and hoarded. He imparted whatever he possessed, material treasures or stores of wisdom and experience, freely to all the land. Every dweller by Whulge came to him for advice how to chase the elk, how to troll or spear the salmon, and how to propitiate Tamanous. He became the Great Medicine Man of the siwashes, a benefactor to his tribe and his race.

"Within a year after he came down from his long nap on the side of Tacoma, a child, my father, was born to him. The sage lived many years, beloved and revered, and on his deathbed, long before the Boston tilicum or any blanketeers were seen in the regions of Whulge, he told this history to my father, as a lesson and a warning. My father, dying, told it to me. But I, alas! have no son; I grow old, and lest this wisdom perish from the earth, and Tamanous be again obliged to interpose against avarice, I tell the tale to thee, O Boston tyee. Mayest thou and thy nation not disdain this lesson of an earlier age, but profit by it and be wise."

So far Hamitchou recounted his legend without the palisades of Fort Nisqually, and motioning, in expressive pantomime, at the close, that he was dry with big talk, and would gladly wet his whistle.

8. Sowee House—Loolowcan

I had not long, that noon of August, from the top of La Tete, to study Tacoma, scene of Hamitchou's wild legend. Humanity forbade dalliance. While I fed my soul with sublimity, Klale and his comrades were wretched with starvation. But the summit of the pass is near. A few struggles more, Klale the plucky, and thy empty sides shall echo less drum-like. Up stoutly, my steeds; up a steep but little less than perpendicular, paw over these last trunks of the barricades in our trail, and ye have won!

So it was. The angle of our ascent suddenly broke down from ninety to fifteen, then to nothing. We had reached the plateau. Here were the first prairies. Nibble in these, my nags, for a few refreshing moments, and then on to superlative dinners in lovelier spots just beyond.

Let no one, exaggerating the joys of campaigning, with Horace's "Militia potior est,"[1] deem that there is no compensating pang among them. Is it a pleasant thing, O traveler only in dreams, envier of the voyager in reality, to urge tired, reluctant, and unfed mustangs up a mountain pass, even for their own good? In such a case a man, the humanest and gentlest, must adopt the manners of a brute. He must ply the whip, and that cruelly; otherwise, no go. At first, as he smites, he winces, for he has struck his own sensibilities; by and by he hardens himself, and thrashes without a tremor. When the cortege arrives at an edible prairie, gastronomic satisfaction will put Lethean[2] freshness in the battered hide of every horse.

We presently turned just aside from the trail into an episode of beautiful prairie, one of a succession along the plateau at the crest of the range. At this height of about five thousand feet, the snows remain until June. In this fair, oval, forest-circled prairie of my nooning, the grass was long and succulent, as if it grew in the bed of a drained lake. The horses, undressed, were allowed to plunge and wallow in the deep herbage. Only horse heads soon could be seen, moving about like their brother hippopotami, swimming in sedges.

To me it was luxury enough not to be a whip for a time. Over and above this, I had the charm of a quiet nooning on a bank of emerald turf, by a spring, at the edge of a clump of evergreens. I took my luncheon of cold salt pork and doughy biscuit by a well of brightest water. I called in no proxy of tin cup to aid me in saluting this sparkling creature, but stooped and kissed the spring. When I had rendered my first homage thus to the goddess of the fountain, Ægle[3] herself, perhaps, fairest of Naiads,[4] I drank thirstily of the medium in which she dwelt. A bubbling dash of water leaped up and splashed my visage as I withdrew. Why so, sweet fountain, which I may name Hippocrene,[5] since hoofs of Klale have caused me thy discovery? Is this a rebuff? If there ever was lover who little merited such treatment it is I. "Not so, appreciative stranger," came up in other bubbling gushes the responsive voice of Nature through sweet vibrations of the melodious fount. "Never a Nymph of mine will thrust thee back. This sudden leap of water was a movement of sympathy, and a gentle emotion of hospitality. The Naiad there was offering thee her treasure liberally, and saying that, drink as thou wilt, I, her mother Nature, have commanded my winds and sun to distil thee fresh supplies, and my craggy crevices are filtering it in the store-houses, that it may be offered to every welcome guest, pure and cool as airs of dawn. Stoop down," continued the voice, "thirsty wayfarer, and kiss again my daughter of the fountain, nor be abashed if she meets thee half-way. She knows that a true lover will never scorn his love's delicate advances."

In response to such invitation, and the more for my thirsty slices of pork, I lapped the aerated tipple in its goblet, whose stem reaches deep into the bubble laboratories.[6] I lapped,—an excellent test of pluck in the days of Gideon son of Barak;[7]—and why? For many reasons, but among them for this;—he who lying prone can with stout muscular gullet swallow water, will be also able to swallow back into position his heart, when in moments of tremor it leaps into his throat.

When I had lapped plenteously, I lay and let the breeze-shaken shadows smooth me into smiling mood, while my sympathies overflowed to enjoy with my horses their dinner. They fed like schoolboys home for Thanksgiving, in haste lest the present banquet, too good to be true, prove Barmecide.[8] A feast of colossal grasses placed itself at the lips of the breakfastless stud. They champed as their nature was;—Klale like a hungry gentleman,—Gubbins like a hungry clodhopper,—Antipodes like a lubberly oaf. They were laying in, according to the Hudson's Bay Company's rule, supply at this

meal for five days; without such power, neither man nor horse is fit
to tramp the Northwest.

I lay on the beautiful verdant bank, plucking now dextrously and
now sinistrously of strawberries, that summer, climbing late to these
snowy heights, had just ripened. Medical men command us to swallow twice a day one bitter pill confectioned of all disgust. Nature
doses us, by no means against our will, with many sweet boluses of
delight, berries compacted of acidulated, sugary spiciness. Nature,
tenderest of leeches,—no bolus of hers is pleasanter medicament
than her ruddy strawberries. She shaped them like Minie-balls,[9]
that they might traverse unerringly to the cell of most dulcet digestion. Over their glistening surface she peppered little golden dots to
act as obstacles lest they should glide too fleetly over the surfaces of
taste, and also to gently rasp them into keener sensitiveness. Mon-
gers of pestled poisons may punch their pills in malodorous mor-
tars, roll them in floury palms, pack them in pink boxes, and send
them forth to distress a world of patients:—but Nature, who if she
even feels one's pulse does it by a gentle pressure of atmosphere,—
Nature, knowing that her children in their travels always need lively
tonics, tells wind, sun, and dew, servitors of hers, clean and fine of
touch, to manipulate gay strawberries, and dispose them attractively
on fair green terraces, shaded at parching noon. Of these lovely
fabrics of pithy pulpiness, no limit to the dose, if the invalid does
as Nature intended, and plucks for himself, with fingers rosy and
fragrant. I plucked of them, as far as I could reach on either side
of me, and then lay drowsily reposing on my couch at the summit
of the Cascade Pass, under the shade of a fir, which, outstanding
from the forest, had changed its columnar structure into a pyrami-
dal, and had branches all along its stalwart trunk, instead of a mere
tuft at the top.

In this shade I should have known the tree which gave it, without looking up,—not because the sharp little spicular leaves of the fir, miniatures of that sword Rome used to open the world, its oyster, would drop and plunge themselves into my eyes, or would insert their blades down my back and scarify,—but because there is an influence and sentiment in umbrages, and under every tree its own atmosphere.[10] Elms refine and have a graceful elegiac effect upon those they shelter. Oaks drop robustness. Mimosas will presently make a sensitive-plant of him who hangs his hammock beneath their shade. Cocoa-palms will infect him with such tropical indolence, that he will not stir until frowzy monkeys climb the tree and pelt him away to the next one. The shade of pine-trees, as anyone can prove by a journey in Maine, makes those who undergo it wiry, keen, trenchant, inexhaustible, and tough.

When I had felt the influence of my fir shelter, on the edge of the wayside prairie, long enough, I became of course keen as a blade. I sprang up and called to Loolowcan, in a resinous voice, "Mamook chaco cuitan; make come horse."

Loolowcan, in more genial mood than I had known him, drove the trio out from the long grass. They came forth not without backward hankerings, but far happier quadrupeds than when they climbed the pass at noon. It was a pleasure now to compress with the knees Klale, transformed from an empty barrel with protuberant hoops, into a full and elastic cylinder, smooth as the boiler of a locomotive.

"Loolowcan, my lad, my experienced guide, cur nesika moosum; where sleep we?" said I.

"Copa Sowee house,—kicuali. Sowee, olyman tyee, memloose. Sia-a-a-h mitlite;—At Sowee's camp—below. Sowee, oldman chief,—dead. It is far, far away," replied the son of Owhhigh.

Far is near, distance is annihilated this brilliant day of summer, for us recreated with Hippocrene, strawberries, shade of fir and tall snow-fed grass. Down the mountain range seems nothing after our long laborious up; "the half is more than the whole." "Lead on, Loolowcan, intelligent brave, toward the residence of the late Sowee."

More fair prairies linked themselves along the trail. From these alpine pastures the future will draw butter and cheese, pasturing migratory cattle there, when summer dries the scanty grass upon the macadamized prairies of Whulge. It is well to remind ourselves sometimes that the world is not wholly squatted over. The plateau soon began to ebb toward the downward slope. Descent was like ascent, a way shaggy and abrupt. Again the Boston hooihut intruded. My friends the woodsmen had constructed an elaborate inclined plane of very knobby corduroy down the steepest steep. Klale sniffed at this novel road, and turned up his nose at it. He was competent to protect that feature against all the perils of stumble and fall on trails he had been educated to travel, but dreaded grinding it on the rough bark of this unaccustomed highway. Slow-footed oxen, leaning inward and sustaining each other, like two roysterers unsteady after wassail, might clumsily toil up such a road as this, hauling up stout, white-cotton-roofed wagons, filled with the babies and Lares of emigrants; but quick-footed ponies, descending and carrying light loads of a wild Indian and an untamed blanketeer, chose rather to whisk along the aboriginal paths.

As we came to the irregular terraces after the first pitch, and scampered on gayly, I by and by heard a welcome whiz, and a dusky grouse (*Tetrao obscurus*)[11] lifted himself out of the trail into the lower branches of a giant fir. I had lugged my double-barrel thus far, a futile burden, unless when it served a minatory[12] purpose among the drunken Klalams. Now it became an animated machine, and uttered a sharp exclamation of relief after long patient silence. Down came tetrao,—down he came with satisfactory thud, signifying pounds of something not pork for supper. We bagged him joyously and dashed on.

"Kopet," whispered Loolowcan turning, with a hushing gesture, "hin kullakullie nika nanitch;—halt, plenty birds I see." He was so eager that from under his low brows and unkempt hair his dusky eyes glared like the eyes of wild beast, studying his prey from a shadowy lair.

Dismounting, I stole forward with assassin intent, and birds, grouse, five noble ones I saw, engaged in fattening their bodies for human solace and support. I sent a shot among them. There was a flutter among the choir,—one fluttered not. At the sound of my right barrel one bird fell without rising; another rose and fell at a hint from the sinister tube. The surviving trio were distracted by mortal terror. They flew no farther than a dwarf tree hard by. I drew my revolver, thinking that there might not be time to load, and fired in a hurry at the lowermost.

"Hyas tamanous!" whispered Loolowcan, when no bird fell or flew,—"big magic," it seemed to the superstitious youth. Often when sportsmen miss, they claim that their gun is bewitched, and avail themselves of the sure silver bullet.

A second ball, passing with keener aim through the barrel, attained its mark. Grouse third shook off his mortal remains, and sped to heaven. The two others, contrary to rule, for I had shot the lower, fled, cowardly carrying their heavy bodies to die of cold, starvation, or old age. "The good die first,"—ay, Wordsworth![13] among birds this is verity; for the good are the fat, who, because of their avoirdupois, lag in flight, or alight upon lower branches and are easiest shot.

Loolowcan bagged my three trophies and added them to the first. Henceforth the thought of a grouse supper became a fixed idea with me. I dwelt upon it with even a morbid appetite. I rehearsed, in prophetic mood, the scene of plucking, the scene of roasting, that happy festal scene of eating. So immersed did I become in gastronomic revery, that I did not mind my lookout, as I dashed after Loolowcan, fearless and agile cavalier. A thrust awoke me to a sense of passing objects, a very fierce, lance-like thrust, full at my life. A wrecking snag of harsh dead wood, that projected up in the trail, struck me, and tore me half off my horse, leaving me jerked, scratched, disjointed, and shuddering. Pachydermatous leggins of buckskin, at cost of their own unity, had saved me from impalement. Some such warning is always preparing for the careless.

I soon had an opportunity to propitiate Nemesis[14] by a humane action. A monstrous trunk lay across the trail. Loolowcan, reckless steeplechaser, put his horse at it, full speed. Gubbins, instead of going over neatly, or scrambling over cat-like, reared rampant and shied back, volte face. I rode forward to see what fresh interference of Tamanous was here,—nothing Tamanous but an unexpected sorry object of a horse. A wretched castaway, probably abandoned by the exploring party, or astray from them, essaying to leap the tree, had fallen back beneath the trunk and branches, and lay there entangled and perfectly helpless. We struggled to release him. In vain. At last a thought struck me. We seized the poor beast by his tail, fortunately a tenacious member, and, heaving vigorously, towed him out of prison.

He tottered forlornly to his feet, looking about him like one risen from the dead. "How now, Caudal?"[15] said I, baptizing him by the name of the part that saved his life; "canst thou follow toward fodder?" He debated the question with himself awhile. Solitary confinement of indefinite length, in a cramped posture, had given the poor skeleton time to consider that safety from starvation is worth one effort more. He found that there was still a modicum of life and its energy within his baggy hide. My horses seemed to impart to him some of their electricity, and he staggered on droopingly. Lucky Caudal, if life is worth having, that on that day, of all days, I should have arrived to rescue him. Strange deliverances for body and soul come to the dying. Fate sends unlooked-for succor, when or horses or men despair.

Luckily for Caudal, the weak-kneed and utterly dejected, Sowee's prairie was near,—near was the prairie of Sowee, mighty hunter of deer and elk, terror of bears. There at weird night Sowee's ghost was often seen to stalk. Dyspeptics from feather-beds behold ghosts, and are terrified, but nightwalkers are but bugbears to men who have ridden from dawn to dusk of a long summer's day over an Indian trail in the mountains. I felt no fear that any incubus in the shape of a brassy-hued Indian chief would sit upon my breast that night, and murder wholesome sleep.

Nightfall was tumbling down from the zenith before we reached camp. The sweet glimmers of twilight were ousted from the forest, sternly as mercy is thrust from a darkening heart. Night is really only beautiful so far as it is not night,—that is, for its stars, which are sources of resolute daylight in other spheres, and for its moon, which is daylight's memory, realized, softened, and refined.

Night, however, had not drawn the pall of brief death over the world so thick but that I could see enough to respect the taste of the late Sowee. When he voted himself this farm, and became seized of it in the days of unwritten agrarian laws, and before patents were in

vogue, he proved his intelligent right to suffrage and seizure. Here
in admirable quality were the three first requisites of a home in the
wilderness, water, wood, and grass. A musical rustle, as we galloped
through, proved the long grass. All around was the unshorn forest.
There were columnar firs making the Sowee house a hypaethral[16]
temple on a grand scale.

There had been here a lodge. A few saplings of its framework
still stood, but Sowee had moved elsewhere not long ago. Wake
siah memloose,—not long dead was the builder, and viator[17] might
camp here unquestioned.

Caudal had followed us in inane, irresponsible way. Patient now
he stood, apparently waiting for farther commands from his pre-
servers. We unpacked and unsaddled the other animals. They knew
their business, namely, to bolt instantly for their pasture. Then a
busy uproar of nipping and crunching was heard. Poor Caudal
could not take the hint. We were obliged to drive that bony estray
with blows out to the supper-field, where he stood aghast at the
appetites of his new comrades. Repose and good example, however, soon had their effect, and eight equine jaws instead of six made
play in the herbage.

"Alki mika mamook pire, pe nesika klatawah copa klap tsuk; now
light thou a fire, and we will go to find water," said Loolowcan. I
struck fire,—fire smote tinder,—tinder sent the flame on, until a
pyre from the world's free wood-pile was kindled. This boon of
fire,—what wonder that men devised a Prometheus greatest of demi-
gods as its discoverer? Mortals, shrinking from the responsibility of
a high destiny and dreading to know how divine the Divine would
have them, always imagine an avatar of some one not lower than
a half-god when a gift of great price comes to the world. And fire
is a very priceless and beautiful boon,—not, as most know it, in

imprisonment, barred with iron, or in sooty chimneys, or in mad revolt of conflagration,—but as it grows in a flashing pyramid out in camp in the free woods, with eager air hurrying in on every side to feed its glory. In the gloom I strike metal of steel against metallic flint. From this union a child is born. I receive the young spark tenderly in warm "tipsoo," in a soft woolly nest of bark or grass tinder. Swaddled in this he thrives. He smiles; he chuckles; he laughs; he dances about, does my agile nursling. He will soon wear out his first infantile garb, so I cover him up in shelter. I feed him with digestible viands, according to his years. I give him presently stouter fare, and offer exhilarating morsels of fatness. All these the hearty youth assimilates, and grows healthily. And now I educate him to manliness, training him on great joints, shoulders, and marrowy portions. He becomes erelong a power and a friend able to requite me generously for my care. He aids me in preparing my feast, and we feast together. Afterward we talk,—Flame and I,—we think together strong and passionate thoughts of purpose and achievement. These emotions of manhood die away, and we share pensive memories of happiness missed, or disdained, or feebly grasped and torn away; regrets cover these like embers, and slowly over dead fieriness comes a robe of ashy gray.

Fire in the forest is light, heat, and cheer. When ours was nurtured to the self-sustaining point, we searched to find where the sage Sowee kept his potables. Carefully covered up in sedges was a slender supply of water, worth concealing from vulgar dabblers. Its diamond drops were hidden away so thoroughly that we must mine for them by torchlight. I held a flaring torch, while Loolowcan lay in wait for the trickle, and captured it in a tin pot. How wild he looked, that youth so frowzy by daylight, as, stooping under the tall sedges, he clutched those priceless sparkles.

Upon the *carte du jour* at Restaurant Soweee was written Grouse. "How shall we have them?" said I, cook and convive, to Loolowcan, marmiton and convive.[18] "One of these cocks of the mountain shall be fried, since gridiron is hot," responded I to myself, after meditation. "Two shall be spitted, and roasted; and, as Azrael may not want us before breakfast to-morrow, the fourth shall go upon the *carte de dejeuner.*"[19]

"O Pork! what a creature thou art!" continued I, in monologue, cutting neat slices of that viand with my bowie-knife, and laying them fraternally, three in a bed, in the frying-pan. "Blessed be Moses! who forbade thee to the Jews, whereby we, of freer dispensations, heirs of all the ages, inherit also pigs more numerous and bacon cheaper. O Pork! what could campaigners do without thy fatness, thy leanness, thy saltness, thy portableness?"

Here Loolowcan presented me the three birds plucked featherless as Plato's man.[20] The two roasters we planted carefully on spits before a sultry spot of the fire. From a horizontal stick, supported on forked stakes, we suspended by a twig over each roaster an automatic baster, an inverted cone of pork, ordained to yield its spicy juices to the wooing flame, and drip bedewing on each bosom beneath. The roasters ripened deliberately, while keen and quick fire told upon the fryer, the first course of our feast. Meanwhile I brewed a pot of tea, blessing Confucius for that restorative weed, as I had blessed Moses for his abstinence from porkers.

Need I say that the grouse were admirable, that everything was delicious, and the Confucian weed first chop? Even a scouse[21] of mouldy biscuit met the approval of Loolowcan. Feasts cooked under the greenwood tree, and eaten by their cooks after a triumphant day of progress, are sweeter than the conventional banquets of languid Christendom. After we had paid our duty to the brisk fryer and

the rotund roaster grouse, nothing remained but bones to propitiate Sowee, should he find short commons in Elysium, and wander
back to his lodge, seeking what he might devour.

All along the journey I had been quietly probing the nature of
Loolowcan, my most intimate associate thus far among the unalloyed copper-skins. Chinook jargon was indeed but a blunt probe,
yet perhaps delicate enough to follow up such rough bits of conglomerate as served him for ideas. An inductive philosopher, tracing the laws of developing human thought *in corpore viti*[22] of a
frowzy savage, finds his work simple,—the nuggets are on the surface. Those tough pebbles known to some metaphysicians as innate
ideas, can be studied in Loolowcan in their process of formation
out of instincts.

Number One is the prize number in Loolowcan's lottery of life.
He thinks of that number; he dreams of it alone. When he lies down
to sleep, he plots what he will do in the morning with his prize and
his possession; when he wakes, he at once proceeds to execute his
plots. Loolowcan knows that there are powers out of himself; rights
out of himself he does not comprehend, or even conceive. I have
thus far been very indulgent to him, and treated him Republicanly,
mindful of the heavy mesne profits[23] for the occupation of a continent, and the uncounted arrears of blood-money owed by my race
to his; yet I find no trace of gratitude in my analysis of his character. He seems to be composed, selfishness, five hundred parts; *nil
admirari*[24] coolness, five hundred parts;—a well-balanced character, and perhaps one not likely to excite enthusiasm in others. I
am a steward to him; I purvey him also a horse; when we reach the
Dalles, I am to pay him for his services;—but he is bound to me by
no tie of comradery. He has caution more highly developed than any
quadruped I have met, and will not offend me lest I should resign

my stewardship, retract Gubbins, refuse payment, discharge my
guide, and fight through the woods, where he sees I am no stranger,
alone. He certainly merits a "teapot" for his ability in guidance. He
has memory and observation unerring; not once in all our intricate
journey have I found him at fault in any fact of space or time. He
knows "each lane and every alley green" here, accurately as Comus
knew his "wild wood."[25]

Moral conceptions exist only in a very limited degree for this type
of his race. Of God he knows somewhat less than the theologians;
that is, he is in the primary condition of uninquisitive ignorance,
not in the secondary, of inquisitive muddle. He has the advantage
of no elaborate system of human inventions to unlearn. He has no
distinct fetishism. None of the North American Indians have, in the
accurate sense or the term; their nomad life and tough struggle with
instructive Nature in her roughness save them from such elaborate
fetishism as may exist in more indolent climes and countries.

Loolowcan has his tamanous. It is Talipus, the Wolf, a "hyas
skookoom tamanous, a very mighty demon," he informs me. He
does not worship it; that would interfere with his devotions to his
real deity, Number One. It, in return, does him little service. If he
met Talipus, object of his superstition, on a fair morning, he would
think it a good omen; if on a sulky morning, he might be somewhat
depressed, but would not on that account turn back, as a Roman
brave would have done on meeting the matinal wolf. In fact, he
keeps Talipus, his tamanous, as a kind of ideal hobby, very much as
a savage civilized man entertains a pet bulldog or a tame bear, a link
between himself and the rude, dangerous forces of nature. Loolowcan has either chosen his protector according to the law of likeness,
or, choosing it by chance, has become assimilated to its character-
istics. A wolfish youth is the *protege* of Talipus,—an unfaithful, sin-

ister, cannibal-looking son of a horse-thief. Wolfish likewise is his appetite; when he asks me for more dinner, and this without stint or decorum he does, he glares as if, grouse failing, pork and hard-tack gone, he could call to Talipus to send in a pack of wolves incarnate, and pounce with them upon me. A pleasant companion this for lamb-like me to lie down beside in the den of the late Sowee. Yet I do presently, after supper and a pipe, and a little jargoning in Chinook with my Wolf, roll into my blankets, and sleep vigorously, lulled by the gratifying noise of my graminivorous horses cramming themselves with material for leagues of lope to-morrow.

No shade of Sowee came to my slumbers with warnings against the wolf in guise of a Klickatat brave. I had no ghostly incubus to shake off, but sprang up recreate in body and soul. Life is vivid when it thus awakes. To be is to do.

And to-day much is to be done. Long leagues away, beyond a gorge of difficulty, is the open rolling hill country, and again far beyond are the lodges of the people of Owhhigh. "To-day," said Loolowcan, "we must go copa nika iliheo, to my home, to Weenas."

Forlorn Caudal is hardly yet a frisky quadruped. Yet he is of better cheer, perhaps up to the family-nag degree of vivacity. As to the others, they have waxed fat, and kick. Klale, the Humorous, kicks playfully, elongating his legs in preparatory gymnastics. Gubbins, the average horse, kicks calmly at his saddler, merely as a protest. Antipodes, the spiteful Blunderer, kicks in a revolutionary manner, rolls under his pack-saddle, and will not budge without maltreatment. Ill-educated Antipodes views mankind only as excoriators of his back, and general flagellants. Klickatats kept him raw in flesh and temper; under me his physical condition improves; his character is not yet affected.

Before sunrise we quitted the house of Sowee.

9. Via Mala

I was now to enter the world east of the Cascades, emerging from
the dense forest of the mountain-side. Pacific winds sailing inland
leave most of their moisture on the western slopes of the range. Few
of the cloudy battalions that sweep across the sea, and come, not like
an invading horde of ravagers, but like an army of generous allies,—
few of these pass over the ramparts, and pour their wealth into the
landward valleys. The giant trees, fattened in their cells by plenteous draughts of water, are no longer found. The land is arid. Slopes
and levels of ancient volcanic rock are no longer fertilized by the secular deposit of forests, showering down year by year upon the earth
liberal interest for the capital it has lent.

Through this drier and airier region we now hastened. An arrowy
river, clear and cold, became our companion. Where it might, the
trail followed the Nachchese valley,—a rough rift often, and hardly
meriting the gentle name of valley.[1] Precipices, stiff, uncrumbling
precipices, are to be found there, if anyone is ambitious to batter

his brains. Cleft front on the right bank answers to cleft front on
the left,—fronts cloven when the earth's crust, cooling hereabouts,
snapped, and the monsters of the period heard the rumble and roar
of the earthquake, their crack of doom. Sombre basalt walls in the
fugitive river, great, gloomy, purple heights, sheer and desperate as
suicide, rise six hundred feet above the water. Above these downright mural breaks rise vast dangerous curves, of mountain-side,
thousands of feet on high, just at such angle that slide or no slide
becomes a question. A traveler, not desponding, but only cautious,
hesitates to wake Echo, lest that sweet nymph, stirring with the
tremors of awakening, should set air vibrating out of its condition
of quiet pressure, and the enormous mountain, seizing this instant
of relief, should send down some cubic miles in an avalanche to
crush the traveler.

A very desolate valley, and a harsh defile at best for a trail to
pursue. At best the way might wind among *debris*, or pass over
hard plates of sheeny, igneous rock, or plunge into the chill river,
or follow a belt of sand, or struggle in swampy thickets,—this at
best it did. But when worst came, when the precipices neared each
other, narrowing the canon[2] pathless, and there were deep, still,
sunless pools, brimming up to the giant walls of the basin, then
the trail must desert the river, and climb many hundreds of feet
above. I must compel my horses, with no warranty against a stumble or a fall, along overhanging verges, where one slip, or even one
ungraceful change of foot, would topple the stumbler and his burden down to be hashed against jutting points, and tossed fragmen-
tary, food for fishes, in the lucid pool below. For there were salmon
there, still working upstream, seeking the purest and safest spots
for their future families.

Now all of this was hard work, some of it dangerous. It was well that, in the paddock of Sowee, my horses had filled themselves with elastic grass, parent of activity and courage. Caudal, though bearing no burden but himself, was often tempted to despair. Society, example, and electric-shocks of friendly castigation aroused him. We rode hard along this wild gorge, down these dreary vistas, up and down these vast barren bulks of mountain. Forlorn yellow pines, starveling children of adversity, gnarled and scrubby, began to appear, shabby substitutes for the prosperous firs and cedars behind. But any gracefulness of vegetation, any feeling of adornment, would be out of place among those big, unrefined grandeurs. Beauty and grace, and all conceivable delicacy of form and color, light and shade, belong to the highest sublimities of Nature. Tacoma is as lovely with all the minor charms, as it is divinely majestic by the possession of the greater, and power of combining and harmonizing the less. But there is a lower kind of sublimity, where the predominant effect is one merely of power, bigness, the gigantesque and cyclopean, rude force acting disorderly, and producing a hurly-burly almost grotesque. Perhaps sublimity is too noble a word to apply to these results of ill-regulated frenzy; they are grand as war, not noble as peace. Such qualities of Nature have an educational value, as legends of giants may prepare a child to comprehend histories of heroes. The volcanic turbulence of the region I was now traversing might fitly train the mind to perceive the want of scenes as vast and calmer;—Salvator Rosa[3] is not without significance among the teachers of Art.

No Pacific Railroad in the Nachchese Pass,—that my *coup d'oeil*[4] assured me. Even the Boston hooihut, with all its boldness in the forest, here could do little. Trees of a century may be felled in an hour; crags of an aeon baffle a cycle. The Boston hooihut must worm its modest way in and out the gorge, without essaying to toss down precipices into chasms. My memory and my hasty road-book alike fail me in artistic detail to make pictures of that morning's Via Mala.[5] My chief emotion was expressed in a sigh for release. It was one of those unkindly days of summer when sunlight seems not a smile, but a sneer. Cruel heat was reflected back from wall to wall of the pass, palpitating to and fro between baked, verdure-less, purple cliff on this side, and the hot harshness of opponent purple cliff across the stream. I breathed a sirocco-like air without pabulum, without constituents of blood. I could fabricate a pale fury, an insane nervous energy, out of this unwholesome, fiery stuff, but no ardor, no joyousness, no doffing aside of troublous care. I could advance, and never flinch, because needs must; but it seemed a weary, futile toil, to spur my horse over the ugly pavements of unyielding rock, up over the crumbling brown acclivities, by perilous ways along the verge of gulfs, where I could bend to the right from my saddle, and see the river a thousand feet below. I felt in this unlifting atmosphere, unwavering except where it trembled over the heated surfaces, no elation, as I overcame crest after crest of mountain along the path,—no excitement, as Klale, the unerring, galloped me down miles of break-neck declivity,—my thundering squadron hammering with sixteen legs on the echoing crust of this furnace-cover.

Ever, "Hyack," cried Loolowcan; "sia-a-ah mitlite Weenas;— Speed," cried the Frowzy; "far, far lieth Weenas."[6]

We were now, just after noon, drawing out of the chasms into a more open valley, when, as we wound through a thicket of hazels near the river, Loolowcan suddenly halted, and motioned me mysteriously.

"What now, O *protege* of Talipus? Is it bear or Boston man?"

"Pasaiooks,—halo cuitan;—Blanketeer,—no horse!" said Loolowcan, with astonishment.

And there indeed was a horseless gentleman,—tossing pebbles into the Nachchese, as quietly as if he were on the Hudson. What with little medicine Klickatats, exploring parties, Boston hooihuters, stray Caudals, and unhorsed loungers, the Nachchese trail was becoming quite a thoroughfare.

The stranger proved no stranger; hardly even horseless, for his mule, from a patch of grass in the thicket, presently brayed welcome to my nags. The gentleman was one of Captain McClellan's party, come up from their camp some leagues farther down. He was waiting at this rendezvous for the Captain, who was exploring another branch of the river. To a patroller of crowded city avenues, it may not seem a significant fact that a man in a solitary trail met a man. But to me, a not unsociable being, travelling with a half-insolent, half-indifferent, jargoning savage, down a Via Mala of desolation, toward a realm of possibly unbrotherly nomads, an encounter by the wayside with a man and a brother was a fact to enjoy and an emotion to chronicle.

But human sympathy was not dinner for my horses. I must advance toward that unknown spot where, having full confidence in Nature, I believed that a table would be spread for them in the wilderness. "Nature never did deceive the heart that loved her";[7] for a true lover becomes a student of his mistress's character enough not to demand impossibilities. And soon did that goddess, kindly and faithful object of my life-long devotion, verify my trust, providing not only fodder for my cavalry, but a bower for my nooning, a breeze from above to stir the dead, hot air, and a landscape appropriate to a banquet, and not like the cruel chasms I had passed.

In a patch of luxuriant wild-pea vines my horses had refreshing change of diet, befitting the change of region. No monotony of scene or action for man or beast thus far in this journey, no stagnation of mind or body from unexciting diet. For me, from the moment when my vain negotiations began with King George of the Klalams, life had been at its keenest, its readiest, its fleetest. Multitudinously besprent[8] also with beauty like a bed of pansies had been these days of dash and charge. My finer and coarser aesthetic faculties had been so exercised that, if an uneducated traveller, I might have gone bewildered with phantasmagoria. But bewilderment comes from superficialness; type thoughts stripped of surface cloaking are compact as diamonds.

My camp for present nooning was a charming little Arcady,[9] shady, sunny, and verdant. Two dense spruces made pleasant twanging to the newly-risen breeze. These were the violins of my festival orchestra with strings self-resinous, while down the canon roared the growing gale, and, filling all pauses in this aerial music, the Nachchese tinkled merrily, or dashed boisterously, or rattled eagerly.

"On, on with speed!" was the lesson hinted to me by wind and water. Yet as I cooked for dinner a brace of grouse, my morning's prey, I might have allowed myself to yield to vain glorious dalliance. The worser half of my scamper was behind me. "Try not the pass," people had said; "you cannot put your space into your time," said they, hinting also at dangers of solitary travel with one of the crafty. But I had taken the risk, and success was thus far with me. Let me now beware of too much confidence. Who can say what lurks in the heart of Loolowcan? He who persuades himself that his difficulties are fought through, is but at threshold of them. When he winds the

horn of triumph, perhaps the sudden ogre will appear; then woe be
to the knight, if he has taken the caps off his revolver.

Loolowcan and I were smoking our pipes of tobacco, when the
tramp of hoofs was heard along the trail, and, with the late skipper
of stones and a couple of soldiers, Captain McClellan rode up. In
vain, through the Nachchese Canon, had the Captain searched for a
Pacific Railroad. He must search elsewhere, along Snoqualme Pass
or other. Apart from a pleasant moment of reciprocal well-wishing,
the chief result of this interview was, that I became disembarrassed
of my treasure-trove Caudal. I seized the earliest chance of restoring this chattel to Uncle Sam, whose initials were branded upon his
flank. No very available recruit to my squadron of light horse was
this debilitated keterrypid,[10] whom Good Samaritanism compelled
me to humanely entreat. Besides, I had erred in his baptism; I had
called him Caudal, and he naturally endeavored to take his place in
the rear. If I had but thought to name him Headlong!

Rest in the shade of the spruces by the buzzing river was so sweet,
after the severity of my morning's ride, that I hesitated for myself
and for my unwilling mustangs to renew the journey. To pace on an
ambling mule over level greensward, like a fat papal legate[11] travelling, in mediaeval times, from refectory to refectory,—that seems
as much as one would wish to do on a hot afternoon of August. I
shook off such indolent thoughts, and mounted. Exertion is its own
reward. The joy in the first effort overbalances the delight of sloth,
and the joy in perpetual effort is clear gain. And really never an
ambling palfrey, slow-footed potterer under an abbot, interfered less
with his rider's quietude than Klale, the gentle loper. We dragged
ourselves from the shade and the pea-vines, and went dashing at
full speed along the trail, no longer encumbered by fallen trunks
and hurdles of bush and brier. Merely rough, meagre, and stony was

the widening valley, and dotted over its adust soil with yellow pines, standing apart in scraggy isolation.

At five I reached Captain McClellan's camp of two tents. He was not yet returned from prying into some other gorge, some purple cavernous defile for his railroad route. Loolowcan's "far to Weenas" the sergeant in charge interpreted to mean still twenty-five miles. Their own main body was encamped in the Weenas valley. Twenty-five miles is a terrible supplement, my horses, after the labors of one day; but ye still seem fresh, thanks to the paddock of Sowee, and the pea-vines at noon, and to-morrow who knows but ye may be running free over the plains, while I with fresh nags go on toward the Dalles. We may not therefore accept the hospitality of the camp, but must on lustily down the broad valley this windy evening of summer.

Every appogiatura[12] of Klale's galloping forefeet and hind-feet seemed doubly musical to me now. I had escaped; I was clear of the stern mountains; I was out upon the great surging prairie-land. Before me all was open, bare, and vast. To the south, pine woods stretched, like helmet crests, along the tops and down to the nodding fronts of brown hills; behind, the gloomy mass of the lower Cascades rose up, anticipating sunset. Distance and dimness shut up the clefts, and made the whole background one great wall, closing avenues of return, and urging me forward upon my eastward way.

The sun had gone down behind the mountains, had paused on the tides of Whulge, had sunk in ocean. Twilight came, and the wind grew mightier, roaring after us like the voice of the storm that baffled the hunter of hiaqua. The gale lifted us up over the tremendous wide rolling bulk of grassy surges, and we swept scudding into billowy deeps below.

In the thickening dusk I discerned an object,—not a tree, not a rock; but a mobile black object, scuttling away for a belt of thicket near the river.

"A bear!" I cried. "Itshoot!" echoed Loolowcan.

Nothing but grouse-shot in my double-barrel,—that I handed to the Frowzy; six leaden peppercorns in my eight-inch revolver,—that I kept. Now, Klale, it is whether Itshoot or thou wilt first touch cover. Klale leaped forward like an adult grasshopper. Bruin, hearing hoofs, lurched on like a coal-barge in a tide bobbery.[13] I was within thirty feet of him when he struck the bushes. I fired. He felt it, and with a growl stopped and turned upon us. Klale swerved from those vicious claws, so that I merely heard and felt them rattle on my stirrup, as I fired again right into the bear's vacant hug. Before I could check and turn my horse, Bruin had concluded the unwelcome interview. He had disappeared in the dense thicket. In vain Loolowcan and I beat about in the dusk. The ursine dodger did not profit by his chances of ambuscade to embrace one of us and that chance together. He was not to be found. Perhaps I am the slayer of a bear. One shot at thirty feet, and one across the breadth of a handkerchief, might possibly discontinue the days of such shaggy monster.

When we were upon the trail again, and galloping faster under the stars, I found that I had a new comic image in my mind. I roared with jolly laughter, recalling how that uncouth creature had clumsily pawed at me, missing laceration by an inch. Had Klale swerved but a little less, there would have been tragi-comedy in this farce. In place of the buckskins torn yesterday, I wore a pair of old corduroys, with scarlet cloth leggings; Destiny thought these did not need to be farther incarnadined, nor my shins, much abused along the briery trail, to be torn by any crueller thorniness of bears' claws.

There was, however, underlying too extravagant fun, this sense of escape from no fun. Nature will not allow even her grotesque creatures to be quite scoffed at. Bears may be laughable, but they are not ridiculous. I have been contiguous to an uncaged bear in free clutching trim but this once, and I respect him too much to laugh at him to his face. With him I could laugh when he is in humorous mood, but at Bruin I laugh no more.[14]

By the time I had thus reasoned out the lesson of my bear-fight, darkness had come. The exhilaration of night-air revived my horses. They guided themselves bravely along the narrow way, and bravely climbed the lift and sway of land surges. Yet over these massive undulations we could travel but slowly. When it might, the trail followed the terrace above the Nachchese. Often wherever the trail might choose to follow, we might not follow it in the dark. Stony arroyos would cut it in twain, or a patch of wild-sage bushes or a belt of hazels and alders send it astray. Then would Loolowcan open wide his dusky eyes, to collect every belated glimmer of twilight, and zigzag until again he found the clew of our progress. While he searched, Klale and Antipodes took large morsels of epicurean bunchgrass, in convenient tufts, a generous mouthful in each.

It grew harder and harder to find the permanent narrow wake of voyagers beforetime over the great ground-swells of this unruly oceanic scope of earth. Mariners may cut their own hooihut over the hilly deep by the stars. Terrene travellers cannot thus independently reject history; they must humble themselves to be followers where tribes have tramped before. Even such condescension may not avail when night is master. Loolowcan, though eager as I to press on, finally perforce admitted that we lost our way in the thickets and over the gravel oftener than we found it; that the horses flagged sadly, and we must stop.

It was one of those cloudless gales, when it seems as if the globe is whirring on so fast beneath the stars, that air must use its mightiest force of wing lest it be left a laggard. In moments of stillness, while the flapping of these enormous pinions ceased, and the gale went gliding on by impetus, we could hear the far-away rumble of the river. Sound is only second to sight as a guide out of darkness. The music of a stream, singing with joy that it knows its way, is pleasanter guidance than the bark of village cur, who, though he bite not because he bark, may have a brother deputed to do that rougher mouthing. Following, then, the sound, we presently came upon the source of sound, the Nachchese.

Sky and stars are a peaceful shelter over a bivouac; yet when between the would-be sleeper and that friendly roof there is a tumultuous atmosphere misbehaving itself, sleep is torn up and whirled away in tatters. We must have some bulwark against the level sweep of the gale; and must pay for getting it by losing something else. Upon the bank we could have a bed level and earthy, but wind-battered; under the bank we could lie sheltered, but must lie on pebbles. On pebble boulders we must make our couch, where water at higher stages had washed away all the soft packing of earth.

We left the horses to occupy the bank above, where they could sup on succulent bunch-grass, firm and juicy as well-cured hay. Much as we regretted abridging their freest liberty of repose, we were obliged to hobble them lest they should go with the wind down the valley, and at morn be leagues away. If a man wishes speed, he must take precautions that speed do not fly away from him. Civilization without its appliances is weaker than barbarism.

No gastronomic facts of our camp below the Nachchese; supper was much lower than secondary to rest. We had been full sixteen difficult hours in the saddle. Nights of my life, not a few, have been

wretched in feather beds for too much softness; stern hardness was
to be the cause of other misery here. This night cobble-stones must
be my bed, a boulder pillow for my head. My couch was uneven as
a rippled lake suddenly congealed. A being not molluscous, but
humanly bony, and muscular over bonyness, cannot for hours beat
upon pebbles unbruised. So I had a night of weary unrest. The wild
rush of the river and noise of the gale ran through my turbid sleep
in dreams of tramping battalions,—such as a wounded and fevered
man, lying unhelped on a battle-field, might dream.

Yet let us always be just. There are things to be said in behalf of
cobble-stone beds by rivers of the Northwest. I was soft to the rocks,
if not they to me. I have heard of regions where one may find that
he slept cheek by jowl with a cobra di capella.[15] These are absent
from the uninviting bed of cobble-stones by the Nachchese, and so
are mosquitos, rattlesnakes, burglars, and the cry of fire. Negative
advantages these. Consider also the positive good to a man, that,
having been thoroughly toughened by hardness, he knows what
the body of him is strong to be, to do, and to suffer. Furthermore,
one after experience of a pummelling couch, like this, will sympa-
thize sufficiently, and yet not morbidly, with the poor bedless. So
I slept, or did not sleep, while the gale roared wildly all night, and
was roaring still at dawn.

10. Treachery

People cloddish, stagnant, and mundane, such as most of us are, pretend to prefer sunset to sunrise, just as we fancy the past greater than the present, and repose nobler than action. Few are radical enough in thought to perceive the great equalities of beauty and goodness in phenomena of nature or conditions of life. Now I saw a sunrise after my night by the Nachchese, which, on the side of sunrise, it is my duty to mention.

Having therefore put in my fact, that on a morning of August, in the latter half of the nineteenth century, sunrise did its duty with splendor, I have also done my duty as an observer. The simple statement of a fact is enough for the imaginative, who will reproduce it for themselves, according to their experience; the docile unimaginative will buy alarm-clocks and study dawns. Yet I give a few coarse details as a work of supererogation.

If I had slept but faintly, the cobble-stones had purveyed me a substitute for sleep by hammering me senseless; so that when the

chill before dawn smote me, and I became conscious, I felt that
I needed consolation. Consolation came. I saw over against me,
across the river, a hill blue as hope, and seemingly far away in the
gray distance. Light flushed upward from the horizon, meeting no
obstacles of cloud, to be kindled and burnt away into white ashi-
ness. Light came up the valley over the dark, surging hills. Full in
the teeth of the gale it came, strong in its delicacy, surely victorious,
as a fine scymitar against a blundering bludgeon. Where light and
wind met on the crest of an earth-billow, there the grass shook like
glittering spray. Meanwhile the hill opposite was drawing nearer,
and all the while taking a fuller blue. Blue passed into deep scintil-
lating purple, rich as the gold-powdered robe of an Eastern queen.
As daylight grew older, it was strong enough to paint detail without
sacrificing effect; the hill took its place of neighborhood, upright
and bold, a precipitous front of warm, brown basalt, with long cav-
ities, freshly cleft, where prisms had fallen, striping the brown with
yellow. First upon the summit of this cliff the sunbeams alighted.
Thence they pounced upon the river, and were whirled along upon
its breakers, carrying light down to flood the valley. In the vigorous atmosphere of so brilliant a daybreak I divined none of the difficulties that were before sunset to befall me.

By this we were in the saddle, following the sunlight rush of the
stream. Stiffish, after passing the night hobbled, were the steeds,
as bruised after boulder beds were the cavaliers. But Loolowcan,
the unimpassioned, was now aroused. Here was the range of his
nomad life. Anywhere hereabouts he might have had his first prac-
tice-lessons in horse-stealing. His foot was on his native bunch-
grass. Those ridges far away to the northeast must be passed to
reach Weenas. Beyond those heights, to the far south, is Atinam

and "Le Play House," the mission.[1] Thus far time and place have made good the description of the eloquent Owhhigh.

Presently in a small plain appeared a horse, hobbled and lone as a loon on a lake. Have we acquired another masterless estray? Not so. Loolowcan uttered a peculiar trilobated yelp,[2] and forth from an ambush, where he had dodged, crept the shabbiest man in the world. Shabby are old-clo' men in the slums of Brummagem;[3] shabbier yet are Mormons at the tail of an emigration. But among the seediest ragamuffins in the most unsavory-corners I have known, I find no object that can compare with this root-digging Klickatat, as at Loolowcan's signal-yelp he crept from his lair among the willows. His attire merits attention as the worst in the world.

The moccasins of Shabbiest had been long ago another's, probably many another Klickatat's. Many a cayote had appropriated them after they were thrown away as defunct, and, after gnawing them in selfish solitude, every cayote had turned away unsatisfied with their flavor. Then shabbiest stepped forward, and claimed the treasure-trove. He must have had a decayed ingenuity; otherwise how with thongs, with willow twigs, with wisps of grass and persistent gripe of toe, did he compel those tattered footpads to remain among his adherents?

Breeches none had Shabbiest; leggins none; shirt equally none to speak of. But a coat he had, and one of many colors.

Days before, on the waters of Whulge, I had seen a sad coat on the back of that rusty and fuddled chieftain, the Duke of York. Nature gently tempers our experience to us as we are able to bear. The Duke's coat was my most deplorable vision in coats until its epoch, but it had educated me to lower possibilities. Ages ago, when this coat was a new and lively snuff-color, Garrick[4] was on the stage, Goldsmith was buying his ridiculous peach-blossom, in shape like

this, if this were ever shapely. In the odors that exhaled from it there
seemed an under stratum of London coffee-houses. Who knows
but He of Bolt Court, slovenly He of the Dictionary,[5] may not have
been guilty of its primal grease-spot? And then how that habiliment
became of a duller snuff-color; how grease-spots oozed each into its
neighbor's sphere of attraction; how one of its inheritors, after famil-
iarizing it with the gutter, pawned it one foggy November day, when
London was swallowing cold pea-soup instead of atmosphere; how,
the pawner never coming to redeem, the pawnee sold it to an American prisoner of the Revolution, to carry home with him to Boston,
his native village; how a degraded scion of the family became the
cook of Mr. Astor's ill-fated ship, the Tonquin,[6] and swopped it with
a Chinook chief for four otter-skins; and how from shabby Chinook
to shabbier it had passed, until Shabbiest got it at last;—all these
adventures, every eventful scene in this historic drama, was written in multiform inscription all over this time-stained ruin, so that
an expert observer might read the tale as a geologist reads eras of
the globe in a slab of fossiliferous limestone.

Such was the attire of Shabbiest, and as such he began a powwow
with Loolowcan. The compatriots talked emphatically, with the dull
impulsiveness, the calm fury, of Indians. I saw that I, my motions,
and my purposes were the subject of their discourse. Meanwhile I
stood by, somewhat bored, and a little curious.

At last, he of the historical coat turned to me, and, raising his
arms, one sleeveless, one fringed with rags at the shoulder, delivered at me a harangue in the most jerky and broken Chinook. Given
in broken English, corresponding, its purport was as follows.

Shabbiest *loquitur*, in a naso-guttural choke:—

"What you white man want get 'em here? Why him no stay Boston country? Me stay my country; no ask you come here. Too much

soldier man go all round everywhere. Too much make pop-gun. Him say kill bird, kill bear,—sometime him kill Indian. Soldier man too much shut eye, open eye at squaw. Squaw no like; s'pose squaw like, Indian man no like nohow. Me no understand white man. Plenty good thing him country; plenty blanket; plenty gun; plenty powder; plenty horse. Indian country plenty nothing. No good Weenas give you horse. No good Loolowcan go Dalles. Bad Indian there. Small-pox there. Very much all bad. Me no like white man nohow. S'pose go away, me like. Me think all same pretty fine good. You big chief, got plenty thing. Indian poor, no got nothing. Howdydo? Howdydo? Want swop coat? Want swop horse? S'pose give Indian plenty thing. Much good. Much very big good great chief white man!"

"Indignant sagamore," replied I, in mollifying tones, "you do indeed misunderstand us blanketeers. We come hither as friends for peace. No war is in our hearts, but kindly civilizing influences. If you resist, you must be civilized out of the way. We should regret your removal from these prairies of Weenas, for we do not see where in the world you can go and abide, since we occupy the Pacific shore and barricade you from free drowning privileges. Succumb gracefully, therefore, to your fate, my representative redskin. Do not scowl when soldier men, searching for railroads, repose their seared and disappointed eyeballs by winking at your squaws. Do not long for pitfalls when their cavalry plod over your kamas swamps. Believe all same very much good. Howdydo? Howdydo? No swop! I cannot do you the injustice of swopping this buckskin shirt of mine, embroidered with porcupine-quills, for that distinguished garment of yours. Nor horse can I swop in fairness; mine are weary with travel, and accustomed for a few days to influences of mercy. But, as a memorial of this pleasant interview and a testimonial to your eloquent speech, I should be complimented if you would accept a couple of charges of powder."

And, suiting act to word, I poured him out powder, which he received in a buckskin rag, and concealed in some shabby den of his historic coat. Shabbiest seemed actually grateful. Two charges of powder were like two soup-tickets to a starving man,—two dinners inevitably, and possibly, according to the size of his mark, many dinners, were in that black dust. He now asked to see my six-shooter, which Loolowcan had pointed at during their vernacular confidence. He examined it curiously, handling it with some apprehension, as a bachelor does a baby.

"Wake nika kumtun ocook tenas musket. Pose mika mamook po, ikta mika memloose;—I no understand that little musket. Suppose you make shoot, how many you kill?" he asked.

"Hin, pose moxt tahtilum;—Many, perhaps two tens," I said, with mild confidence.

This was evidently impressive. "Hyas tamanous; big magic," said both. "Wake cultus ocook; no trifler that!"

We parted, Shabbiest to his diggings, we to our trail. Hereupon Loolowcan's tone changed more and more. His old terrors, real or pretended, awoke. He feared the Dalles. It was a long journey, and I was in such headlong haste. And how could he return from the Dalles, had we once arrived? Could the son of Owhhigh foot it? Never! Would I give him a horse?

Obviously not at all would I give a horse to the new-fledged dignitary, I informed him, cooling my wrath at these bulbous indications of treachery, nurtured by the talk of Shabbiest, and ready to grow into a full-blown Judas-tree if encouraged. At last, by way of incitement to greater diligence in procuring fresh horses for me from the bands at Weenas, I promised to hire one for his return journey. But

Loolowcan the Mistrusted, watching me with disloyal eyes from under his matted hair, became doubly doubted by me now.

We turned northward, clomb[7] a long, rough ridge, and viewed, beyond, a valley bare and broad. A strip of cotton-wood and shrubs in the middle announced a river, Weenas. This was the expected *locale*; would the *personnel* be as stationary? Rivers, as it pleases nature, may run away forever without escaping. Camps of nomad Klickatats are more evasive. The people of Owhhigh, driving the horses of Owhhigh, might have decamped. What then, Loolowcan, son of a horse-thief? Can your talents aid me in substituting a fresher for Gubbins drooping for thy maltreatment.

Far away down the valley, where I could see them only as one sees lost Pleiads with telescopic vision, were a few white specks. Surely the tents of Boston soldier tilicum, winkers at squaws and thorns in the side of Shabbiest,—a refuge if need be there, thought I. Loolowcan turned away to the left, leading me into the upper valley.

We soon discovered the fact, whatever its future worth might be, that horses were feeding below. Presently a couple of lodges defined themselves rustily against the thickets of Weenas. A hundred horses, roans, calicos, sorrels, iron-grays, blacks and whites, were nipping bunch-grass on the plain. My weary trio, wearier this hot morning for the traverse of the burnt and shaggy ridge above Weenas, were enlivened at sight of their fellows, and sped toward them companionably. But the wild calvacade, tossing disdainful heads and neighing loudly, dashed off in a rattling stampede; then paused curiously till we came near, and then were off again, the lubberly huddling along far in the rear of the front caracolers.

We dismounted, and tethered our wayfarers each to a bush, where he might feed, but not fly away to saddleless freedom with the wild prairie band. We entered the nearer and larger of the two lodges.

Worldlings, whether in palaces of Cosmopolis[8] or lodges of the siwashes, do not burn incense before the absolute stranger. He must first establish his claims to attention. No one came forth from the lodges to greet us. No one showed any sign of curiosity or welcome as we entered. Squalid were these huts of squalid tenancy. Architecture does not prevail as yet on the American continent, and perhaps less among the older races of the western regions than among the newer comers Bostonward. These habitations were structures of roughly split boards, leaning upon a ridge-pole.

Five foul copper heads and bodies of men lurked among the plunder of that noisome spot. Several squaws were searching for gray hairs in the heads of several children. One infant, evidently malcontent, was being flat-headed. This fashionable martyr was papoosed in a tight-swathing wicker-work case. A broad pad of buckskin compressed its facile skull and brain beneath. If there is any reason why the North-west Indians should adopt the configuration of idiots, none such is known to me. A roundhead Klickatat woman would be a pariah. The ruder sex are not quite so elaborately beautified, or possibly their brains assert themselves more actively in later life against the distortion of childhood. The Weenas papoose, victim of aboriginal ideas in the plastic art, was hung up in a corner of the lodge, and but for the blink of its beady black eyes, almost crowded out of its head by the tight pad, and now and then a feeble howl of distress, I should have thought it a laughable image, the pet fetish of these shabby devotees. Sundry mats, blankets, skins, and dirty miscellanies furnished this populous abode.

Loolowcan was evidently at home among these compatriots, frowzier even than he. He squatted among them, *sans gene*, and lighted his pipe. One of the ladies did the honors, and motioned me to a seat upon a rusty bear-skin. It instantly began biting me virulently through my corduroys; whereat I exchanged it for a mat, soon equally carnivorous. Odors very villanous had made their settlement in this congenial spot. An equine fragrance such as no essence could have overcome, pervaded the masculine group. From the gynaeceum[9] came a perfume, hard to decipher, until I bethought me how Governor Ogden, at Fort Vancouver of the Hudson's Bay Company, with a cruelly waggish wink to me, had persuaded the commissary of the railroad party to buy twelve dozen quarts of Macassar,[10] as presents for the Indians.

"Fair and softly" is the motto of a siwash negotiation. Why should they, in their monotonous lives, sacrifice a new sensation by hurry? The five copper-skins "first eyed me over" with lazy thoroughness. They noted my arms and equipment. When they had thus taken my measure by the eye, they appealed to my guide for historical facts; they would know my whence, my whither, my wherefore, and his share in my past and my future.

Loolowcan droned a sluggish tale, to whose points of interest they grunted applause between puffs of smoke. Then there was silence and a tendency toward slumber declared itself among them; their minds needed repose after so unusual a feast of ideas. Here I protested. I expressed my emphatic surprise to Loolowcan, that he was not urgent in fulfilling the injunctions of my friend the mighty Owhhigh, and his own agreement to procure horses. The quadrupeds were idle, and I was good pay. A profitable bargain was possible.

The spokesman of the party, and apparently owner of the lodge and horses, was an olyman siwash, an old savage, totally unwashed from boyhood up, and dressed in dirty buckskin. Loolowcan, in response to my injunctions, appealed to him. Olyman declined expediting me. He would not lend, nor swop, nor sell horses. There was no mode for the imparting of horses, temporarily or perma-

nently, that pleased him. His sentiments on the subject of Boston
visitors were like those of Shabbiest. All my persuasions he qualified
as "Cultus wah wah; idle talk." Not very polite are thy phrases, Olyman head man of Stenchville on Weenas. At the same time he and
the four in chorus proposed to Loolowcan to abandon me. Olyman
alone talked Chinook jargon; the other four sat, involved in their
dirty cotton shirts, waiting for interpretation, and purred assent or
dissent,—yea, to all the insolence of Olyman; nay, to every suggestion of mine. Toward me and my plans the meeting was evidently
sulky and inclement.

Loolowcan, however, did not yet desert his colors. He made the
supplementary proposition that Olyman should hire us a sumpter
horse,[11] on which he the luxurious Loolowcan, disdainer of pedes-
trians, might prance back from the far-away Dalles. I was very willing on any conditions to add another quadruped to my trio. They
all flagged after the yesterday's work, and Gubbins seemed ready
to fail.

While this new question was pending, a lady came to my aid.
The prettiest and wisest of the squaws paused in her researches,
and came forward to join the council. This beauty of the Klickatats
thought hiring the horse an admirable scheme. "Loolowcan," said
she, "can take the consideration-money, and buy me 'ikta,' what not,
at the Dalles." This suggestion of the Light of the Harem touched
Olyman; he rose, and commanded the assistance of the shirt-clad
quartette. They loungingly surrounded the band of horses, and
with whoops and throwing of stones drove them into a corral, near
the lodges. Olyman then produced a hide lasso, and tossed its loop
over the head of a roan, the stereoscopic counterpart of Gubbins.

Meantime Loolowcan had driven up my horses. I ordered him
to tie Antipodes and Gubbins together by the head, with my long

hide lariat. The manner of all the Indians was so intolerably insolent, that I still expected trouble. My cavalry, I resolved, should be
well in hand. I flung the bight[12] of the lariat with a double turn over
the horn of my saddle and held Klale, my quiet friend, by his bridle.
My three horses were thus under complete control.

The roan was brought forward. But again an evil genius among
the Indians interfered, and growled a few poisonous words into
the ear of Olyman. Olyman doubled his demand for his horse. I
refused to be imposed upon, with an incautious expression of opinion on the subject. The Indians talked with ferocious animation for
a moment, and then retired to the lodge. The women and children
who had been spectators immediately in a body marched off, and
disappeared in the thickets. Ladies do not leave the field when amicable entertainment is on the cards.

But why should I tarry after negotiation had failed? I ordered
Loolowcan to mount and lead the way. He said nothing, but stood
looking at me, as if I were another and not myself, his recent friend
and comrade. There was a new cast of expression in his dusky
eyes.

At this moment the Indians came forth from the lodge. They came
along in a careless, lounging way, but every ragamuffin was armed.
Three had long single-barrel guns of the Indian pattern. One bore a
bow and arrows. The fifth carried a knife, half concealed, and, as he
came near, slipped another furtively into the hand of Loolowcan.

What next? A fight? Or a second sham-fight, like that of
Whulge?

I stood with my back to a bush, with my gun leaning against my
left arm, where my bridle hung; my bowie-knife was within convenient reach, and I amused myself during these instants of expec-
tancy by abstractedly turning over the cylinder of my revolver.

"Another adventure," I thought, "where this compact machine will be available to prevent or punish."

Loolowcan now stepped forward, and made me a brief, neat speech, full of facts. Meanwhile those five copper-heads watched me, as I have seen a coterie of wolves, squatted just out of reach, watch a wounded buffalo, who made front to them. There was not a word in Loolowcan's speech about the Great Spirit, or his Great Father, or the ancient wrongs of the red man, or the hunting-grounds of the blest, or fire-water, or the pipe of peace. Nor was the manner of his oration lofty, proud, and chieftainly, as might befit the son of Owhhigh. Loolowcan spoke like an insolent varlet, ready to be worse than insolent, and this was the burden of his lay.

"Wake nika klatawah copa Dalles; I won't go to Dalles. Nika mitlite Weenas; I stay Weenas. Alta mika payee nika chickamin pe ikta; now you pay me my money and things."

This was the result then,—my plan shot dead, my confidence betrayed. This frowzy liar asking me payment for his treachery, and backing his demand with knives and guns!

Wrath mastered me. Prudence fled.

I made my brief rejoinder speech, thrusting into it all the billingsgate[13] I knew. My philippic ran thus:—

"Kamooks, mika klimminwhet; dog, you have lied. Cultus siwash, wake Owhhigh tenas; paltry savage, no son of Owhhigh! Kallapooya; a Kallapooya Indian, a groveller. Skudzilaimoot; a nasty varmint. Tenas mika tum tum; cowardly is thy heart. Quash klatawah copa Dalles; afraid to go to Dalles. Nikli mamook paper copa squally tyee pe spose mika chaco yaquah yaka skookoom mamook stick; I shall write a paper to the master of Nisqually (if I ever get out of this), and suppose you go there, he will lustily apply the rod."

Loolowcan winced at portions of this discourse. He seemed ready to pounce upon me with the knife he grasped.

And now as to pay, "Hyas pultin mika; a great fool art thou, to suppose that I can be bullied into paying thee for bringing me out of my way to desert me. No go, no pay."

"Wake nika memloose; I no die for the lack of it," said Loolowcan, with an air of unapproachable insolence.

Having uttered my farewell, I waited to see what these filthy braves would do, after their scowling looks and threatening gestures. If battle comes, thou, O Loolowcan, wilt surely go to some hunting-grounds in the other world, whether blest or curst. Thou at least never shalt ride Gubbins as master; never wallop Antipodes as brutal master; nor in murderous revelry devour the relics of my pork, my hardtack, and my tongues. It will be hard if I, with eight shots and a slasher, cannot make sure of thee to dance before me, as guide, down the defiles of purgatory.

There was an awkward pause. All the *apropos* remarks had been made. The spokesmen of civilization and barbarism had each had their say. Action rather halted. No one was willing to take the initiative. Whether the Stenchvillians proposed to attack or not, they certainly would not do it while I was so thoroughly on my guard. Colonel Colt, quiet as he looked, represented to them an indefinite slaughter power.

I must myself make the move. I threw Klale's bridle over his neck, and, grasping the horn, swung myself into the saddle, as well as I could with gun in one hand and pistol in the other.

The Klickatats closed in. One laid hold of Antipodes. The vicious-looking Mephistophiles with the knife leaped to Klale's head and made a clutch at the rein. But Colonel Colt, with Cyclopean eyeball, was looking him full in the face. He dropped the bridle, and fell back a step. I dug both spurs into Klale with a yell. Antipodes whirled and lashed at his assailant with dangerous hoofs. Gubbins started. Klale reared and bolted forward.

We had scattered the attacking party, and were off.

11. Kamaiakan

Towing a horse on each side, by a rope turned about my saddle-horn, I moved but slowly. For a hundred yards I felt a premonitory itching in my spine, as if of arrow in the marrow. I would not deign to turn. If *vis a tergo*[1] came, I should discover it soon enough. I felt no inclination to see anything more of any Indians, ever, anywhere. I was in raging wrath; too angry as yet to be at a loss for the future; too furious to despond.

Whatever might now befall, I was at least free of Loolowcan the Frowzy. As to mutual benefit, we were nearly quits. He had had from me a journey home and several days of banqueting: I from him guidance hither. He had at last deserted me, shabbily, with assassination in his wishes; but I had not paid him, had vilipended[2] him, and taken myself off unharmed. Withal I was disappointed. My type Indian, one in the close relations of comrade, had failed me. It is a bitter thing to a man to find that he has thrown away even a minor measure of friendship or love upon a meaner nature. I could see what the traitor influences were, but why could he not resist, and be plucky, honorable, and a fine fellow? Why cannot all the pitiful be noble?

What saved me from massacre by the citizens of Weenas was not, I suppose, my six-shooter, not my double-barrel, not my bowie,— though each had its influence on the minds of Indians,—but the neighborhood of the exploring camp. Much as Shabbiest and Olyman disliked these intruders, they feared them more. Loolowcan also felt that he was responsible for my safety, and that, if I disappeared, some one would ask him the inevitable question, where he had put me. The explorers, not having had much success in finding a railroad, would be entertained with an opportunity for other researches. Yet the temptation to six siwashes to butcher one Boston man, owner of three passable horses and valuable travelling gear, is so great, and siwash power to resist present temptation so small, that I no doubt owed something to my armament, and something to my evident intention to use it.

I now made for the exploring camp as best I might. Gubbins and Antipodes were disposed to be centrifugal, and, as I did not wish to weary Klale with pursuits, I held to my plan of towing the refractory steeds. At times the two would tug their lengths of rope isosceles, and meet for biting each other. When this happened, I, seated just behind the apex of the triangle, was wellnigh sawed in twain by the closing sides. After such encounter, Antipodes would perhaps lurch ahead violently, while Gubbins, limping from a kick, would be a laggard. Klale would thus become the point where two irregular arms of a diagonal met, and would be sorely unsteadied, as are those who strive to hold even control between opponent forces.

Thus I jerked along, sometimes tugging, sometimes tugged, until I discerned a distant flicker in the air, which soon defined itself as the American flag, and through the underwood I saw the tents of the exploring party, a welcome refuge.

I was tired, hot, excited, and hateful, disgusted with Indians and horses, and fast losing my faith in everything; therefore the shelter of a shady tent was calming, and so was the pleasant placidity of the scene within. Lieutenant M. was reclining within, buying of a not uncleanly Indian long, neat potatoes and a silver salmon. Dewiness of his late bath in the melted snows of the Weenas sparkled still on the bright scales of the fish. It was a tranquillizing spectacle after the rough travel and offensive encounters of the day. Almost too attractive to a man who, after a few moments of this comparatively Sybaritic[3] dalliance, must renew, and now alone, his journey, fed with musty hardtack, and must again whip tired nags over plains bristling with wild sage, and over the aggravating backbones of the earth.

The camp could give me, as it did, a hospitable meal of soldiers' fare; but, with friendliest intentions, the camp could do little to speed me. It could advise me that to launch out unguided into the unknown is perilous; but I was resolved not to be baffled. Le Play House, the mission where Loolowcan should have guided me in the morning, was somewhere. I could find it, and ask Christian aid there. The priests would probably have Indian retainers, and one of these would be a safer substitute for my deserter. I would not prognosticate failure; enough to meet it if it come.

Le Play House is on the Atinam, twenty miles in a bee-line from camp. Were one but a bee, here would be a pleasant flight this summer's afternoon. But how to surely trace this imaginary route across pathlessness, over twenty miles of waste, across two ranges of high scorched hills? Two young Indians, loungers about the camp, offered to conduct me for a shirt. Cheap but inadmissible; I am not now, my young shirtless, in the mood for lavishing a shirt of civilization on any of the siwash race. Too recent are the injuries and insults of Loolowcan and the men of Stenchville. I am still in an imprudent rage,—I rashly scorn the help of aborigines. Thereaway is Atinam,—I will ride thither alone this pleasant afternoon of summer.

I could not fitly ask the fusillade for Loolowcan, Olyman, and his gang. Their action had been too incomplete for punishment so final. I requested Lieutenant M. to mamook stick[4] upon my ex-comrade should he present himself. I fear that the traitor escaped unpunished, perhaps to occupy himself in scalping my countrymen in the late war. Owhhigh in that war was unreasonably hung; there are worse fellows than Owhhigh, in cleaner circles, unhung, and not even sent to Coventry.[5]

Before parting, Lieutenant M. and I exchanged presents of our most precious objects, after the manner of the Homeric heroes. Hardshell remainder biscuits he gave, jaw-breakers, and tough as a pine-knot, but more grateful than my hardtack, well sprouted after its irrigation by the S'kamish. I bestowed, in return, two of my salted tongues, bitter as the maxims of La Rochefoucauld.[6]

Gubbins and Antipodes were foes irreconcilable,—a fact of immense value. Therefore, that they might travel with less expense of scamper to me, I tied their heads together. I felt, and so it proved, that, whenever Antipodes begged to pause and feed, Gubbins would be impelled to keep up a steady jog-trot, and whenever Gubbins wished to inspect a tuft of bunch-grass to the right, his companion would stolidly decline compliance, and plod faithfully along the ideal bee-line. There must be no discursiveness in my troop henceforth.

Then I resolutely said adieu to the friendly camp, and, pointing my train for a defile in the hard hills upon the southern horizon, started, not very gayly, and very lonely. We did not droop, horses or man, but the visionary Hope that went before was weak in the knees, and no longer bounded gallantly, beckoning us onward. The two light-loaded horses, in their leash, were rarely unanimous to halt, but their want of harmony often interfered with progress, and Owh-high's whip must often whirr about their flanks, hinting to them not to be too unbrotherly. Toiling thus doggedly on over the dry levels and rolling sweeps of prairie, Klale and I grew weary with the remorseless sunshine, and our responsibility of the march.

As I rounded a hillock, two horsemen, galloping toward me, drew up at a hundred yards to reconnoitre. One of them immediately rode forward. What familiar scarecrow is this? By that Joseph coat I recognize him. It is Shabbiest, pleased evidently to see that Loolowcan has taken his advice, and I am departing alone.

"Kla hy yah? Howdydo?" said the old man, "Whither now, O Boston tyee ?"

"To Le Play House," answered I, short and sour, feeling no affinity for this rusty person, the first beguiler of my treacherous guide.

"Not the hooihut," said he. "Nanitch ocook polealy; behold this powder,"—the powder I had given him. For this gift, within his greasy garb there beat a grateful heart, or possibly a heart expectant of more, and he volunteered to guide me a little way into the trail. Moral: always give a testimonial to dreary old grumblers in ole clo', when you meet them in the jolly morning,—possibly they may requite you when you meet at sulky eve.

First, Shabbiest must ask permission of his companion. "My master," he said; "I am elaita, a slave." The master, a big, bold Indian of Owhhigh type, in clothes only second-hand, gave him free permission. The old man's servitude was light.

Shabbiest led off on his shambler in quite another direction from mine, and more southerly. After a mile or so we climbed a steep hill, whence I could see the Nachchese again. I saw also behind me a great column of dust, and from it anon two galloping riders making for us.

They dashed up, the same two youths who at camp had offered to guide me to Le Play House for a shirt. I was humbler now than when I refused them before noon, having over-confidence in myself and my power of tracing bee-lines. We must, perhaps, be lost in our younger and prodigal periods, before our noon, that we may be taught respect for experience, and believe in co-operation of brother-men.

Now, I possessed two shirts of faded blue-check calico, and was important among savages for such possession. One of these, much bedimmed with dust, at present bedecked my person,—buckskin laid aside for the heat. There was no washerwoman within many degrees of latitude and longitude,—none probably between the Cascades and the Rockys. Why not, then, disembarrass myself of a valueless article,—a shirt properly *hors du combat*,[7]—if by its aid I might win to guide me two young rovers, ambitious of so much distinction on their Boulevards as a checked calico could confer?

Young gallopers, the shirt is yours. Ho for Le Play House!

Adieu, Shabbiest, unexpected re-enterer on this scene! Thy gratitude for two charges of powder puts a fact on the merit side of my book of Indian character. Receive now, with my thanks, this my last spare dhudeen, and this ounce of pigtail, and take away thyself and thy odorous coat from between the wind and me. Shabbiest rode after his master.

Everything now revived. Horses and men grew confident, and Hope, late feeble in the knees, now with braced muscles went turning somersets of joy before us. Antipodes and Gubbins, unleashed, were hurried along by the whoops and whips of my younker guides;[8] and Klale, relieved of responsibility, and inspired by gay companions, became sprightly and tricksy. Sudden change had befallen my prospects, lately dreary. Shabbiest had come as forerunner of good fortune. Then, speeding after him, appeared my twin deliverers, guiding me for the low price of a shirt totally buttonless.

It was worth a shirt, nay, shirts, merely to be escorted by these graceful centaurs.[9] No saddle intervened between them and their horses. No stirrup compelled their legs. A hair rope twisted around the mustang's lower lip was their only horse furniture. "Owhhigh tenas," one of Owhhigh's boys, the younger claimed to be. Nowhere have I seen a more beautiful youth. He rode like an Elgin marble.[10] A circlet of otter fur plumed with an eagle's feather crowned him. His forehead was hardly perceptibly flattened, and his expression was honest and merry, not like the sombre, suspicious visage of Loolowcan, disciple of Talipus.

Neither of my new friends would give me his name. After coquetting awhile, they pretended that to tell me would be tamanous of ill omen, and begged me to give them pasaiooks' names. So I received them into civilization under the titles of PRINCE and POINS.[11] These they metamorphosed into U'PLINT'Z and K'PAWINT'Z, and shouted their new appellatives at each other in glee as they galloped. Prince, my new Adonis, like Poins, his admiring and stupid comrade, was dressed only in hickory shirt of the Hudson's Bay Company and some nondescript raggedness for leggins. Deer are not abundant in this arid region, and buckskin raiment is a luxury for chiefs.[12]

With these companions, the journey, just now dismal, became a lark. Over the levels the horses dashed freshly,—mine as if they wished to show how much I had undervalued their bottom, and how needless had been my detour, under my false leader, to exchange these trusty and tried fellow-travellers for unknown substitutes. Over the levels they dashed, and stout of heart, though not quite so gayly, they clambered the hills Macadamized with pebbles of trap.

Antipodes, loping in the lead, suddenly shied wildly away from a small rattlesnake coiled in the track. The little stranger did not wait for our assault. He glided away into a thick bush, where he stood on the defensive, brandishing his tongue, and eying us with two flames. His tail meanwhile recited cruel anathemas, with a harsh, rapid burr. He was safe from assault of stick or stone, and I was about to call in my old defender, the revolver, when Uplintz prayed me to pause. I gave him the field, while Kpawintz stood by, chuckling with delight at the ingenuity of his friend and hero.

Uplintz took from a buckskin pouch at his belt his pipe, and, loosening from the bowl its slender reed stem, he passed through it a stiff spire of bunch-grass. A little oil of tobacco adhered to the point. He approached the bush carefully, and held the nicotinized straw a foot from the rattlesnake's nose. At once, from a noisy, threatening snake, tremulous with terror and rage from quivering fang to quivering rattle,—a snake writhing venomously all along its black and yellow ugliness,—it became a pacified snake, watchful, but not wrathful.

Uplintz, charmer of reptiles, proceeded with judicious coolness. Imperceptibly he advanced his wand of enchantment nearer and nearer. Rattler perceived the potent influence, and rattled no more. The vixenish twang ceased at one end of him; at the other, his tongue became gently lambent. The narcotic javelin approached, and finally touched his head. He was a lulled and vanquished rattlesnake. He followed the magic sceptre, as Uplintz withdrew it,—a very drunken serpent "rolled to starboard, rolled to larboard," staggering with the air of a languidly contented inebriate.[13] He swayed feebly out upon the path, and squirmed there, while the charmer tickled his nose with the pleasant opiate, his rattles uttering mild plaudits.

At last Kpawintz, the stolid, whipping out a knife, suddenly decapitated our disarmed plaything, and bagged the carcass for supper, with triumphant guffaws. Kpawintz enjoyed his solution of the matter hugely, and acted over the motions of the snake, laughing loudly as he did so, and exhibiting his tidbit trophy.

We had long ago splashed across the Nachchese. The sun, nearing the western hills, made every opening valley now a brilliant vista. The rattlesnake had died just on the edge of the Atinam ridges, and Kpawintz was still brandishing his yellow and black prey, and snapping the rattle about the flanks of his wincing roan, when Uplintz called me to look with him up into the streaming sunshine, and see Le Play House.

A strange and unlovely spot for religion to have chosen for its home of influence. It needed all the transfiguring power of sunset to make this desolate scene endurable. Even sunset, lengthening the shadow of every blade of grass, could not create a mirage of verdant meadow there, nor stretch scrubby cottonwood-trees to be worthy of their exaggerated shade. No region this where a Friar Tuck would choose to rove, solacing his eremite days with greenwood pleasures. Only ardent hermits would banish themselves to such a hermitage. The missionary spirit, or the military religious discipline, must be very positive, which sends men to such unattractive heathen as these,—to a field of labor far away from any contact with civilization, and where no exalting result of converted multitudes can be hoped.

The mission was a hut-like structure of adobe clay, plastered upon a frame of sticks. It stood near the stony bed of the Atinam.[14] The sun was just setting as we came over against it, on the hill-side. We dashed down into the valley, that moment abandoned by sunlight. My Indians launched forward to pay their friendly greeting to the priests. But I observed them quickly pause, walk their horses, and noiselessly dismount.

As I drew near, a sound of reverent voices met me,—vespers at this station in the wilderness. Three souls were worshipping in the rude chapel attached to the house. It was rude indeed,—a cell of clay,— but a sense of the Divine presence was there, not less than in many dim old cathedrals, far away, where earlier sunset had called worshippers of other race and tongue to breathe the same thanksgiving and the same heartfelt prayer. No pageantry of ritual such as I had often witnessed in ancient fanes of the same faith; when incense filled the air and made it breathe upon the finer senses; when from the organ tones large, majestical, triumphant, subduing, made my being thrill as if music were the breath of a new life more ardent and exalting; when inward to join the throngs that knelt there solemnly, inward to the old sanctuary where their fathers' fathers had knelt and prayed the ancestral prayers of mankind for light and braver hope and calmer energy, inward with the rich mists of sunset flung back from dusky walls of time-glorified marble palaces, came the fair and the mean, the desolate and the exultant,—came beauty to be transfigured to more tender beauty with gentle penitence and purifying Hope,—came weariness and pain to be soothed with visions of joy undying, celestial,—came hearts wellnigh despairing, self-scourged or cruelly betrayed, to win there dear repentance strong

with tears, to win the wise and agonized resolve;—never in any temple of that ancient faith, where prayer has made its home for centuries, has prayer seemed so mighty, worship so near the ear of God, as
vespers here at this rough shrine in the lonely valley of Atinam.[15]

God is not far from our lives at any moment. But we go for days
and years with no light shining forth from kindling heart to reveal
to us the near divineness. With clear and cultivated perception we
take in all facts of beauty, all the wonderment of craft, cunning adap-
tation, and subtile design in nature; we are guided through thick
dangers, and mildly scourged away from enfeebling luxury of too
much bliss; we err and sin, and gain the bitter lessons of penance;
and all this while we are deeming or dreaming ourselves thoughtfully religious, and are so up to the measure of our development. But
yet, after all these years, coming at last to a wayside shrine, where
men after their manner are adoring so much of the Divine as their
minds can know, we are touched with a strange and larger sympathy, and perceive in ourselves a great awakening, and new and wider
perception of God and the godlike, and know that we have entered
upon another sphere of spiritual growth.

Vespers ended. The missionaries, coming forth from their service, welcomed me with quiet cordiality. Visits of men not savage
were rare to them as are angels' visits to worldlings. In winter they
resided at a station on the Yakimah in the plains eastward. Atinam
was their summer abode, when the copper-colored lambs of their
flock were in the mountains, plucking berries in the dells, catching
crickets on the slopes.

Messrs. D'Herbomez and Pandosy had been some five years
among the different tribes of this Yakimah region, effecting of
course not much. They had become influential friends, rather than
spiritual guides. They could exhibit some results of good advice in

potato-patches, but polygamy was too strong for them. Kamaiakan, chiefest of Yakimah or Klickatat chiefs, sustained their cause and accepted their admonitions in many matters of conduct, but never asked should he or should he not invite another Mrs. Kamaiakan to share the honors of his lodge. Men and Indians are firm against clerical interference in domestic institutions. Perhaps also Kamaiakan had a vague notion of the truth, that polygamy is not a whit more unnatural than celibacy.[16]

Whether or not these representatives of the Society of Jesus have persuaded the Yakimahs to send away their supernumerary squaws, for fear of something harsher than the good-natured amenities of purgatory, one kindly and successful missionary work they have done, in my reception and entertainment. Their fare was mine. Salmon from the stream and potatoes from their own garden spread the board. Their sole servant, an old Canadian lay brother, cared for my horses,—for them and for me there was perfect repose.

By no means would Uplintz and Kpawintz allow me to forget their promised reward. Each was an incomplete dandy of the Yakimahs until that shirt of blue had been tried on by each, and contrasted with the brown cuticle of each. They desired to dress after my mode; with pasaiooks' names and an exchangeable shirt between them, they hoped to become elegant men of Boston fashion. Twilight was gloom to their hearts until I had condescended to lay aside that envied garment, until it had ceased to be mine, and was the joint property of two proud and happy young braves, and until each, wearing it for a time and seeing himself reflected in the admiring eyes of his fellow, felt that he was stamped with the true *cachet*[17] of civilization. Alas, that the state of my kit did not permit me to double the boon, and envelope the statuesque proportions of Uplintz with a clean calico, rich in pearl buttons. For there came an obtruding question, how the two juvenals[18] would distribute the one mantle. Would they appear before the critical circles of Weenas only on alternate days? Would they cleave the garment into a dexter[19] and a sinister portion, one sleeve and half a body to each? Or would they divide the back to one, and the front to the other, and thenceforth present, the one an obverse, the other a reverse to the world? It is my hope that their tenancy in common of this perishable chattel did not sunder companionship. Kpawintz would infallibly give up his undivided half to Uplintz, if that captivating young Adonis demanded it. But I trust that the latter was content with grace, beauty, and rattlesnakes, and yielded the entire second-hand shirt to his less accomplished friend. Elaborate toilettes are a necessity of ugliness. Uplintz, fair as Antinoius,[20] would only deteriorate under frippery.

It had a fresh flavor of incongruity to talk high civilization on the Atinam, in a mud chamber twelve feet square, while two dusky youths of Owhhigh's band, squatted on the floor, eyed us calmly, and, when their pipe was out, kept each other awake with monotonous moaning gutturals. The mountain gale of tonight was strong as the mistral of Father D'Herbomez's native Provence.

We talked of that romantic region, comparing adobe architecture of the Northwest with the Palace of Avignon, the Amphitheatre of Nismes, the Maison Carree, and the Pont du Gard.[21] Kamaiakan's court lost by contrast with King Rene's, and no Petrarch[22] had yet arisen among the Yakimahs. Then, passing over the Maritime Alps into the plains of Piedmont, we measured Monte Rosa, dominant over Father Pandosy's horizon of youth, with St. Helen's, queen of the farthest West, and rebuilt in fancy, on these desert plains, sunny Milan and its brilliant dome.

It is good to have the brain packed full of images from the wealthy past; it is good to remember and recall the beautiful accumulations of human genius from earliest eld to now. For with these possessions a man may safely be a comrade of rudest pioneers, and toughen himself to robust manliness, without dislinking himself from refinement, courtesy, and beauty of act and demeanor. Nature indeed, wise, fair, and good, is ever at hand to reintroduce us to our better selves; but sometimes, in moods sorry or rebellious, Nature seems cold and slow and distant, and will not grant at once to our eagerness the results of long, patient study. Then we turn to our remembrances of what brother men have done, and standing among them, as in a noble amphitheatre, we cannot be other than calm and patient; we cannot fall back into barbarism and be brutal, though our present society be Klalams or Klickatats; and even when treachery has exasperated us in the morning, in the evening, under the quieting influence of Art and History, we can forgive the savage, and think of pacifying themes.

A roof crushes and fevers one who has been long wont to sleep beneath the stars. I preferred my blankets without the cabin, sheltered by its wall from the wind that seemed to prophesy a storm of terrors growing on the mountains and the sea, to the luxury of a bunk within. The good fathers were lodged with more than conventual simplicity. Discomfort, and often privation, were the laws of missionary life in this lonely spot. It was camp life with none of the excitement of a camp. Drearily monotonous went the days of these pioneers. There was little intellectual exercise to be had, except to construct a vocabulary of the Yakimah dialect,—a hardly more elaborate machine for working out thought than the babbling Chinook jargon. They could have inevitably but small success in proselyting, and rarely any society except the savage dignity of Kamaiakan,

the savage vigor of Skloo, and the savage cleverness of Owhhigh.[23]
A tame lustrum for my hosts, varied only by summer migrations
to the Atinam and winter abode on the Yakimah. If the object of a
man's life were solely to produce effect upon other men, and only
mediately upon himself, one would say that the life of a cultivated
and intellectual missionary, endeavoring to instruct savages in the
complex and transitional dogmatisms of civilization, was absolutely
wasted.

When I woke, late as sunrise, after the crowded fatigues and difficulties of yesterday, I found that already my hosts had despatched
Uplintz and Kpawintz to a supposed neighbor camp of their brethren, to seek me a guide. Also the old servitor, a friendly grumbler,
was off to the mountains on a similar errand. Patience, therefore,
and remember, hasty voyager, that many are the chances of savage life.

Antipodes had shaken to pieces whatever stitched bag he bore. I
seized this moment to make repairs. Among my traps were needles
and thread of the stoutest, for use and for presents. The fascinating
squaw of Weenas, if she had but known it, was very near a largess
of such articles. But the wrong-doing of Sultan Olyman lost her the
gift, and my tailor-stock was undiminished. I made a lucky thrust at
the one eye of a needle, and began my work with severe attention.

While I was mending, Uplintz, with his admiring Orson,
Kpawintz, came galloping back. Gone were the Indians they had
sought; gone—so said their trail—to gad nomadly anywhere. And
the two comrades, though willing to go with me to the world's end
for the pleasure of my society and the reward of my shirts, must
admit to Father Pandosy, cross-examining, that they had never
meandered along the Dalles hooihut.

The old lay brother also returned bringing bad luck. Where he had looked to find populous lodges, he met one straggling squaw, left there to potter alone, while the Bedouins were far away. The many chances of Indian life seemed chancing sadly against me. Should I despair of farther progress, and become an acolyte of the Atinam mission?

Just then I raised my eyes, and lo! a majestic Indian in Lincoln green! He was dismounting at the corral from a white pacer. Who now?

"Le bon Dieu l'envoie," said Father Pandosy; "c'est Kamaiakan meme."[24]

Enter, then, upon this scene Kamaiakan, chiefest of Yakimah chiefs. He was a tall, large man, very dark, with a massive square face, and grave, reflective look. Without the senatorial coxcombry of Owhhigh, his manner was strikingly distinguished, quiet and dignified. He greeted the priests as a Kaiser might a Papal legate. To me, as their friend, he gave his hand with a gentlemanly word of welcome.

All the nobs[25] I have known among Redskins have retained a certain dignity of manner even in their beggarly moods. Among the plebeians, this excellence degenerates into a gruff coolness or insolent indifference. No one ever saw a bustling or fussy Indian. Even when he begs of a blanketeer gifted with chattels, and beg he does without shame or shrinking, he asks as if he would do the possessor of so much trumpery an honor by receiving it at his hands. The nauseous, brisk, pen-behind-the-ear manner of the thriving tradesman, competitor with everything and everybody, would disgust an Indian even to the scalping point. Owhhigh, visiting my quarters at Squally with his fugue of beggars, praying me to breech his breechless, shirt his shirtless, shoe his shoeless child, treated me with a calm loftiness, as if I were merely a steward of his, or certainly nothing more than a co-potentate of the world's oligarchy. He showed no discomposure at my refusal, as unmoved as his request. Fatalism, indolence, stolidity, and self-respect are combined in this indifference. Most of a savage's prayers for bounty are made direct to Nature; when she refuses, she does so according to majestic laws, of which he, half reflectively, half instinctively, is conscious. He learns that there is no use in waiting and whining for salmon out of season, or fresh grasshoppers in March. According to inevitable laws, he will have, or will not have, salmon of the first water, and aromatic grasshoppers sweet as honey-dew. Caprice is out of the question with Nature, although her sex be feminine. Thus a savage learns to believe that power includes steadiness.

Kamaiakan's costume was novel. Louis Philippe, dodging the police as Mr. Smith, and adorned with a woolen comforter and a blue cotton umbrella, was unkingly and a caricature.[26] He must be every inch a king who can appear in an absurd garb and yet look full royal. Kamaiakan stood the test. He wore a coat, a long tunic of fine green cloth. Like the irregular beds of a kitchen garden were the patches, of all shapes and sizes, combined to form this robe of ceremony. A line, zigzag as the path over new-fallen snow trodden by a man after toddies too many,—such devious line marked the waist. Sleeves, baggy here, and there tight as a bandage, were inserted somewhere, without reference to the anatomical insertion of arms. Each verdant patch was separated from its surrounding patches by a rampart or a ditch of seam, along which stitches of white threads strayed like vines. It was a gerrymandered coat,—gerrymandered according to some system perhaps understood by the operator, but to me complex, impolitic, and unconstitutional.

Yet Kamaiakan was not a scarecrow. Within this garment of disjunctive conjunction he stood a chieftainly man. He had the advantage of an imposing presence and bearing, and above all a good face, a well-lighted Pharos[27] at the top of his colossal frame. We generally recognize whether there is a man looking at us from behind what he chances to use for eyes, and when we detect the man, we are cheered or bullied according to what we are. It is intrinsically more likely that the chieftainly man will be an acknowledged chief among simple savages, than in any of the transitional phases of civilization preceding the educated simplicity of social life, whither we now tend. Kamaiakan, in order to be chiefest chief of the Yakimahs, must be clever enough to master the dodges of salmon and the will of wayward mustangs; or, like Fine-Ear,[28] he must know where kamas-bulbs are mining a passage for their sprouts; or he must be able to tramp farther and fare better than his fellows; or, by a certain tamanous that is in him, he must have power to persuade or convince, to win or overbear. He must be best as a hunter, a horseman, a warrior, an orator. These are personal attributes, not heritable; if Kamaiakan Junior is a nature's nobody, he takes no permanent benefit by his parentage.

Chieftainly Kamaiakan seated himself and his fantastic coat in the hut. He had looked in to see his friends, the good fathers, and to counsel with them what could be done for Mrs. Kamaiakan the third. That estimable lady had taken too much salmon,—very far too much, alas!—and Kamaiakan feared that he was about to become a widower, *pro tanto*.[29] Such a partial solution of the question of polygamy was hardly desired by the missionaries. It were better to save Mrs. K. the third; for doubtless already, knowing of her illness, many a maiden of Yakimah high fashion was wishing that her locks might glisten more sleekly attractive; many a dusky daughter of the tribe was putting on the permanent blush of vermilion to win a look from the disconsolate chief. The fathers feared that he would not content himself with one substitute, but, not to give offence, would accept the candidates one and all. Therefore one of the gentlemen busied himself with a dose for the surfeited squaw,—a dose in quantity giant, in force dwarf,—one that should make itself respected at first sight, and gain a Chinese victory by its formidable aspect alone.

While one compounded this truculent bolus,[30] the other imparted my needs to the chief.

Kamaiakan himself could not profit by this occasion to make a trip to the Dalles and cultivate my society. Not only domestic trials, but duties of state prevented. Were he absent at this critical epoch, when uninvited soldier-men were tramping the realm and winking at its ladies without respect to rank, who would stand forward as champion? Who pacify alike riotous soldier-man and aggrieved savage? Kamaiakan could not leave the field to Skloo the ambitious, nor to Owhhigh the crafty, when he returned from Squally rich with goods, the proceeds of many a horse-theft. Absent a week, and Kamaiakan might find that for another, and not for him, were the tawny maids. Kamaiakan must stay. A nobleman on the climb must keep himself always before the vulgar.

But a follower of the chief had just ambled up on a pony, leading his sumpter horse. Him Kamaiakan despatched up the Atinam, where he had heard that a camp of his people had halted on their way to the mountain berry-patches. Among them was a *protege* of the chief, who knew every trail of the region and had horses galore.

Many are the chances of nomad life. Enter now, in the background, a siwash soon to be a personage in this drama, if the last legs of his flea-bitten white Rosinante can but convey him to the foreground to announce himself.

Enter Ferdinand on the scene, in an Isabella yellow[31] shirt,—he and his garments alike guiltless of the soap of Castile, or any soap of land less royal.

Ferdinand was a free companion, a cosmopolite of his world. He was going somewhere, anywhere, nowhere. He had happened in with dinner in view. So long as the legs of Rosinante lasted, Ferdinand could be a proud cavalier. Now, those legs failing, he drooped. He would soon become a peon, a base footman, and possibly, under temptation, a footpad.[32] Better, then, quarter himself on his friends and former masters, the priests, until in the free pastures of Atinam Rosinante should grow bumptious again.

As his name imported, this new-comer claimed to be identified with civilization. "No Indian name have I," he said, "I am Fudnun, a blanketeer." He was a resolved renegado from Indian polity and sociality. He had served with the Hudson's Bay Company. He had even condescended to take lessons in cookery from the pale-face squaws of the Willamette.

While Ferdinand was thus announcing himself, and communicatively making good his claim as a blanketeer, the envoy of Kamaiakan returned. He had hastened up the Atinam, and come to Camp No-camp. The able-bodied siwashes had all vanished, leaving only a few children, recently out of the papoose period, and a few squaws far on toward second childhood. Only such were left as had no more than power enough to chase and bag the agile grass-hopper and far-bounding cricket, and to pounce upon and bag every tumbling beetle of the plain.

Such industry the messenger had found at the camp; but the able-bodied, capable of larger duties, had vanished up the wild valleys,

and scattered along the flanks of Tacoma, to change their lowland
diet for that of the mountainside;—while the fresh horses I should
have had swam in the verdure of the summit prairies, the guide I
should have had was stuffing by the handful strawberries, raspber-
ries, blackberries, sallal-berries, and his squaws, with only furtive
tribute to their own maw, were bestowing the same fruits into baskets for provident drying.

Again what was to be done, for day grew toward noon, and by to-
morrow night I must be at the Dalles, eighty miles away? My kind
friends of the mission were discussing whether the old sacristan[33]
could be trusted to know the trail and bear the fatigues, when Ferdinand rose, stepped out of the chorus, to become an actor in the
drama, and thus spoke, self-prompted:—

"Fudnun nika, pasaiooks; Ferdinand I, blanketeer. Siks nika
copa Boston tyee; friend I to Boston chief. Nika nanitch cuitan,
closche yakah klatawah; I've seen the horses, they'll go well enough.
Nika kumtux Dalles hooihut, pe tikky hyack klatawah; I know the
Dalles trail, and am ready to go at once."

Excellent Ferdinand! What fine apparition, what quaint Ariel,
doing his spiriting gently, wooed thee to these yellow sands of Atinam, to be my deliverer? Sweet youth, thou shalt have a back-load of
trinkets to carry to thy Miranda when we part.[34] Fudnun the blanketeer, let us go.

My new comrade showed Boston energy. He drove up the three
horses at once. Rest and bunch-grass at discretion had revived
them. A tough journey was before us, but thus far they had not
failed in the face of worse difficulties than we were to meet. For a
supplement, the missionaries lent me a mare of theirs, to be ridden
as far as her foal would follow, and left on the prairie for Ferdinand

to pick up on return. The kindness of these gentlemen went with me after my departure.

Adieu, therefore, to the good fathers, and may they be requited in better regions of earth, or better than earth, for their hospitality. Adieu Kamaiakan, prudent and weighty chief! fate grant thee a coat of fewer patches, a nobler robe of state. Adieu the old lay brother. Uplintz and Kpawintz, my merry pair, continue foes of the rattle-snake, and friends to the blue-shirted Boston men.

12. Lightning and Torchlight

A little before noon we left the hut of blue mud, the mission of Atinam. We forded the shallow river, and Ferdinand cheerily led the way straight up the steep hill-side. From its summit I could overlook, for farewell, the parallel ranges, walls of my three valleys of adventure. There were no forests over those vast arid mounds to narrow the view. Hills of Weenas, hills of Nachchese, valley of Atinam,—I took my last glance over their large monotony.

I might glance over the landscape, and recall my crowded life in it, only while the horses breathed after their climb, and no longer. If not eighty, certainly sixty miles away over the mountains is the Columbia, Achilles of rivers. And, says Ferdinand, "it must be a race all day with time, all night with time, a close race with time to-morrow." If uncertainty of success is a condition of success, we shall win the race. But no dalliance, no staying to study landscape; we must on, steadily as the Princess Parazaide, whatever sermons there be in the stones along our way.[1]

Vast were the hilly sweeps we overcame. Nags of mine, ye had toil that penultimate day of August. But straight from far snow cliffs came electric airs, forerunners of the nightly gale. And the sun, that it might never be deemed a cruel tyrant, had provided remedies against its own involuntary despotism, in streams from the snows of Tacoma, melted not beyond the point of delicious coolness. Snow crystals married with sunbeams came gliding down the valleys on their wedding tour. Down the gorges in the basalt, and so by pool and plunge, the transfigured being, a new element, poured to the pebbly reaches below. Whenever we had climbed the long bulk of a dusty hill-side, dreary with wild sage, a stunted and abortive tree, the mean ensign of barrenness, and then descended the hot, thirsty slopes of a declivity as dreary, down in the valley always we found the antidote to dust, thirst, and sterility, the precious boon of water hidden among grass and trees,—sunshine's gift brought from the snows to cure the pangs of sunshine. Sparkling draughts of water were ready in vale after vale. I had but to stoop from my saddle while Klale drank, and scoop the bright flow in a leather cup long dedicated to Ægle, in classic fountains of historic lands.

Ferdinand's temptation and test of faithfulness befell him before we had gone two leagues on our way. As the fates threw Shabbiest in the path of Loolowcan, now Ferdinand's tempter appeared. One watches his man narrowly at such a moment. Which Janus-face will he turn? the one that sees the past, or the one that looks toward the future? Will he be the bold and true radical, or the slinking conservative? The combat, with its Parthian flights and Pyrrhic victories,[2] is generally more briefly called life, and its result character.

Thus far I had only the coarse public facts on Ferdinand as a theme for analysis. When Mystery takes care that a man shall exist, and have a few years' career in villainy or heroism, Mystery also takes care to set upon the man's front a half-decipherable inscription. Fudnun was attractive, not repulsive, in the traits that mark character. By physiognomy, I deemed him a truish man, a goodish fellow, a wiseish nomad. But how was I to know what education had made of him? what indiscriminate vengeance he might have in his heart? what treachery in return for other blanketeers' treachery? The same spirit of our darksome enlightenment that makes slavery possible, makes maltreatment of Indians certain. Fudnun might feel himself nominated to punish in me the wrong of his race.

The Indian who was to be Fudnun's Mephistophiles was riding seemingly astray and purposeless across the world, like an Indian. But when the stranger, coming full tilt through a bending defile, saw us, it was too late to skulk. He pulled up his wild black horse, noticed me with a cool Howdydo, and opened fire upon Fudnun, with gutturals not at all cheerful. Fudnun informed me that the tenor of the new-comer's oration was like Shabbiest's to Loolowcan, yesterday.

So, then, big Brownskin on a fiery black mustang, inferior chief with shirt and leggins of buckskin reddened with clay, sulky siwash of Skloo's band, armed with gun and knife,—thou too art inhospitable to the parting guest,—thou too art unwilling that by the aid of Fudnun, my friend, I should speed out of the country toward the Columbia. Now, then, none of this! Avaunt! Make tracks!

But he declined to make tracks, and held the too facile Ferdinand in powwow. I questioned in my prudent heart whether I should do what I twitched to do, namely, use the Owhhigh whip upon this scowling interloper. The wristlet of otter-fur tightened in my grasp; I shook the long lash carelessly about the sturdy legs of the wiry horse of Brownskin the Tempter, stinging them restive, horse and man. With revengeful venom of the blackest in his mind, the copper-headed, snaky beguiler continued his solicitations, urging Ferdinand, as that excellent worthy afterwards told me, not merely to desert, but to aid in a scheme of pillage, and whatever outrage might precede or follow pillage.

Ferdinand, as I trusted, was proof against the wily wheedler, though he sputtered poisonously in a language I knew not. Ferdinand at last shook off that serpent influence, and turned toward the trail. Copper-head, baffled, gave me a glance with a bite in it, and galloped away, too much enraged to ask more barbarico for all my valuables as a present.

"Ha, ha!" chuckled Fudnun, shaking his head, showing his white teeth, and seeming as happy as a school-girl with a new conundrum; "ha, ha!" chuckled he, as if this were a joke of the freshest. "Yaka tikky memloose mika pe capsualla conoway ikta; he want kill you and steal all the traps. Halo nika; not at all I. Wake kahquah klimmeriwhit Fudnun,—wake cultus man ocook; not so is Fudnun a liar,—no dastard he."

Certainly not, Fudnun the Trusty! I divined you rightly, then. Your Janus-face points aright. You are not a spoilt Indian. I set you in the scale against Loolowcan the Frowzy, and once more half believe in honesty of barbarians. Having defied temptation, henceforth you are true.

Fudnun had thus far ridden the mission mare, while Gubbins pranced bare-back. Now the foal began to sigh for his native heath, and shrink from strange, wild scenes. We therefore stopped, and turned them out into the wide world. They could wallow in the long sedges there along, and drink of the brook. No Indian of all the country-side would allow his thievish heart to covet an animal with the mission brand. Me, or any other intrusive pasaiooks, he might rob of beast or the burden of beast, but whatever belonged to the priests was taboo. And if mission property could not protect itself, woe be to the thief when the green, gleaming coat of the dread inevitable Kamaiakan was seen along his trail.

Gubbins must again endure a rider more humane than Loolowcan. Antipodes's packs were now ridiculously light, as Æsop's bag at the end of the journey. We could press on fleet over hill and dale, on and on, steadily riding as if we bore tidings of joy, or rode for succor for the beleaguered of a starving city. On, never flagging, we sped, and drew, as day waned, toward the wooded mountains. Never a moment we rested, traversing tenantless wastes, until deep in the afternoon we came to a large, pure well of exquisite water, predicted by Ferdinand, wisest of nomads.

There, in a glade emeralded with richest of grass, I reposed, elaborating strength for my night ride. Meanwhile, my horses, with never a leg the less than when I proved them on the Macadam of Squally, swallowed green landscape fast, as if they feared this feast were a mirage, and the water-sprite would presently roll up her green drapery and vanish. The horses, with or without fancies or forethought, instinctively made ready for the coming trial.

Sweet are such episodes of travel in the fair spots of earth. Sweet, though the fare be but pork toasted on a stick, and hardtack to which mustiness has but slightly penetrated. And if after feast so Spartan, before a night to be sleepless, a siesta propose itself, who will refuse? Not the wise traveler, to whom sleep or food never come amiss. By the Fountain of Fudnun the Jolly, to whom in less busy times life was a long joke, sleep, or repose not quite losing consciousness, might be permitted. For now my doubts of winning the race were beheaded by trenchant intuitions of success, and wriggled away into the background. Such doubts necessarily forecrawl a man on the march toward any object; it is well if he can timely destroy them, lest they trip up the rider's hopeful ardor.

Distance, lying in long coils from Whulge onward, I had nearly trampled to death; its great back showed marks of my victorious hoofs; only the head reared itself, monstrous and unsubdued. One more great rampart of mountains must be stormed, and for this final assault Klale, Antipodes, and Gubbins were still taking in such stuff as courage is made of. Feed on, trusty trio; I love the sound of those jaws. It racks my heart to know that I must still demand much go-ahead of you. But though an exalting, I have been a merciful master. Ye have had long grass, to be digested into leaps, short grass for walking material, and sometimes a prairie-flower for inspiring a demivolt.[3] I have whipped you, Antipodes, but have I whaled you? And now that you have taken your fill of grass, long, short, and flowery, let us away, to climb the great ridges before nightfall.

We came, not long before sunset, to the great mountain range,—another buttress of the Cascade system. Full against the plain rose a bulky earthwork. Klickatats on mustangs had been, ever since Klickatats first learned to ride, forever assaulting this fortress in elaborate zig-zags, engineered with skill. And here, for fifteen hundred feet, we too must climb, driving our horses before us; we bending forward, and they struggling up on tiptoe and consuming energy far too rapidly.

The sun was prematurely gone when we reached the edge of easier slope above this mural front. Where I should have seen, westward, the Cascades and Tacoma bright as sunny cloud, but firmer than cloud, were now no mountains black with pines, was no Tacoma against the rose of sunset. A gloomy purple storm lay over the Cascades, vaster than they. A mass of thunderous darkness had swept in from ocean, and now stayed majestic, overlooking the wide world.

Would it retreat with the sun, to do havoc wherever white sails were strained in hopeless flight, and whirl the spray from wrecking coral-reefs to the calm lagoons within? Or would it take a night of Titanic revelry among the everlasting hills, toppling crag into chasm, shaking down avalanches to drown their roar with roar of louder thunder, tossing great trees over into the torrents to see their strong death-struggle in the foam, by the ghastly beauty of lightning, revealing a spectacle born and dead in an instant? Or must it, with no choice of its own, range with the whirl of the globe, taking giant pleasure or doing giant ruin as the chances of Nature offered? Which of these was to be the destiny of that purple storm, poised and lowering over the hidden mountains? I could divine its decision, or its obedience, by prophetic puffs of roasted air, that ever and anon, in a sudden calm that had now befallen, smote me, as if some impish urchin, one of the pages of Æolus, dancing on a piping wind-bag, was looking my way and smiting his breezy cheeks.

Beside that envelope of storm hiding the west from floor to cope, there was only to be seen, now softened with dull violet haze, the large, rude region of my day's gallop,—thirty miles of surging earth, seamed with frequent valleys of streams flowing eastward, where scanty belts of timber grew by the water-side.

When August's sun, the remorseless, is gone, whether behind the ragged rims of a hurricane or the crest of a sierra, men and horses revive in that long shade. Twilight is sweet and restoring in itself, and also to an unforeseeing trio of mustangs, as promising the period when men encamp and horses are unsaddled. Therefore, now, although the air was heavy and the light lurid, we chased along the trail, mounting slowly ever, and winding on through files of pines;—vigorously we chased on, as if twilight of eve were twilight of dawn, and our day but now begun.

Among the silent pines, deeper into the darkening wood. But the same power that swept darkness forward in a steady growing inundation, banished also silence. The overcoming storm was battling with stillness, and slowly enveloping the strife with thicker and thicker pall, such as hangs over fields trod by the loud agonies of war.

A far forerunner of the gale struck suddenly upon the mountain-front, like an early shot of battle, fired to know the death range. While the roar of this first blast was passing away, and the trees were swaying back to stillness, a fugue of growling winds came following after. The alarmed whispers from leaf to leaf grew thicker now, joining to an undertone of delicate wailing a liquid sound, but sad, like the noise of a water-fall falling all the hours into a sunless pool where one lies drowned because his life and soul could bear life and light no longer. Again, with gush of blacker darkness, came a throng of blasts tramping close; and after them was seeming calm,—calm only in seeming, and filled with the same whispers of alarm, the same dreary, feeble wail, and now with sobs desperate, irrepressible.[4]

Fitful bursts of weeping rain were now coming thicker, until control ceased, and the floods fell with no interval, borne on furiously, dashing against every upright object as great crushing wave-walls smite on walls of cliff by the sea-side. The surges of wind were mightier than the furious rain drift, and with their strength and their roaring came the majesty of thunder, constant as the wind. Long ago, from where the clouds lay solid on the mountains, great booming sounds had come, as if these masses rolling over the summits had struck with illumed crash upon crags below; and when those purple glooms stayed in hesitating poise upon the Cascades, lightnings were passing in among them, calling them together for the march, and signalling on the laggards. Now a great outer continent, a belt of storm world, was revolving over earth, and shaping itself to the region it traversed. In this storm zone, revealed by the scenic flames of neighbor lightning, were mountains huger than any ever heaped by Titanic forces assaulting heaven from earth. There were sudden clefts, and ravines with long sweeping flanks, and chasms where a cloud mountain-side had fallen in, leaving a precipice all ragged and ruinous, ready itself to fall. There were plateaus and surgy sweeps of cloud-land, valleys of gentleness, dells sweet and placid, passes by toppling crags from vale to vale: great stairways up to Alpine levels on high, garden-like Arcadias among horrent[5] heights, realms changefully splendid,—all revealed by the undulations of broad, rosy lightning and lightning's violet hues, where it shone through their gloom of clouds. These clouds so black and terrible, hurrying on a night so black and dreary, were not then terrible and dreary in themselves, but only while there was no light to prove their beauty;—when light gleamed, they shone transcendent.

Lightning, besides its business of revelation, had some gymnastic feats of its own to show the world; to spring at some great round-topped, toppling cloud-crag, and down to the valleys beneath; to shoot through tunnels of darkness, and, across chasms, hanging a bending line of light athwart, like the cable bridges of the Andes.

Lightning was also casting blinding splendors over the permanent world below the storm. Wherever the trail bent toward the vantage edges of the mountain-side, every flash disclosed magnificent breadth of lonely landscape, and then the vision was instantly limited to the dense darkness around, darker to dazzled eyes. But soon there were no such moments of darkness nor any silence. Thunder-tone flowed into thunder-tone, as blasts had thickened to a gale, and lightning made pervading light, flickering and unsteady as fevered pulses.

Such was the machinery of this drama, and as to the actors, I and my party, what of them?

Wet were they all, yea, drenched. And why should not a little biped be drenched? It is an honor to the like of him that splendid phenomena should take the trouble to notice him even with ridicule. And drenching by an August thunder-storm is not chilly misery. Nor are men on a hooihut considering damage to their integuments. On a hooihut, we wear no tiles that to-morrow will be pulp; nor coats with power to shrink and never again be shapely. Therefore, while the air beat upon us with electric thrills, and the furious excitements of the tempest were around us, we dashed along the narrow thread of the trail between the innumerable pines,—dashed along, acting with the might of the storm, as if we were a part of it, and reacting with ardors of our own against its fury.

Ferdinand, wrapped in a white blanket, led the way; Antipodes followed as main body; Klale and I were the third division of my army. Flooded lightning showed us our slender path winding up the illumined vista, and marked more clearly, in the long, coarse mountain grass, by rain pools.

For all the ceaselessness of flashes there would sometimes be moments of utter darkness, when the eyes closed involuntarily, and the look blenched, confounded and dazzled by the sudden gloom. Then the vista would disappear, the path be blotted out, and Ferdinand, white blanketeer, be annulled, so far as vision knew. But before night could gain power from permanence, or my guide could lose his last ocular image of the silver pathway, again flashes went curving above us, the floods of light poured forth, and the forest was betrayed as if clear noon were master.

The path had now bent inward, away from the edge of the mountain. Under the roofing pines we could see no more the stormy pageantry. The straight black trunks opened before us; we were to go on, on, guided by the beautiful ghastliness of lightning, fit illumination of terrible rites in the penetralia[6] of this austere forest. Very wet neophytes we should arrive in the presence of whatever antique hierophant[7] there might be wonder-working within the roofless sanctuary whither the lightning was leading us.

By this time the grandeurs of the storm were ended. Madness and pangs died away into sullen grief. Passion was over; tame realities were coming. There had been a majestic overture crowded with discordant concords, and there was nothing left for the opera but dull recitative. Night became undramatic; sulky instead of inspired; grizzly instead of splendorous. Solid rain now took the place of atmosphere. While the storm rampaged, it was adventurous and heroic to breast it; now our journey became an offensive plod. So long as lightning declared the path, it was exciting to chase therein; our present meaner guide was the sound of our own splashing in the trail.

Ferdinand still led on, finding the way by instinct. He could see naught, and I could see not even him in his white toga, except when some belated flash of the rear-guard turned its lantern hither and thither, seeking its comrades. We kept together by whistling to and fro. Observe this fact; for it is said that Indians do not whistle. Also that they eat no pork. For this latter reason some have connected them with the Lost Tribes.[8] With regard to the latter charge, I can speak from a considerable range of induction. Indians only eat no pork when they have no pork. Not one to whom I have offered that viand of low civilization ever refused it, but clutched it with more or less ardor, proportioned to his state of repletion at the moment. My facts for induction on whistling among the Red Men are fewer. This one, however, I present confidently: Fudnun the Blanketeer whistled tunefully. Ours was but a faint trail, rarely traversed, often illegible, even by full daylight, to untrained eyes, as I learned afterwards. What wonder, then, that we wandered often, and that the keenness of Fudnun's vision was often tried, as he peered about and searched by intelligent zigzags in the darkness of night, under the darkness of pines, along the matted, muffling grass, for the slight clew of our progress? What wonder, then, that at last we erred totally, and searched in vain?

"Halo klap; no find," said Fudnun the Trusty, coming back rather disconsolate.

Perforce of the great controls of Nature, we must submit, and take this night involuntary rest, quite lost in the forest.

Fudnun unsaddled. The horses could show no dislike to their fare. The grass was long, plenteous, and every blade was hung with lubricating rain-drops. Meanwhile, I, groping about, found some bits of punk and dry fuel in a natural fireplace hollowed in an ancient pine, one of the giants. The *genius loci*[9] here, being of monotonous cast of mind, had given himself totally to pine culture. I could see nothing, but I had a sense that immense rough-barked pines were standing all about, watching my movements,—what was I doing, grubbing there at the roots of their big brother?

I was at work to light a fire. Fire was once a thing to be kept safe by vestals;[10] but now we can do without them; fire sacred is cared for on myriads of domestic hearths; fire profane is in our pantaloons pocket. One may evoke it in an instant, as I did now. The tricksy sprite alighted in my tindery tipsoo, and presently involved my punk and my chips and all my larger fuel, as fast as I could seek it, by the growing blaze, among the ruins of the forest.

Fudnun took his supper, and soon was asleep, coiled in a heap among the saddles. As for me, I watched and drowsed, squatted before the fire, mummied in my blankets. Not a position, certainly, for cheerful reveries. A drizzle, thick as metaphysics, surrounded me. In its glowing cavity was my fire, eating its way slowly into the dead old heart of the tree, baking my face, but not drying my back. I was fortunately hungry, and hunger is excellent entertainment. A hungry man has something to think of, and if he is his own cook, something to do. I frizzled my pork and toasted my biscuit-chips; then I ate the same, and that part of the frolic was over. I longed for a tin cup of tea, well boiled and bitter, but it was "water, water everywhere, and not a drop to drink."[11] I could not concentrate the drizzle, nor collect the drops from the grass, nor wring a supply from my wet clothes,—no tea, then, the best friend of the campaigner.[12] In fact, as I could not sleep and recruit, and as I was in rather sorry plight, there was nothing to be done except to endure despondency and be patient.

Such pauses as this, midway in minor difficulty, are profitable, if patience can but come up from the rear, and marshal her sister faculties for steadier future march. In such isolated halts in a man's life, when the future is not so certain as to make him disdain the past, he discovers the lessons there were in empiric days or years, of hurry and dash. In the lonely forest, dark with midnight and storms, where his fire casts but a gloaming light,—in such a solitude a man self-dependent will hear the oracles speak to him if they are to speak. He who would ask his fate at Delphi goes not along the summer-blooming plains, nor in among the vine-clad trellises, nor through the groves of olives, gray and ancient in gentle realms of Arcady. The Delphic gorge is stern and wild, and would affright all but one who is resolute to wring a favorable fate from the cave of prophecy. Poetic visions do not visit beds of roses, and no good thing or thought came out of Sybaris.

So there, "lone upon the mountain, the pine-trees wailing round me,"[13] I seemed to hear some of those great calming words without which life goes restless, and may not dream of peace. For early, thoughtful years and eras of ours are saddened and bewildered by the sting of evil, others' and our own; poisonous bigotries grapple with faith from its cradle; we are driven along the gantlet of selfishness; love, the surest test of nobleness, seems the most hopeless test, discovering only the ignoble; we dwell among comrades of chance, not choice, and cannot find our allies, know not any other law of growth than the unreflecting stir about us. So instinctive faith dies, and because without faith the soul dies, we must seek it, and perhaps wander for it as far and not hopefully,—wander perhaps as far as to the forests of Tacoma.

As I sat by my fire, thinking over the wide world, and feeling that I looked less blindly than once upon its mysteries, suddenly I was visited by a brilliant omen.

All at once the darksome forest became startlingly full of light. A broad glare descended through the lowering night, and shed about me strange, weird lustre. I sprang up, and beheld a pillar of flame hung on high in the gloom.

An omen quite too simply explicable. I had kindled my fire in the hollow of a giant dead trunk. Flame slowly crept up within, burning itself a way through the dry core, until it gained the truncated summit, sixty feet aloft, and leaped outward in a mighty flash. Once escaped, after its stealthy growth, the fire roared furiously up this chimney of its own making. The long flame streamed away from its gigantic torch, lashing, among the trees and tossing gleams, sparks and great red flakes into the inner glooms of the wood. Nobler such an exit for one of the forest primeval than to rot away and be a century in slow dying. His brethren around watched sombrely the funeral pyre of their brother. Their moaning to the wind mingled with the roar of his magnificent death-song.

Trust Nature. None of the thaumaturgists, strong in magical splendors, ever devised such a spectacle as this. I had fought my way, a pressing devotee, into the inner shrine, unbullied by the blare of the tempest, and this was the boon offered by Nature to celebrate my initiation.

The fire roared, and there was another roaring. Ferdinand snored roaringly from his coiled position among the traps. A snore is the expression of gratitude for sleep, not less genuine for its unconsciousness. Every breath is a plaudit to Morpheus,[14] the burlesque of a sigh of joy. Snoring is to sleep what laughter is to waking. Fudnun's snore in the solitary woods, among the great inarticulate facts of nature, was society and conversation. He seemed to utter amens of content in long-drawn cadence.

As I could not take my tall torch in hand and be a path-finder, I patrolled about the woods, admiring it where it stood, a brilliant beacon. The blossom of flame still unfolded, unfading, and as leaf after leaf fell away like the petals of roses, other petals opened about the unconsumed bud. Firelight gave rich greenness to the dark pines. Sometimes a higher quiver of flame would seize an overhanging branch and sally off gayly; but the blast soon extinguished these escapades.

Fire gnaws quicker than the tooth of Time. I was sitting, drowsy and cowering, near my furnace, when a warning noise aroused me. A catastrophe was at hand. Flames grew intenser, and careered with leaps more frantic, as now, with a riving uproar, the giant old trunk cut away at its base, cracked, trembled, swayed, and fell in sublime ruin. At this strange tumult, loud and harsh in the dull dead of night, the horses, affrighted, looked up with the light of the flame in their eyes, and then dashed off furiously.

Fudnun also was startled. He woke; he uncoiled; he stared; he grunted; he recoiled; he slept; he snored.

Mouldering away in cheerless ruin lay the trunk all along in the dank grass. Its glory had quenched itself in time, for now, Aurora[15] being in the sulks, a fusty dawn, the slipshod drudge of her palace, was come as substitute for the rosy goddess, to wake the world to malcontent. Enchantment was perished. My torch, bright flarer through darkness, became mere kitchen fuel. Fudnun awoke to snore no more. He squatted in a mass, warming his musty members after their bedrizzled cramps of the night. Then we toasted our pork over the embers, completing the degradation of the pine. It had had its centuries of dignity, while its juniors, lengthening upward ungainly, envied its fair proportions. Then the juniors had times of rejoicing within their cortex, in their vegetable hearts, when glory of foliage fell away from their senior's crown, and larger share of sunlight came to the hungry youngsters. And now the junior pines were in high feather that an unsightly monument of the past and *memento mori*[16] was gone, and lay a vertebrated skeleton of white ashes in the glade it sheltered so fatherly once.

13. The Dalles—Their Legend

Klale the ardent, Gubbins the punchy, Antipodes the lubberly, had not stampeded far in their panic when the great pine-tree torch fell crashing through the woods. Fudnun easily recovered them by the light of dawn,—three horses well fed and well rested, three sinewy nags, by no means likely to be scant of breath through Falstaffian fatness, but yet stanch, and able to travel the last thirty or forty miles of my journey before nightfall.

Prayerful for sunrise and sun-born ardors in that dull dawn were horses and men. Cold is a bitter foe of courage; hot blood is the only brave blood. All five of us, the grazers three, the snorer one, and the one drowsy watcher, still trembled with the penetrating chill of drizzle on the bleak mountain-top. We might not have the instinctive cheerfulness, child and nursling of sunshine, but we soon, by way of substitute, made an inspiriting discovery,—the trail. Like many an exit from life's labyrinths, it was hidden only for want of searching with more light. We pounced upon its first faint indications, and went at such full speed as a night of damp and cramp permitted, with as much tirra lirra[1] in our matin song of march as might ring through the vocal pipes of knights-errant carrying colds in their heads.

"Nika klap; find um," Fudnun had shouted, with a triumphant burst of laughter, when he caught sight of the trail, lurking serpentine in the grass; and now, having recovered his reputation as a pathfinder, he would not lose it again. With single-handed accuracy he kept this one object in view. He fairly shamed my powers of observation by his quick, unerring glance. Shrewd detective, he was never at fault wherever that eluding path dodged artfully, and became but a shattered clew of escape. If ever the hooihut disappeared totally, like a rivulet sinking under ground, Fudnun, as if he bore a witch-hazel divining-rod, made straight for the spot of its reappearance. Sometimes for a mile there would be no visible way, and I, seeing my guide still galloping on confidently under the pines, over the dry brown carpet of their fallen leaves, would call him, and say,—

"Halo mitlite hooihut; here's no trail." "Nawitka, closche nika nanitch; yes, I see it well," Fudnun would reply, pointing where a root had been scraped by a hoof, or a tuft of moss kicked up, or the brown pine-leaves trodden to a yellower tint; and presently, in softer ground, the path would again declare itself distinctly, like a pleasant association reawakening in moments of tenderness. Thus we hastened on through the open pine woods, gaining distance merely. We fled on between tedious ranks of yellow pines, with a raw wind chasing us and growing icier, as we rode out upon the bare, shelterless slopes of the lower regions.

And by and by, as the trail disentangled itself from forest and mountain, lo, in houseless wilds, a house! an architectural log cabin.

"Whose house, Fudnun? What outpost sentry-box of Boston camps to come?"

It is the house of Skloo, Telamon of the Yakimaks, as Owhhigh is their Diomed, the horse-thief, and Kamaiakan their great-hearted Agamemnon; no advanced post of Boston men, but a refuge of the siwashes, between two fires of pale-faces advancing westward and eastward.

The cabin was deserted. Skloo and the braves of Skloo were gone over moor and fell, gone by canon and prairie, gone after salmon, grasshoppers, berries, kamas,—after all Indian luxuries and wants, including pillage of pasaiooks and foes of their own color, when to be had without peril. The cabin of Telamon Skloo stood, lonely and deserted, in a spot where the world looked large, and yellow prairies rushed out of the forest, billowing broadly southward, toward the desolate ranges, walls of the Columbia. As well, perhaps, that Skloo was an absentee and his house shut; Skloo, with a house on his back and a roof over his head, would have been totally neutralized as a nomad chief. He would have lost Skloo the Klickatat rover, with whatever interest or value he had in that relation, and have been precipitated to the level of any Snooks in Christendom, dweller in villa or box.

I did not envy Skloo his stationary property of house; certain mobile chattels of his I did envy him greatly. A band of his horses were feeding in this spot of the unfenced world. They did not heed our roadster passage as we draggled by, much the worse for wearing travel. They noticed us no more than a wary old grouse notices a gunless man. Antipodes felt the thoughtless dolt stir again within him; he forgot how he had been taught who was his master, and, with packs flapping like rapid pinions, he bolted, to join that free cavalcade. Fudnun instantly educated him severely back into line.

Just then, over a swell of the ripe, yellow prairie, came at full speed, on a coal-black horse, a young Indian, with his long hair uncovered and streaming in the wind as he galloped. On he rode,— a cavalier free and bold, without saddle or stirrups, whirling his lasso with arm outstretched. He made straight for the band of grazing horses, and the unwarning blast blew from them toward him, as they stood curiously watching our slow tramp along the trail. So the untamed horses of Skloo's prairie did not sniff or see or hear the new-comer until he was close upon them and the whiz of his whirling lasso sang in their ears. Then they tossed their proud heads, shook their plumage of mane, and, with a snort of disgust at their unwatchfulness, sprang into full speed of flight. They bent toward us, and crossed the trail not a hundred yards before us. Their pursuer was riding almost parallel with them. As they dashed by, he flung his lasso at a noble black, galloping with head elate and streaming mane and tail.

The loop of the lasso, preserving its circle with geometrical accuracy, seemed to hang an instant in the air, waiting for its certain captive.

Will he be taken? Must he be enthralled?

Not so. A glorious escape! While the loop of the lasso hung poised, the black had sprung through it unerringly—straight through its open circle—touching it only to spurn with his hindmost hoof, and then with the excitement of his success he burst forward, and took the lead of all that wild throng, dashing on like the wind.[2]

But not at all for this failure and overcast did the speed of the headlong chaser lessen. He did not even turn for my applause at the circus-like "act of horsemanship" he had afforded me in this spacious amphitheatre. His powerful coal-black horse still sped on fleet as before, close upon the particolored regiment, and the rider had his lasso quickly in hand, and coiled for a fresh cast, more cautious. Far as we could see over the undulations of the tawny plain, so beautifully boundless, the herd was stretching on, rather in joyous escapade than coward flight; and just apart from them, their pursuer still held tireless and inevitable gallop,—his right arm raised and whirling with imperceptible motion the lasso, now invisible in the distance.

My good-will was with the dappled herd of runaways, rather than with the bronze horseman in chase. The capture of any wild stampeder would begin or renew his history of maltreatment, as some of them already knew from past experience, and were flying now with remembrance of abuse as well as for the instinct of freedom. There are no absolutely wild horses in the Northwest. All the cavalier Indians have their numerous bands of horses, broken and unbroken, and wild enough, following the nomad movements of the tribe. It is a rough, punchy, hardy stock, utterly unkempt and untaught, but capable of taking care of itself, and capable also, according to the law of barbarism, of producing chance individuals of size, strength, and beauty. Bucephalus is the exception; Rosinante the rule. Bucephalus is worth a first-class squaw, or possibly two of those vexatious luxuries of a cheaper grade. Rosinantes go about five to the squaw. Papa gets the price; not as in civilization, where, when a squaw sells herself for a Bucephalus, a brougham, and a black coachman, she keeps and uses the equivalent. And now that I am on the tariff for squaws,—dry goods buy them in Siwashdom as sometimes in Christendom. The conventional price is expressed in blankets. Blankets paid to papa, buy: five, a cheap and unclean article, a drudge; ten, a tolerable article, a cook and basket-maker; twenty, a fine article of squaw, learned in the kamas-beds, and with skull flat as a shingle; fifty, a very superior article, ruddy with vermilion and skilled in embroidering buckskin with porcupine-quills; and one hundred blankets, a princess, with the beauty and accomplishments of her rank. Mothers in civilization will be pleased to compare these with their current rates.

Skloo's prairie and the region thereabouts merits tenants more numerous than stray bands of mustangs. Succulent bunch-grass grows there in plenty for legions of graminivora to fatten on, as they take gentle, wholesome exercise over the hillocks. It was by far the most propitious country I had seen this side the mountains, and will make a valuable cattle range.

At present, exercise, and not grazing, was the business of my cattle. We must hold to our unflagging march for a few hours more. But prostration after my night watch, and straining of mind and body for many days, was overcoming me. I was still wet, cold, and weary, hardly capable of observation, the most instinctive of healthy human faculties. It was now eleven o'clock of the thirty-first of August. The sky began to clear with tumultuous power. Massive black battalions of cloud came rushing by from the reserves of storm that still were encamped upon the mountain strongholds west-ward. Every gloomy cloud trailed a blast, chilling as Sarsar, the icy wind of death. Between these moments of torture, the sun of August came forth through vistas of blinding white vapor, and fevered me. I grew suddenly sick with a despair like death. Fudnun was descending a slope some distance before me, driving Antipodes laboriously along. I essayed to shout to him, but my voice choked with a sneering, fiendish rattle, as if contempt of my soul at its mean jailer, my poor failing, dying body. I clutched vainly at the coil of my lariat by my saddle horn, and fell senseless.

I slept through a brief death to a blissful resurrection. Awaking slowly, I doubted at first whether I were not now released from

earthly trammels, for tireless toil in a life immortal. First, I perceived
that I was conscious; therefore I still was in being. Quickly the tremulous blood, in every fibre and cell, told me that I was still an organized being, possessed of members like those old familiar ones, my
agents in winning undying thoughts. Next, my eyes unclosed, and
I saw the fair sky. With my senses newborn, my first discovery of
external facts was the illimitable heaven, bright with evanescent
wreaths of clouds, white and virginal. Whether, then, this were a
new world where I had awakened, or the world of my ancient tenancy, I knew that the well-known laws of beauty reigned, and I need
not here apostatize from old loves and old faiths. Life went on slowly
reviving, drawing vigor from the air, and action, the token of life,
became a necessity. I stirred feebly, like a child. The rustle of my
first movement called out a sympathetic stir. Another organization
in the outer world took note of me. I felt a warm puff upon my cheek,
and the nose of Klale the Trusty bent over me inquisitively.

The situation was now systematically explained; I was my old self,
on the old earth; wholly satisfactory, whether desirable or not. Let
us at least know where we stand,—what are our facts; then, if there
is anything to be done with ourselves, or made of our facts, we can
make the attempt.

Something toward self-restoration may be done even by a passive, supine weakling, lying among bunch-grass, on a solitary prairie, leagues away from a house,—an unpromising set of circumstances. I was at present a very valueless worldling. But the world
that takes us and mars us has also to make us again. Unless our
breakage is voluntary, determined, and habitual, we shall mend.
Not behind corpulent bottles, purple, crimson, and blue, in a shop
where there is a putty-faced youth with a pestle and a redolence of
rhubarb, are kept the great agents of Nature,—our mother, father,—

who as mother gives us life, and as father warns, flogs, cures, and guides us with severe tenderness. Air, light, and water are the trinity of simple remedies, not sold in the shops, for making a marred man new and whole again. These three medicines were liberally provided near my fainting fit on the prairie.

The first thing I had to do, to be changed from a limp object to a robust man, was only passive action. I was to breathe and to bask. And when I had sufficiently suffered the influence of air and light, Nature's next potent remedy was awaiting me. I heard the welcome trickle of water near at hand,—delicious, winsome sound, hardly less articulate than the tones of a beloved voice calling me to a presence that should be refreshment and full renovation. I could not walk, but I dragged myself along toward the source of sound, Klale following, an uncontrolled friend.

Sweet water-music guided me to a neighbor rivulet. It came singing along the bosomy swells of prairie, fondling its long, graceful fringes of grass, curving and returning, that it might not lose, with too much urgency, the self-possessed delight of motion along the elastic softness of its cushioned bed. If there were anywhere above in this brook's career turmoil and turbulence, it suffered no worse consequence than that it must carry along a reminiscence of riot, quickly soothed, in files of bright bubbles, with their skulls fuller than they could bear of microscopic images of all the outer world. Each bubble was so crowded with reflections from the zenith, that it must share its bursting sympathy, and marry with every bubble it overtook and touched, until it became so full of fantasies that it must merrily explode and be resolved into a drop and a sunbeam.

The countless charm of water, so sweetly shining forth its quality of refreshment, revived me even before I could stoop and taste.

I sank and lapped. I bathed away the fever from my brow, and let the warm, healthy sunshine cherish me.

In eldest days, had I drooped by a Hippocrene like this, a nymph had surely emerged from among the ripples and laid her cooling hand upon me gently, giving me for all my mortal days a guardian vision of immortality. In younger time, then, had I perchance been blessed with healing at the hands of some maiden leech, a Una, unerringly errant hither upon a milk-white palfrey, hither where a knight was sore bestead.[3] Now, Nature nursed me, and I grew strong again.

But let us bethink ourselves, Klale, "my trusty frere." We were five; we are two. Where are the three? Where is Fudnun, the Incorruptible, the Path-finder, the Merry? Where Antipodes? Where Gubbins?

Where? Here! Here, pelting down the slope, overjoyed, comes Fudnun, with whinnying nags. He had advanced sleepily, giving his whole mind to driving Antipodes, until that reluctant steed, pretending to grow unhappy that Klale and I were missing, bolted to the rear; whereupon Fudnun perceived my absence, and turned to recover me, dead or alive.

"Nika kulapi; I wheel about," said he, "halo nanitch; see naught. Cultus nika tum tum; feeble grows my heart. Pose mika memloose; perhaps you dead. Nika mamook stick copa k'Gubns; I ply stick on Gubbins,"—and he continued to describe how he had found the spot of my fall, and my gun lying there, and had followed my trail through the long grass. Not, I am sure, with hopes of my scalp and my plunder without a battle. Fudnun was honest, and, finding me safe, he relieved himself by uproarious laughter.

There is magnetism in society, even a Fudnun's. Strength came quicker to my flaccid tissues. I thought of my journey's end, not far off, and toiled up that dread ascent into my saddle. Klale trudged along, and soon perceiving that I swayed about no more, and, instead of clinging with both hands to my saddle, sat upright and held the bridle, he paced gradually into his cradling lope.

By the hearty aid of noon, the Cascades put their shoulders to the clouds, lifted them and cut them to pieces with their peaks, so that the wind could come in, like a charge of cavalry, and annihilate the broken phalanxes. Mount Adams, Tacoma the Less, was the first object to cleave the darkness. I looked westward, and saw a sunlit mass of white, high up among the black clouds, and baseless but for them. It would have seemed itself a cloud, but, while the dark volumes were heaving and shifting about it, this was permanent. While I looked, the mountain and the sun became evident victors; the glooms fell away, were scattered and scourged into nothingness, and the snow-peak stood forth majestic, the sole arbiter of this realm. The yellow prairies rolled up where the piney Cascades, dwarfed by distance, were a dark ridge upon the horizon, and the overtopping bulk of Tacoma rose directly from them, a silver mountain from a golden sea. No tameness of thought is possible here, even if prairie-land lies dead level for leagues, when on its edge the untamed forces of Nature have set up these stately monuments. More than a hundred miles away on the transcontinental journey, more than a hundred miles away on the sea, these noble isolated snow-peaks are to a traveler memorials of the land he has left, or beacons, firmer than a pillar of cloud, of a land whither he goes.

Again I thought of the influence of this most impressive scenery upon its future pupils among men. The shape of the world has controlled or guided men's growth; the look of the world has hardly yet begun to have its effect upon spiritual progress. Multitudes of agents have always been at work to poison and dwarf poets and artists in those inspiring regions of earth where nature means they shall grow as naturally as water-lilies by a lake, or palms above the thicks of tropic woods. Civilized mankind has never yet had a fresh chance of developing itself under grand and stirring influences so large as in the Northwest.

"Yah wah, enetee," said Fudnun, pointing to a great surging hill a thousand feet high, "mit-lite skookoom tsuk, k'Lumby tsuk; there, across, is the mighty water, Columbia River."

One more charge up this Titanic bastion, and I could fairly shout, Victory! and Time beaten in the race by a length! Up, then, my squad of cavalry. Clamber up the grassy slope, Klale the untiring. Stumble forward, k'Gubns; on thy last legs. Plod on, Antipodes, in the despairing sulks. If ye are weary, am I not wearier ? Have I not died once to-day? Beyond this mighty earthwork is a waste and desolate valley; if I am to perish, let me die on the edge of appropriate, infernal scenery, such as I know of beyond that hill. And that great river, briefest of the master streams of earth, if it be not Styx to us, shall be Lethe. Klale, my jolly imp, k'Gubns, my honest servitor, Antipodes, my recalcitrant Caliban, Lethe is at hand. Across that current an Elysium awaits us, as good an Elysium as the materials permit, and there whatever can be found of asphodel or horse-fodder shall be your meed; and ye shall repose until ye start again.

Such a harangue roused the drooping quadrupeds. We travelled up the steep, right in the teeth of hot blasts, baked in the rocky cells of the valley beyond, and pouring over to meet us like puffs from deadly batteries upon the summit. We climbed for a laborious hour, and paused at last upon the crest.

Behind was the vast, monotonous plain of my morning's march. Distant behind were the rude, difficult mountains I had crossed so painfully; and more distant westward were the main Cascades, with their snow-peaks calm and solemnly radiant. Of all this I was too desperately worn out to take much appreciative notice. The scene before me was in closer sympathy with my mood.

Before me was a region like the Valley of Death, rugged, bleak, and severe. A tragical valley, where the fiery forces of Nature, impotent to attain majestic combination, and build monuments of peace, had fallen into despairs and ugly warfare. A valley of anarchy,—a confession that harmony of the elements was hopeless here, and that the toil of Nature for cycles working a world out of chaos, had failed, and achieved only a relapse into ruin, drearier than chaos.

Racked and battered crags stood disorderly over all that rough waste. There were no trees, nor any masses of vegetation to soften the severities of the landscape. All was harsh and desolate, even with the rich sun of an August afternoon doing what it might to empurple the scathed fronts of rock, to gild the ruinous piles with summer glories, and throw long shadows veiling dreariness. I looked upon the scene with the eyes of a sick and weary man, unable to give that steady thought to mastering its scope and detail without which any attempt at artistic description becomes vague generalization.

My heart sank within me as the landscape compelled me to be gloomy like itself. It was not the first time I had perused the region under desolating auspices. In a log barrack I could just discern far beyond the river, I had that very summer suffered from a villain malady, the smallpox. And now, as then, Nature harmonized discordantly with my feelings, and even forced her nobler aspects to grow sternly ominous. Mount Hood, full before me across the valley, became a cruel reminder of the unattainable. It was brilliantly near, and yet coldly far away, like some mocking bliss never to be mine, though it might insult me forever by its scornful presence.

The Dalles of the Columbia, upon which I was now looking, must be studied by the Yankee Dante, whenever he comes, for imagery to construct his Purgatory, if not his Inferno. At Walla Walah two great rivers, Clark's Fork and the Snake, drainers of the continent north and south, unite to form the Columbia.[4] It flows furiously for a hundred and twenty miles westward. When it reaches the dreary region I was now studying, where the outlying ridges of the Cascade chain commence, it finds a great, low surface paved with enormous polished sheets of basaltic rock. These plates, Gallice *dalles*,[5] give the spot its name. Canadian voyageurs in the Hudson's Bay service had a share in the nomenclature of Oregon. The great river, a mile wide not far above, finds but a narrow rift in this pavement for its passage. The rift gradually draws its sides closer, and at the spot now called the Dalles, subdivides into three mere slits in the sharp-edged rock. At the highest water there are other minor channels, but generally this continental flood is cribbed and compressed within its three chasms suddenly opening in the level floor, each chasm hardly wider than a leap a hunted fiend might take.

In fact, the legend of this infernal spot asserts a diabolical origin for these channels in the Dalles. I give this weird and grotesque attempt at explaining strange facts in Nature, translating it into more modern form.

THE LEGEND OF THE DALLES

The world has been long cycles in educating itself to be a fit abode for men. Man, for his part, has been long ages in growing upward through lower grades of being, to become whatever he now may be. The globe was once nebulous, was chaotic, was anarchic, and is at last become somewhat cosmical. Formerly rude and convulsionary forces were actively at work, to compel chaos into anarchy and anarchy into order. The mighty ministries of the elements warred with each other, each subduing and each subdued. There were earthquakes, deluges, primeval storms, and furious volcanic outbursts. In this passionate, uncontrolled period of the world's history, man was a fiend, a highly uncivilized, cruel, passionate fiend.

The Northwest was then one of the centres of volcanic action. The craters of the Cascades were fire-breathers, fountains of liquid flame, catapults of red-hot stones. Day was lurid, night was ghastly with this terrible light. Men exposed to such dread influences could not be other than fiends, as they were, and they warred together cruelly, as the elements were doing.

Where the great plains of the Upper Columbia now spread, along the Umatillah, in the lovely valley of the Grande Ronde, between the walls of the Grande Coulee, was an enormous inland sea, filling the vast interior of the continent, and beating forever against a rampart of hills, to the east of the desolate plain of the Dalles.

Every winter there were convulsions along the Cascades, and gushes of lava came from each fiery Tacoma, to spread new desolation over desolation, pouring out a melted surface, which, as it cooled in summer, became a fresh layer of sheeny, fire-hardened *dalles*.

Now as the fiends of that epoch and region had giant power to harm each other, they must have of course giant weapons of defence. Their mightiest weapon of offence and defence was their tail; in this they resembled the iguanodons and other "mud pythons" of that period, but no animal ever had such force of tail as these terrible, monster fiend-men who warred together over all the Northwest.

As ages went on, and the fires of the Cascades began to accomplish their duty of expanding the world, earthquakes and eruptions diminished in virulence. A winter came when there was none. By and by there was an interval of two years, then again of three years, without rumble or shock, without floods of fire or showers of red-hot stones. Earth seemed to be subsiding into an era of peace. But the fiends would not take the hint to be peaceable; they warred as furiously as ever.

Stoutest in heart and tail of all the hostile tribes of that scathed region was a wise fiend, the Devil. He had observed the cessation in convulsion of Nature, and had begun to think out its lesson. It was a custom of the fiends, so soon as the Dalles plain became agreeably cool after an eruption, to meet there every summer and have a grand tournament after their fashion. Then they feasted riotously, and fought again until they were weary.

Although the eruptions of the Tacomas had ceased now for three years, as each summer came round this festival was renewed. The Devil had absented himself from the last two, and when, on the third summer after his long retirement, he reappeared among his race on the field of tourney, he became an object of respectful attention. Every fiend knew that against his strength there was no defence; he could slay so long as the fit was on. Yet the idea of combined resistance to so dread a foe had never hatched itself in any fiendish head; and besides, the Devil, though he was feared, was not especially hated. He had never won the jealousy of his peers by rising above them in morality. So now as he approached, with brave tail vibrating proudly, all admired and many feared him.

The Devil drew near, and took the initiative in war, by making a peace speech.

"Princes, potentates, and powers of these infernal realms," said he, "the eruptions and earthquakes are ceasing. The elements are settling into peacefulness. Can we not learn of them? Let us give up war and cannibalism, and live in milder fiendishness and growing love."

Then went up a howl from deviltry. " He would lull us into crafty peace, that he may kill and eat safely. Death! death to the traitor!" And all the legions of fiends, acting with a rare unanimity, made straight at their intended Reformer.

The Devil pursued a Fabian policy, and took to his heels.[6] If he could divide their forces, he could conquer in detail. Yet as he ran his heart was heavy. He was bitterly grieved at this great failure, his first experience in the difficulties of Reform. He flagged sadly as he sped over the Dalles, toward the defiles near the great inland sea, whose roaring waves he could hear beating against their bulwark. Could he but reach some craggy strait among the passes, he could take position and defy attack.

But the foremost fiends were close upon him. Without stopping, he smote powerfully upon the rock with his tail. The pavement yielded to that Titanic blow. A chasm opened and went riving up the valley, piercing through the bulwark hills. Down rushed the waters of the inland sea, churning boulders to dust along the narrow trough.

The main body of the fiends shrunk back terror-stricken; but a battalion of the van sprang across and made one bound toward the heartsick and fainting Devil. He smote again with his tail, and more strongly. Another vaster cleft went up and down the valley, with an earth-quaking roar, and a vaster torrent swept along.

Still the leading fiends were not appalled. They took the leap without craning. Many fell short, or were crowded into the roaring gulf, but enough were left, and those of the chiefest braves, to martyr their chase in one instant, if they overtook him. The Devil had just time enough to tap once more, and with all the vigor of a despairing tail.

He was safe. A third crevice, twice the width of the second, split the rocks. This way and that it went, wavering like lightning eastward and westward, riving a deeper cleft in the mountains that held back the inland sea, riving a vaster gorge through the majestic chain of the Cascades, and opening a way for the torrent to gush oceanward. It was the crack of doom for the fiends. A few essayed the leap. They fell far short of the stern edge, where the Devil had sunk panting. They alighted on the water, but whirlpools tripped them up, tossed them, bowled them along among floating boulders, until the buffeted wretches were borne to the broader calms below, where they sunk. Meanwhile, those who had not dared the final leap attempted a backward one, but wanting the impetus of pursuit, and shuddering at the fate of their comrades, every one of them failed and fell short; and they too were swept away, horribly sprawling in the flood.

As to the fiends who had stopped at the first crevice, they ran in a body down the river to look for the mangled remains of their brethren, and, the undermined bank giving way under their weight, every fiend of them was carried away and drowned.

So perished the whole race of fiends.

As to the Devil, he had learnt a still deeper lesson. His tail also, the ensign of deviltry, was irremediably dislocated by his last life-saving blow. In fact, it had ceased to be any longer a needful weapon! its antagonists were all gone; never a tail remained to be brandished at it, in deadly encounter.

So, after due repose, the Devil sprang lightly across the chasms he had so successfully engineered, and went home to rear his family thoughtfully. Every year he brought his children down to the Dalles, and told them the terrible history of his escape. The fires of the Cascades burned away; the inland sea was drained, and its bed became fair prairie, and still the waters gushed along the narrow crevices he had opened. He had, in fact, been the instrument in changing a vast region from a barren sea into habitable land.

One great trial, however, remained with him, and made his life one of grave responsibility. All his children born before the catastrophe were cannibal, stiff-tailed fiends. After that great event, every new-born imp of his was like himself in character and person, and wore but a flaccid tail, the last insignium of ignobility. Quarrels between these two factions imbittered his days and impeded civilization. Still it did advance, and long before his death he saw the tails disappear forever.

Such is the Legend of the Dalles,—a legend not without a moral.

So in this summer afternoon I rested awhile; looking over the brown desolateness of the valley where the Devil baffled the fiends, and then slowly and wearily I wound along down the enormous hill-side by crumbling paths, and then between scarped cliffs of fired rock or shattered conglomerate down to the desert below. The Columbia was still two or three cruel miles away, but at last, turning to the right, away from the pavement and channels of the Dalles, I came to the cliffs over the river.

Over against me, across the unfordable whirls of gray water, still furious after its compression in the rifts above, was the outermost post of Occidental civilization. My countrymen were backing from the Pacific across the continent, and to protect their advancing rear had established a small garrison here at the Dalles. There were the old log barracks on the terrace a mile from the river. My very hospital, where I had suffered, and received the kindliest care, and where to my fevered dreams had come visions of Indians, antic, frantic, corybantic, circling about me with hatchets because I had brought the deadly pest into their tribe,—that log cabin, vacated by its occupant, the officer in command, that I might be well lodged through my illness, was still there among the rough, yellow pines, unaltered by one embroiling summer. There was the sutler's[7] shop near the shore, and, grouped about it, tents of the first-comers of the overland emigration, each with its gypsy supper-fire. Truly an elysium of civilization as elysian as one could desire, and Mount Hood standing nobly in the background, no longer chill and unsympathizing. But between me and elysium flows the Styx, gray and turbulent, and Charon, where is he? There are no canoes on this side. How shall we cross, Fudnun, the Blanketeer?

"Kloneas; dunno. Pose mika mamook po; suppose you fire a shot," said Fudnun, "pesiwash chaco copa canim; and Indian come with canoe."

I fired shots, nay, impatient volleys, and very petty popgun noise it seemed by the loud river in this broad, rough bit of earth. No one appeared to ferry me. I waved a white blanket. No one heeded. I fired more shots, more volleys. It would be farcical, or, worse, should we be forced to stay here "dum defluat amnis,"[8] to wait until this continental current run driblets. Are we to repeat, with variations, the trials of Tantalus?[9] No, for I see a figure stirring near a log on the beach. At this distance I cannot distinguish, but I can fancy the figure to be one of the Frowzy, and the log a canoe. It is so. He launches, and comes bravely paddling across the stream. We scuffled down the craggy bank to meet him.

"Howdydo! Howdydo!" said Olyman Charon, landing his canoe, and lounging bow-leggedly up to shake hands. A welcoming howdydo, said I in return, and for a fitting number of oboli[10] he agreed to ferry me and mine in two detachments. I would cross first with the traps, swimming Klale; Fudnun would come afterward with k'Gubns and Antipodes. I upheld Klale's head in the bow while

Charon paddled and steered aft. The river proved indeed almost a Styx to poor Klale. It was a long half-mile of stemming a furious current, and once or twice the stout-hearted little nag struggled as if his death-moment had come. But Charon paddled lustily, and we safely touched the farther shore.

It was sunset of the last of August. I had won the day, and not merely the day. Across the tide-ways of Whulge, the Squally prairies, the wooded flanks and buttresses of Tacoma, by the Nachchese canon and valley, from traitors on Weenas, from the Atinam mission, from the camp of the flaring torch, across Sklool's domains, and at last over the region of the Devil's race-course here at the Dalles;—over all these stages of my route I had hastened, and my speed was not in vain. I had seen new modes of savage life. I had proved Indian treachery and Indian friendship. I knew the glory and the shame of Klalam and Klickatat. Among many types of character were some positively distinct and new ones; Dooker Yawk, the drunken; Owhhigh, the magisterial; Loolowcan, the frowzy; Shabbiest, the not ungrateful; merry Uplintz, and hero-worshipping Kpawintz; Kamaiakan, the regal and courteous; Fudnun, the jocund;—all these had been in some way intimately associated with my destiny. I had conquered time and space by just so little as to feel respect for my antagonists, and some satisfaction in myself as victor. My allies in the contest, my three quadrupeds, had borne them nobly. I had a serene sense of new and large experience, and of some qualities in myself newly tested. Of all my passages of wild life, this was the most varied and concentrated. There had been much grandeur of nature, and vigorous dramatic scenes, crowded into this brief journey. As a journey, it was complete with a fortunate catastrophe after the rapidity of its acts, to prove the plot well conceived. I had rehearsed my longer march, and was ready to begin to enact it.

I left Klale to shake himself free of the waters of his Lethe, and nibble at what he could find of the promised asphodel, until his comrades came over, and myself moved about to greet old friends. My two comrades of the morrow were in a tent, hard by, playing poker with Pikes of the emigration, and losing money to the said crafty Pikes.

So, when the morrow came, I mounted a fresh horse, and went galloping along on my way across the continent. With my comrades, a pair of frank, hearty, kindly roughs, I rode over the dry plains of the Upper Columbia, beyond the sight of Mount Hood and Tacoma the Less, across John Day's river and the Umatillah, day after day, through throngs of emigrants with their flocks and their herds and their little ones, in great patriarchal caravans, with their white-roofed wagons strewed over the surging prairie, like sails on a populous sea, moving away from the tame levels of Mid-America to regions of fresher and more dramatic life on the slopes toward the Western Sea. I climbed the Blue Mountains, looked over the lovely valley of the Grande Ronde, wound through the stern defiles of the Burnt River Mountains, talked with the great chiefs of the Nez Perces at Fort Boisee, dodged treacherous Bannacks along the Snake, bought salmon, and otter-skins for finery, of the Shoshonees at the Salmon Falls, shot antelope, found many oases of refreshing beauty along the breadth of that desolate region, and so, after much adventure, and at last deadly sickness, I came to the watermelon patches of the Great Salt Lake Valley, and drew recovery thence.[11] I studied the Utah landscape, Oriental, simple, and severe. I talked with Brother Brigham, a man of very considerable power, practical sense, and administrative ability. I chatted with the buxom thirteenth of a boss Mormon, and was not prose-lyted. And then, in delicious October, I hastened on over the South Pass, through the buffalo over prairies on fire, quenched at night by the first snows of autumn. For two months I rode with days sweet and cloudless, and every night I bivouacked beneath the splendors of unclouded stars.

And in all that period while I was so near to Nature, the great lessons of the wilderness deepened into my heart day by day, the hedges of conventionalism withered away from my horizon, and all the pedantries of scholastic thought perished out of my mind forever.

Notes

1. An Entrance
1. Indian word for Port Townsend, spelled "Kah Tai" in James G. McGurdy, *By Juan de Fuca's Strait: Pioneering along the Northwestern Edge of the Continent* (Portland OR: Metropolitan, 1937), 16.

2. A Klalam Grandee
1. The Duke of York, namely Chits-a-mah-han, or Chet-ze-moka (ca. 1808–1883), later chief of the S'Klallams, was well respected in his time. A peacemaker, he signed a treaty with Washington Territorial governor Isaac I. Stevens on January 26, 1855, ceding most of Puget Sound and the Olympic Peninsula to the United States. At the mouth of Hood Canal, 3,840 acres were reserved, where all the tribes were to settle within one year. As a familiar form of ridicule, white settlers bestowed the name Duke of York. His wives See-hem-itza and Chill'lil received the names Queen Victoria and Jenny Lind; his son, the Prince of Wales.

2. Assyrian king Ashurbanipal or Sardanapalus (ca. 668–627 BC), a favorite of Romantic artists. Lord Byron wrote a tragedy, Delacroix did a painting, and Berlioz composed a cantata about this cross-dressing physician who assembled in Nineveh the first systematically organized library in the ancient Middle East.

3. Sans Souci: fine lodgings. Winthrop is being sarcastic about King George's lodge. Brighton Pavilion, also known as the Royal Pavilion, was built in 1784 and purchased in the early nineteenth century for the Prince Regent. Between 1815 and 1821 the pavilion was rebuilt under the direction of architect John Nash, who employed a mixture of classical and Indian styles that has been named "Hindoo-Gothic."

4. Originally a tribal group in Afghanistan, the Bashi Bazouks were mercenary troops in the Ottoman Empire.

5. Calapooya: a member of the Indian people of the Willamette Basin including present-day Salem, Oregon.

6. "Because they lack a sacred poet." In *A Defence of Poetry* (1821), Percy Bysshe Shelley used this clause in his discussion of poetry and imperialism (part 1, paragraph 21, sentence 165).

7. Fit reward or dividend.

8. Jenny Lind was a Swedish singer (1820–1887) whom impresario P. T. Barnum brought to the United States in 1850 as "the Swedish Nightingale." Winthrop lived in New York during the same time Lind did.

9. Literally, painted; here, painting or makeup.

10. The state barge of Venice.

11. Nauseous from consuming alcohol.

12. Torture in which a person is lifted off the ground by a rope tying his hands behind his back.

13. A stiff hat.

14. A person who travels about selling books.

15. A "Pike," as Winthrop wrote in his novel *John Brent*, is a southern migrant "from Pike County, Missouri," *John Brent* (Boston: Ticknor and Fields, 1862), 118. Connotatively, though, Pike was "a byword for all that was ruffianly in the frontier life," Van Wyck Brooks, *The Times of Melville and Whitman* (New York: E. P. Dutton, 1947), 76.

16. In the Greenpoint district of Brooklyn, New York, Webb and Bell's shipyard was the institution that laid the keel for the first ironclad of the Civil War, the *Monitor.*

17. Native canoes were typically made of the western red cedar, although "pine-tree" in this case might be a common mistake for the Douglas fir (*Pseudotsuga menziesii*).

18. A bugbear or baseless fear, like today's boogeyman, an imaginary specter used to frighten children.

19. From the Chinook Jargon, *siwash* derives from the French *sauvage,* for "forest dweller."

3. Whulge

1. Soldiered, a loan word from Scots-Gaelic; Winthrop glosses it below to denote "sham vehemence" [37].

2. Bottle, in Chinook Jargon.

3. Neal Dow (1804–1897), best known as a temperance reformer, was mayor of Portland, Maine, from 1851 to 1858 and originator of the 1851 "Maine Law," the toughest statute against alcohol sales and consumption in the world. In his day Portland was a center of the rum trade with the West Indies.

4. Winthrop's "six-shooter" was likely a .36 caliber Colt Model 1851 Navy, a cap-and-ball revolver.

5. The Olympic Mountains of the Olympic Peninsula.

6. German for leader, especially a military or political leader.

7. Painter Michaelangelo da Caravaggio (1573–1610) was renowned for the use of chiaroscuro, the skillful use of intermingled areas of light and dark in paintings.

8. The lazzaroni were homeless idlers of Naples, who lived by chance work or begging, so called from the Hospital of St. Lazarus, which served as their refuge.

9. Bulbs of the camas lily (*Camassia quamash*), widely used by Indian tribes for food.

10. The common harbor seal (*Phoca vitulina*), the only species of seal that breeds along Puget Sound.

11. Fishermen, above, who invoked their tamanous or spirit-guide by wearing special hats while fishing.

12. Turbid, muddy, from the Scots-Gaelic.

13. Short for aristocrats.

14. An allusion to *Bubbles from the Brunnen of Nassau*, a humorous travel account published in 1833 by Sir Francis Bond Head, British administrator in Canada.

15. A parr is a salmon up to two years of age, with dark spots and transverse bands.

16. Palinurus, his life exacted by the god Neptune in exchange for the crew's safe passage, steered for Aeneas in Virgil's *Aeneid* till he was overcome by the curse of sleep and drowned.

17. References to the operas *La Favorita* by Gaetano Donizetti (1843) and *La Traviata* by Giuseppe Verdi (1853).

18. As a punishment for stealing fire from Zeus and giving it to humans,

Prometheus was bound and had his liver eaten away each day by a bird of prey, only for it to grow back before the bird visited again the next day.

19. Tobacco pipe.

20. In potential, in abeyance.

21. The white fur of the winter weasel, here perhaps used metaphorically for the office or functions of a judge, whose ermine-lined robe represented purity and honor.

22. Literally, "out of the deep," possibly alluding to the Renaissance-era madrigal by Thomas Morley.

23. Cyclops is the one-eyed monster who makes captives of Odysseus and his crew.

24. *Arbutus menziesii*, a broadleaf evergreen, more commonly known today in the United States as the madrone, is a rare deciduous tree that sheds its bark instead of its leaves.

25. An allusion to Shakespeare's *The Tempest* (ca. 1611). Caliban is a "savage and deformed slave" of Prospero, the magician, and Stefano is the drunken butler.

26. A kenning or epithet often applied to Zeus.

27. On May 8, 1792, Capt. George Vancouver of the British Royal Navy viewed the mountain from present-day town of Port Townsend and named it after his friend, Rear Admiral Peter Rainier.

28. The many volumes of Murray's *Handbook for Travellers*, with their signature red covers, were published from 1836 to 1913. Britons, especially Cockneys, are known for the elision of the letter "h" (e.g., pronouncing "his" as " 'is").

29. At 11,239 feet (3426 meters), Mount Hood is the highest point in today's state of Oregon; Tacoma or Mount Rainier, the highest glaciated mountain in the lower forty-eight states, stands 14,411 feet (4,392 meters). Mont Blanc, compared below, the highest peak in Europe, is 15,781 feet (4807 meters).

30. Victuals or supplies.

31. The eighth labor of Hercules was to fetch the flesh-eating mares of Diomedes, which Diomedes originally had stolen.

32. The western red cedar (*Thuja plicata*) still is referred to today as the western arborvitae.

4. Owhhigh

1. Road surface, so called after John Loudon McAdam (1756–1836), Scottish civil engineer who invented a way of paving roads with gravel.

2. Burned or scorched. "Mount Rainier is known to have erupted as

recently as in the 1840s," Thomas W. Sisson, "History and Hazards of Mount Rainier, Washington." USGS Open-File Report 95–642. 1995.

3. Traps, things, property, according to the Chinook Jargon as Winthrop learned it.

4. Entrance.

5. Fort Nisqually, founded in 1833, headquartered the Hudson's Bay Company farming subsidiary called the Puget Sound Agricultural Company. It oversaw hundreds of cultivated acres and produced all kinds of foods—meat, potatoes, wheat, oats, and peas—for sale to travelers and settlers as far away as Alaska. William Fraser Tolmie (1812–1886) served there as medical officer, trader, and superintendent beginning in 1843; in 1855, he became its chief factor. Edward Huggins (1832–1907), the "Mr. H." of this chapter, arrived on April 13, 1850, to work under the direction of Tolmie. A bartizan is an overhanging turret.

6. King Philip or Metacomet, son of Massasoit and chief of the Wampanoag tribe, died in 1676 at Mt. Hope, now Bristol, Rhode Island, in the war named for him. His body was drawn and quartered and his head paraded and displayed on a stake in Plymouth, Massachusetts. Philip's wife and son were sold into slavery in the West Indies.

7. Owhi, a chief of the Yakama tribe, was imprisoned and shot while trying to escape at Fort Dalles, now The Dalles, Oregon, in 1858. Owhi's son Qualchan (brother of Lo-kout, Winthrop's guide whom he knew as Loolowcan) was hanged earlier that same year near Spokane, Washington.

8. Winthrop is contrasting natural male beauty with the peacock elegance of Alfred Guillaume Gabriel, Count D'Orsay (1801–1852), a French artist and dandy who much impressed Lord Byron.

9. Winthrop "incorrectly charged" the Duke of York, Cantwell wrote, "with having murdered a couple of palefaces," and in fact the Duke "kept his tribe from joining the Indian war." Robert Cantwell, *The Hidden Northwest* (Philadelphia: J. B. Lippincott, 1972), 163.

10. Hussars were members of ornately uniformed European units of light cavalry.

11. King of Naples, the flamboyant Marshal Joachim Murat (1767–1815) served under Napoleon.

12. A purple dye originally extracted from shellfish.

13. Rigorously just and severe. Rhadamanthus, a son of Zeus and Europa, in reward for his exemplary sense of justice, was made a judge of the underworld after his death.

14. Today the S'Kamish is the White River, so named for its milky color, caused by glacial flour and volcanic silt. It is fed by Winthrop Creek, which flows out of Winthrop Glacier, both named for the author.

15. The identity of this "oldman chief" (113) is untraced.

16. The Naches River. Owhi's narrative describes the route over historic Naches Pass.

17. St. Joseph's Mission on Ahtanum Creek, founded in 1852 to teach religion to the Yakamas, is now the site of a museum.

18. The opposite side of the world in some constructions; otherwise, Hell.

19. Something whose name is either forgotten or not known.

20. Bucephalus: Alexander the Great's war horse. Rosinante: A wretched jade of a riding horse, the name of Don Quixote's steed.

21. Native to Central America and Mexico, lignum vita (*Guaiacum officinale*) is the densest and hardest of hardwoods. Fort Steilacoom, where Winthrop bought his pork and hardtack biscuits, was founded in 1849.

22. Apparel.

23. A civil or military authority in Egypt or Turkey.

24. Small cans or cups.

25. A stone is a unit of weight in Great Britain, 14 pounds (6.4 kilograms), thus putting Winthrop's weight at roughly 126 pounds (57.6 kilograms).

26. A Muslim beggar.

27. Face or visage, from "physiognomy."

28. As Owhi died in 1858, this detail places composition of *The Canoe and the Saddle* at late 1858 or 1859.

29. Compare this passage with the painting *The Giant's Chalice* (1833) by Thomas Cole.

30. Astoria, Oregon, was named for German immigrant and fur tycoon John Jacob Astor (1763–1848). Washington Irving's *Astoria; or Anecdotes of an Enterprise Beyond the Rocky Mountains* was first issued in 1836. The Chinook chief Comcomly gave his daughter as wife to Duncan M'Dougal of Astor's crew.

31. A phrase used by Alfred Lord Tennyson (1809–1892) in his 1832 poem "The Lotos-Eaters" to describe those drugged characters of Homeric legend. The lotus flower was fabled to bring forgetfulness of one's homeland or loss of desire to return to it.

5. Forests of the Cascades

1. The two preceding paragraphs are perhaps the most compelling examples of Winthrop's forays into Hudson River School aesthetics and its analog in literary Transcendentalism. Winthrop's publisher, Ticknor and Fields, also had published works by both Emerson and Thoreau.

2. Winthrop's language in this sentence, especially the plural "artists," suggests more than literary fancy. It is in keeping with an animism that suggests gods and spirits shape and inhabit everything in nature: trees, animals, and mountains. As he writes below, "Solitude became to me personal, and pregnant with possible emanations, as if I were a faithful pagan in those early days when gods were seen of men, and when, under Grecian skies, Pan and the Naiads whispered their secrets to the lover of Nature" [72–73]. The next paragraph concludes, though, on a note that harmonizes instead with the conventional religiosity of his friend Frederic Edwin Church and with Winthrop's own Puritan ancestry. That paragraph yields to allegorical imagery, as if *The Faerie Queene*—which Winthrop indicates in chapter 13 that he had read—were mediating Winthrop's account of his experiences in the Pacific Northwest forests.

3. A seventy-four-gun man-of-war, the kind of ship Herman Melville described in *Billy Budd* (1891).

4. Another allusion to the *Iliad*. Wise old Nestor is counselor to the Greeks at Troy.

5. French for kitchen boys or chef's helpers.

6. Insatiable hunger, abnormal craving for food, related to today's bulimia.

7. To pleach is to braid, weave or interlock.

8. An allusion to the Old Testament story of King David and his son Absalom (Samuel 2:13–18). Routed in a battle to dethrone his father, Absalom was entangled among tree boughs and slain by his pursuers.

9. Canonicus was a Narragansett chief who lived from 1562 to 1647; Chickatawbut, a chief of the Massachusetts born circa 1600, died in 1633 of smallpox; Passaconnaway (ca. 1610–1669), chief of the Pennacook tribe in the 1620s, lived most of his life in the Merrimack River Valley.

10. In the book of Joshua, God intervened in a battle to make the sun stand still and allow Joshua to defeat his enemies in a battle.

11. A barrier of felled or live trees with branches sharpened or entwined with wire.

12. In 1846 at Chapultepec castle, otherwise known as the Halls of Mon-

tezuma, Gen. Winfield Scott's forces overwhelmed the Mexican army, the last bastion of resistance in Mexico City, during the Mexican-American War (1846–1848), which was the first major U.S. conflict fueled by Manifest Destiny.

13. George B. McClellan (1826–1885) was assigned in April 1853 to the Pacific Railroad Survey. At the same time, as superintendent of Indian affairs he was also empowered to clear Indians from the route of his railroad and from lands needed by new settlers. Kent D. Richards, "The Young Napoleons: Isaac Stevens, George McClellan and the Northern Railroad Survey," *Columbia* 3, no.4 (1989): 21–28.

14. Peter Skene Odgen (1794–1854), chief trader with the Hudson's Bay Company, led numerous trapping expeditions in the northern Rockies between 1824 and 1830.

15. An alternate spelling of pom-pom: a ball or tuft.

16. Estray is a legal term for any loose domestic animal whose owner is unknown.

6. "Boston Tilicum"

1. Erebus in Greek mythology is the embodiment of primordial darkness, the son of Chaos.

2. Grapeshot, or bits of iron sometimes used for cannon loads.

3. An allusion to the biblical parable of the rich man Dives and the beggar Lazarus outside his door in Luke 16:19–31; also perhaps to a painting by Heinrich Aldegrever, *Lazarus Begging for Crumbs from Dives's Table* (1552). In Winthrop's variation Clodpole, a type of country bumpkin, robustly fails to observe social graces at table.

4. A tutelary deity, often a deceased ancestor, regarded as protector of the family.

5. Corybantic dances, meant to honor Bacchus, were accompanied with music and noise produced by the clashing of swords and spears against shields.

6. Corpses.

7. Tacoma

1. Before noon; here, during one's youth.

2. A lavish place of honor; literally, the palace of Nestor at Englianos in Greece.

3. From "Ode: Intimations of Immortality from Recollections of Early

Childhood" (section 9, lines 25–27) by English poet William Wordsworth (1770–1850).

4. A vestal is a virgin goddess of the hearth.

5. In the legends of the Ojibway and other people, Manito was the creator. Socrates' daimon would warn him if he were doing something wrong, remaining silent if he followed goodness.

6. The shell of a scaphopod (*Dentalium neohexagonum*), known as hiaqua, came to be replaced as currency by the blankets and clothing the Northwest Indians demanded and the furs the Europeans sought. Hamitchou's legend, with its theme of avarice, compares to "The Pardoner's Tale" in *The Canterbury Tales* of Geoffrey Chaucer.

7. Bearberry or kinnikinnick (*Arctostaphylos uva-ursi*), a ground cover related to heather.

8. A gentle slope or incline.

9. Penelope, here used as a type, was the faithful wife of Odysseus who thwarted suitors for twenty years while awaiting his return from the Trojan War.

8. Sowee House—Loolowcan

1. From Horace, the first book of *Satires*, this Latin translates "Warfare is preferable."

2. Lethe, the river of forgetfulness in Hades, allowed weary travelers to make fresh beginnings.

3. Aegle is the most beautiful of the nymphs of fresh water in Greek mythology.

4. The Naiads were nymphs of bodies of fresh water, sex symbols of the ancient world, both seducer and the seduced. The sun god, Helios, mated with the Naiad Aegle, renowned as the most beautiful of the Naiads, to produce the Charites or Graces.

5. The fountain of the Muses on Mount Helicon, Hippocrene arose from a stroke of the hoof of Pegasus.

6. Compare, again, the painting *The Titan's Goblet* (1833) by Thomas Cole.

7. God chose each of the three hundred men, who lapped the water "with his tongue, as a dog lappeth" (Judges 7:5), to prevail in battle against the Midianites under Gideon.

8. Illusory and therefore disappointing. Originally the patronymic of a line of princes in Baghdad, one of whose story is told in the Arabian

Nights, Barmecide puts a succession of imaginary dishes before a beggar, pretending that they are courses of a lavish feast. He is in turn beaten by the beggar, who feigns intoxication with the imaginary wine.

9. Conical rifle bullets designed with a hollow base that expanded when fired, named after Claude Étienne Minié (ca. 1814–1879), French army officer. Minié's patent for the bullet was purchased and adopted by the British government for the Enfield rifle in 1851.

10. A close parallel to the doctrine of correspondence developed by Emmanuel Swedenborg, who argued that the correspondence of nature to transcendental reality is functionally immanent in creation.

11. Tetrao is the genus of many grouses and ptarmigans, most of them European. Winthrop got the species right but not the genus of what was probably the blue grouse, today *Dendragapus obscurus*.

12. Minatory: menacing, ominous, threatening.

13. "Oh, Sir! the good die first, / And they whose hearts are dry as summer dust / Burn to the socket." The quotation comes from William Wordsworth's 1814 poem *The Excursion* (book 1, lines 500–502).

14. Nemesis: retribution, righteous anger. Originally a female Greek deity whose mother was Nox (Night).

15. The name caudal hails from Latin *cauda*, for tail.

16. Wholly or partly open to the sky.

17. Viator is Latin for wayfarer, traveler.

18. A guest at a banquet.

19. That is, the lunch menu. Azrael, the angel of death, watches over and takes the soul from the dying body.

20. Plato defined a man as an animal, bipedal and featherless. Diogenes plucked a chicken and declared, "Here is Plato's man."

21. A culinary concoction resembling a stew.

22. In the flawed body (Latin).

23. A legal term for profits that accrue during a dispute over land ownership.

24. To be astonished at nothing.

25. From Puritan poet John Milton's "Comus, a Mask" (1634).

9. Via Mala

1. Today, the Naches Valley.

2. Canyon.

3. Salvator Rosa was an Italian Baroque-era painter, 1615–1673.

4. Intuition.

5. A source of the Rhine River, one of the most wild and picturesque gorges in Switzerland, the Via Mala is walled by vertical limestone cliffs. Winthrop's points of reference for his travels in the American West often are European in origin.

6. Today, Wenas, site of the city of Selah, Washington.

7. Slightly misquoted, the lines are from Wordsworth's "Tintern Abbey" (1798): "And this prayer I make, / Knowing that Nature never did betray / The heart that loved her" (lines 122–23).

8. Sprinkled.

9. A mountain region of the Greek Peloponnesus, Arcady was imagined as the ideal place of shepherds, nymphs, and pastoral poetry.

10. An untraced epithet or name, keterrypid in this book is used identically in *John Brent* as kettrypid.

11. Emissary or representative, in this case of the pope.

12. Appoggiatura: a grace note or ornamental note in music.

13. A disturbance, tumult, uproar.

14. Having wounded the bear for no good reason, Winthrop here "reasoned out the lesson," as he says below, and practices self-examination suggestive of William Wordsworth respecting his relationship with nature.

15. A species of cobra native to southern Africa.

10. Treachery

1. In 1847, Jesuit missionaries Charles Pandosy and Louis d'Herbomez built a mission on Ahtanum Creek in what would become known as the Yakima Valley. They named the mission Sainte Croix, the sainted cross. Yakama chief Kamiakin (ca. 1800–1877) used this site as his main summer camp. Soldiers burned down the mission during the Yakima Indian War of 1855 when they discovered gunpowder there.

2. A yelp of three notes.

3. For Birmingham, England, this phonetic transcription duplicates the way some locals pronounce the city's name. In the sixteenth century's thriving slave trade, Birmingham became a center for the production of cheap trinkets or "Brummagem ware"—shiny jewelry, mirrors, beads and knives—that was exchanged for slaves in Africa.

4. David Garrick (1717–1779) was the renowned actor at Drury Lane Theatre in England. Irish-born author Oliver Goldsmith (ca. 1730–1774) died deeply in debt.

5. English author and lexicographer Samuel Johnson (1709-1784) died in his residence at Bolt Court.

6. John Jacob Astor's *Tonquin* was burned and sunk off Vancouver Island in June 1811.

7. Now archaic, *clomb* is a poetic past participle of *climb*.

8. An imagined or utopian society, as rationally ordered as the Newtonian view of nature.

9. Gynaeceum: women's quarters.

10. Macassar oil: popular as men's hair dressing in the nineteenth century, was named after the Indonesian port where the oil purportedly originated.

11. A horse that carries packs or baggage.

12. Loop or slack part in a rope.

13. Billingsgate: coarse, foul or abusive language, from the name of a former market in London.

11. Kamaiakan

1. Latin for "a push from behind."

2. Treated with contempt, disparaged.

3. A sybarite is a person devoted to luxury and pleasure, from Sybaris, an ancient Greek city.

4. Take a stick to.

5. To send to Coventry is to ostracize. Late in 1858, one of Col. George Wright's men reportedly shot Owhi while he was trying to escape. Owhi's son, Loolowcan's (Lo-kout's) brother Qualchan, was hanged by Wright earlier that same year.

6. Duc de la Rochefoucauld (1613-1680), an aristocratic Frenchman famous for his collection of some five hundred epigrams or maxims that betray the selfishness behind supposedly honorable motives.

7. Outside of combat.

8. A young man or boy, an obscure Dutch term also used by Spenser in *The Faerie Queene* (1590-96).

9. Centaur: a fabulous being with the head, arms, and torso of a man and the lower body of a horse.

10. An Elgin marble is part of the collection of marble sculptures brought to Britain in 1803 by Thomas Bruce, Seventh Earl of Elgin, who had removed them from the Parthenon in Athens. They are housed in

the British Museum, London. Keats wrote poems about them, and Byron strongly objected to their removal.

11. Poins is one of Prince Hal's drinking companions in Shakespeare's plays about King Henry.

12. An important ecological observation. Deer now are abundant in this region, a result perhaps of irrigation, agriculture, and the expanding range of the whitetail deer where mule deer once were dominant.

13. The quotation comes from Alfred, Lord Tennyson, "The Lotos-Eaters," line 151.

14. Ahtanum Creek drains a watershed of 171 square miles, discharging into the Yakima River near the city of Yakima. Salmon and steelhead migrated in large numbers to Ahtanum Creek, but those runs mostly died out with the advent of large-scale irrigation. Today, coho salmon reintroduced by the Yakama Indian Nation are spawning again in the lower reaches of the creek.

15. This epic sentence, 212 words, measures both Winthrop's hunger for civilization during his sojourn and his nostalgia for Europe where "ancient fanes"—temples or sanctuaries—were more commonly found.

16. This perception echoes Winthrop's novel *John Brent*, set amid the Mormon immigration to Utah and published posthumously in 1862. There, the narrator observes, "The Pope and Brigham Young are the rival bidders for such weaklings in the nineteenth century. Brigham with polygamy is the complement of Pio with celibacy," *John Brent*, 163. Where he refers in the same novel to "that monstrous ogre of Mormonism" (199), his language recalls Sir Edmund Spenser's on Catholicism.

17. An indication of superior status.

18. Jokers, satirists.

19. On or starting from the wearer's left.

20. Perhaps a misprint for Antonius, for Marcus Antonius, representing one who loves luxury.

21. The Meison Carree is a temple and the Pont du Gard, a Roman aqueduct, both in Nimes, France. In 1852, the Oblate fathers D'Herbomez and Pandosy had dug irrigation canals with shovels near the mission.

22. Petrarch was an Italian poet of love lyrics. Rene D'Anjou, influential in the European Renaissance, rode at Jeanne d'Arc's side in her crusade to Orleans and gave Christopher Columbus his first commission.

23. Skloom was brother to Chief Kamiakin, and Owhi was his uncle.

24. "The good God sends him; it is Kamaiakin himself." Chief Kamia-

kin was the most prominent Yakama chief of his time and the major political and military leader in the area. He reluctantly signed the Yakama
Treaty of 1855, and he fought in the Yakama War of 1855–58.

25. A nob is an elegantly dressed man.

26. On February 24, 1848, King Louis-Philippe, fearful of what had
happened to Louis XVI and Marie Antoinette, abdicated the throne by
disguising himself and fleeing Paris. In an ordinary cab, under the name
of "Mr Smith," he escaped to England.

27. A beacon, originally an Egyptian lighthouse classed among the
Seven Wonders of the World.

28. The fairy-tale character Fine Ear reputedly could hear grass grow
and moles work underground.

29. Legal terminology meaning "only to that extent," that is, Kamiakin had other wives if this one died.

30. A large pill.

31. Isabella yellow: a brownish yellow, after the Spanish princess Isabella, daughter of King Philip II, referring to the color assumed by a dress
she wore without change from 1601 to 1604, a consequence of a vow she
made.

32. That is, a robber.

33. A church officer in charge of sacred objects.

34. Ariel: a water spirit in the Hebrew Cabala and in Shakespeare's play
The Tempest. Miranda is the heroine in the same play.

12. Lightning and Torchlight

1. Rushing to get to The Dalles to make his meeting, Winthrop thought
of these lines from Shakespeare:

> "Sweet are the uses of adversity,
> Which like the toad, ugly and venomous,
> Wears yet a precious jewel in his head;
> And this our life, exempt from public haunt,
> Finds tongues in trees, books in the running brooks,
> Sermons in stones, and good in every thing."
>
> *As You Like It*. act ii, scene. 1, lines 12–17

The reference to "Princess Parazaide" is untraced.

2. A Parthian flight is one delivered in or as if in retreat; a Pyrrhic victory is one offset by great losses.

3. An equestrian term, demivolt is a half vault, one of the seven artificial motions of a horse, a raising of the forelegs in a particular manner.

4. This storm interlude comprises one of the finest examples of the Hudson River school sensibility Winthrop brought to his narrative. Compare Frederic Edwin Church, *Storm in the Mountains* (1847). Both Church and Thomas Cole painted stormy scenes and trunks of blasted trees, a common Romantic motif.

5. Covered with bristling points; standing erect.

6. Recesses, secrets, hidden things.

7. A neophyte is a new convert or new participant. A hierophant is a presiding teacher or priest, especially of ritual magic in honor of Ceres.

8. In 1837 Mordechai Manuel Noah, a founder of New York University, published his *Discourse on the Evidence of the American Indians Being the Descendants of the Lost Tribes of Israel.* The idea had had wide currency before Noah's publication, however.

9. A genius loci is a guardian or presiding spirit of a place.

10. In Roman mythology, princesses who kept sacred fires.

11. From "The Rime of the Ancient Mariner," by Samuel Taylor Coleridge, the quotation should read: "Water, water every where / Nor any drop to drink" (lines 121–22).

12. That is, member of an expedition.

13. The source of this quotation is untraced.

14. The god of sleep or dreams.

15. The Roman goddess of the dawn, counterpart of Greek Eos.

16. A reminder of mortality.

13. The Dalles—Their Legend

1. Tirra lirra: Tennyson used this nonce lyric in "The Lady of Shalott" (1832) to show Lancelot's light-heartedness; Shakespeare in *Winter's Tale* (ca. 1610) created "The lark that tirra-lirra chants" (IV, ii, 9).

2. This image—a horse leaping through lasso—is developed more fully in Winthrop's *John Brent.*

3. To be bestead is to be put in peril. Una, above, is the heroine of *The Faerie Queene,* whom the Red Crosse Knight labors to gain the hand of in that epic poem by Edmund Spenser.

4. At the Tri-Cities—Kennewick, Pasco, and Richland—the Snake River joins the Columbia in present-day Washington State. The Clark Fork River drains into Lake Pend Oreille in north Idaho.

5. From the Canadian French (or Gallic), *dalles* means flagstone, although here it connotes a stretch of a river with rapids and dangerous currents between high rock walls.

6. A Fabian policy, after Roman general Quintus Fabius Maximus Verrucosus, is one that cautiously avoids direct confrontation.

7. A sutler is a supplier or purveyor of food to an army.

8. The Latin is from the *Epistles* of Horace, part of a longer quotation thus: "He who postpones the hour of living is like the rustic who waits for the river to pass along before he crosses."

9. Zeus punished Tantalus for a transgression by having him hang from a tree over a pool of water. When he bent to drink, the water would recede.

10. An obolus is a small silver Greek coin.

11. Winthrop's unspecified illness, while returning home on the Oregon Trail, prompted him to buy baking soda and powerful laudanum—opium suspended in alcohol—from travelers along the way.

Bibliography

American Council of Learned Societies, comp. *Dictionary of American Biography*. 10 vols. New York: Scribner's, 1928–58.

American Memory: Historical Collections of the American Digital Library. The Library of Congress. http://memory.loc.gov/. July 16, 2002.

Bergthaller, Hannes. "Staking Claims—Literatur und Landnahme im Pazifischen Nordwesten." Master's thesis. University of Bonn, 2000.

Brooks, Van Wyck. *The Times of Melville and Whitman*. New York: E. P. Dutton, 1947.

Cantwell, Robert. *The Hidden Northwest*. Philadelphia: J. B. Lippincott, 1972.

Carr, Gerald L. "Frederic Edwin Church as a Public Figure." In *The Early Landscapes of Frederic Edwin Church, 1845–1854*. Edited by Franklin Kelly and Gerald L. Carr. Fort Worth TX: Amon Carter Museum, 1987.

Colby, Elbridge. *Theodore Winthrop*. New York: Twayne, 1965.

Curtis, George William. "Biographical Sketch of the Author." In *Cecile Dreeme,* by Theodore Winthrop, 5–19. Boston: Ticknor and Fields, 1861.

Datasegment.com. Online Dictionary. http://onlinedictionary.
     datasegment.com/. July 16, 2002.

Duberman, Martin, Martha Vicinus, and George Chauncey Jr., eds.
     Hidden from History: Reclaiming the Gay and Lesbian Past.
     New York: Meridian Penguin, 1989.

Egan, Timothy. *The Good Rain: Across Time and Terrain in the Pacific
     Northwest.* New York: Vintage, 1990.

Emerson, Ralph Waldo. "The American Scholar." In *Emerson: Essays
     and Poems.* New York: Library of America, 1996. 51–71.

Encyclopedia Mythica. http://www.pantheon.org/mythica.html. July
     16, 2002.

Evans, Ivor H., comp. *Brewer's Dictionary of Phrase and Fable.* 14th ed.
     New York : Harper Collins, 1989.

Fresonke, Kris. *West of Emerson: The Design of Manifest Destiny.*
     Berkeley: University of California Press, 2003.

Garraty, John A., and Mark C. Carnes, eds. *American National
     Biography.* 10 vols. New York: Oxford University Press, 1999.

Irving, Washington. *A Tour on the Prairies.* 1835. Reprint, Norman:
     University of Oklahoma Press, 1956.

Harmon, Alexandra. *Indians in the Making: Ethnic Relations and
     Indian Identities around Puget Sound.* Berkeley: University of
     California Press, 1999.

Howells, William Dean. *The Cambridge History of English and
     American Literature in 18 Volumes.* Vol. 17. Excerpted at http://
     www.bartleby.com/227/0403.html. Irving, Washington.

Lape, Noreen Groover. *West of the Border: The Multicultural Literature
     of the Western American Frontiers.* Athens: Ohio University
     Press, 2000.

Library of Congress, comp. *National Union Catalog.* 141 vols. New
     York: Roman and Littlefield, 1958–1983.

Lichatowich, Jim. *Salmon without Rivers: A History of the Pacific
     Salmon Crisis.* Covelo CA: Island, 1999.

Lyman, William Denison. *Indian Myths of the Northwest.* Worcester MA
     American Antiquarian Society, 1915.

Matthiessen, Peter. *Wildlife in America.* New York: Viking, 1959.

McGurdy, James G. *By Juan de Fuca's Strait: Pioneering along the
     Northwestern Edge of the Continent.* Portland: Metropolitan,
     1937.

Nisbet, Jack. *Sources of the River: Tracking David Thompson across Western North America.* Seattle: Sasquatch, 1990.

Peltier, Jerome. *Warbonnets and Epaulets.* Montreal: Payette Radio Limited, 1971.

Powers, Alfred, ed. *Canoe and the Saddle by Theodore Winthrop.* Portland: Binford and Mort, 1957.

Propst, H. Dean. "Theodore Winthrop: His Place in American Literary and Intellectual History." PhD diss. George Peabody College for Teachers, 1964.

Richards, Kent D. "The Young Napoleons: Isaac Stevens, George McClellan and the Northern Railroad Survey." *Columbia* 3, no. 4 (1989): 21–28.

Rosowski, Susan J. *Birthing a Nation: Gender, Creativity, and the West in American Literature.* Lincoln: University of Nebraska Press, 1999.

Ruby, Robert H., and John A. Brown. *A Guide to the Tribes of the Pacific Northwest.* Norman: University of Oklahoma Press, 1986.

Sisson, Thomas W. "History and Hazards of Mount Rainier, Washington." usgs Open-File Report 95-642. 1995.

Slotkin, Richard. *Regeneration through Violence: The Mythology of the American Frontier, 1600–1860.* Middleton CT: Wesleyan University Press, 1973.

———. *The Fatal Environment: The Myth of the Frontier in the Age of Industrialization.* New York: Atheneum, 1992.

Splawn, A. J. *Ka-mi-akin: Last Hero of the Yakimas.* 1917. Reprint, Portland: Binford and Mort, 1944.

Stephanson, Anders. *Manifest Destiny: American Expansion and the Empire of Right.* New York: Hill and Wang, 1995.

Strong, George Templeton. *The Diary of George Templeton Strong.* Vol. 2: 1850–1859. Edited by Allan Nevins and Milton Halsey Thomas. New York: Macmillan, 1952.

Thwaites, Reuben Gold, ed. *Early Western Travels, 1748–1846.* 32 vols. Cleveland: A. H. Clark, 1904–07.

Wilton, Andrew, and Tim Barringer. *American Sublime: Landscape Painting in the United States, 1820–1880.* Princeton NJ: Princeton University Press, 2002.

Winthrop, Theodore. *A Companion to "The Heart of the Andes."* New York: Appleton, 1859.

———. *John Brent*. Boston: Ticknor and Fields, 1862.

———. *The Canoe and the Saddle, Adventures among the Northwestern Rivers and Forests, and Isthmiana*. Boston: Ticknor and Fields, 1863.

———. *The Canoe and the Saddle; or Klalam and Klickitat, to Which Are Now First Added His Western Letters and Journals*. Edited by John H. Williams. Tacoma: John H. Williams, 1913.

———. *The Canoe and the Saddle*. Edited by Alfred Powers. Portland: 1957.

———. *Saddle and Canoe: An Early 19th Century Ride through the Pacific North-West*. Glasgow KY: Long Riders' Guild, 2001.

White, Richard. *The Middle Ground: Indians, Empires, and Republics in the Great Lakes Region, 1650–1815*. New York: Cambridge University Press, 1991.

Woolf, Eugene T. *Theodore Winthrop: Portrait of an American Author*. Washington DC: University Press of America, 1981.

Index